I0094082

# Hubbard's Guide

# to

# Moosehead Lake

# and

# Northern Maine

BY LUCIUS L HUBBARD

Author of

"Woods and Lakes of Maine – A Trip from Moosehead
Lake to New Brunswick in a Birch-Bark Canoe."

## Maine Bicentennial

## Annotated Edition

*based on the fifth edition, 1893, to which earlier edition advertisements
and information have been added.*

**new content by:**
**Tommy Carbone, Ph.D.**
**&**
**Frederick T. Wilcox, Forester**

# ANNOTATED EDITION

Cover photo, and newly added interior illustrations, and photos from the collection of Tommy Carbone, or as otherwise noted.

Cover design by Tommy Carbone.


Authors of the 2020 annotated edition:
> Tommy Carbone, PhD
> Frederick T. Wilcox, Forester

Use of <u>newly added</u> material (text and photos) from this book, other than short passages for review purposes or used within quotations, requires prior written permission be obtained by contacting the publisher at info@tommycarbone.com. Thank you for your support.

***Burnt Jacket Publishing***
Greenville, Maine


Library of Congress Control Number: 2020911598

*20210726 ISPB*

ISBN: 978-1-954048-01-0


www.tommycarbone.com

# Hubbard's Guide

## to

## Moosehead Lake

### and

## Northern Maine

For those who have discovered the Maine North

Woods, you will appreciate this guide.

For those who have yet to visit, this guide will give

you plenty of ideas off the beaten path.

For those who only venture up and down our coast,

and it is a beautiful coast, this guide is here to help

you discover some of the many places to explore in

the interior of the Pine Tree State.

Pick a tour and go.

The fifth edition of *Hubbard's Guide to Moosehead Lake and Northern Maine* was published in 1893. The guide was based on shorter books that Hubbard expanded into one complete volume. Hubbard also published a popular memoir titled, *Woods and Lakes of Maine – A Trip from Moosehead Lake to New Brunswick in a Birch-Bark Canoe,* in 1884.

In this travel guide to a wicked big chunk of northern Maine, Hubbard has provided a list of trips for exploring the north woods by paddle, or on foot. Within, there are excursions north, south, east, and west of Moosehead Lake. Admittedly, reaching the starting point of many of these locations is easier today than in Hubbard's time.

If you are not sure about mapping your own path, many outfitters offer river trip excursions in this area for an inclusive backwoods experience. However, those that want to venture deeper, to places where few travel, will find Hubbard's Guide a valuable addition to a Maine map.

For others who want to explore through the written word, those readers will find this an interesting and historical look-back to what was, and yet what still remains in Maine's northern forest.

*Tommy and Fred are pleased to bring you the*

**Annotated Edition**

*of*

**Hubbard's Guide to Moosehead Lake and Northern Maine**

A

Burnt Jacket Publishing

Classic Release

## Annotated Edition Introduction

*"The book, aside from its illustrations, is not meant to be entertaining, and they who seek in its pages any elaborate or detailed descriptions of scenery will be disappointed."*

*Lucius L Hubbard*

I would, if I could, tell Hubbard I found this book quite entertaining. I found myself using *The Maine Atlas and Gazetteer* to follow the itineraries he provided. I enjoyed researching many of the remote places for the first time. The pages provided hours of entertainment as I discovered names of ponds, streams, bogs, and more "dead-waters," than I can recall. I made a list and marked places I intend to visit. I spent hours on the internet researching the 'then and now' differences of some of the locations. Although, entertainment, I suppose, depends on your perspective.

I imagine Hubbard made the comment as a comparison to his earlier book, *"Woods and Lakes of Maine – A Trip from Moosehead Lake to New Brunswick in a Birch-Bark Canoe."* (From herein noted as **"Woods and Lakes of Maine."**) In that book he elaborated on his exploration in a day-by-day memoir with descriptive prose on the Maine woods. Within that text he describes scenery in enhanced detail, and includes many facts on animals and Maine geography. Thus, maybe, he considered readers would find **"Woods and Lakes of Maine,"** the more entertaining of his books.

Personally, I found both of Hubbard's books informative and entertaining. Through the process of editing these Maine classics I learned a great deal about Maine, and I am pleased to bring the history in these books to a new generation of readers.

My exploration of the tours, as Hubbard has called the itineraries, led to the idea of re-issuing this book which has been out of print for many decades. While many people may turn to the internet to search for hiking and paddling suggestions, there are several good reasons for having this book in print.

First, when you go to the north woods, there is no internet signal. Not yet anyway, and I can only wish that's the way it remains. It is nice to disconnect, even for a short time. So, relying on an electronic device to find directions, or hoping to read a blog post to find a trailhead, is a sure way to be disappointed, or worse – to get lost.

Second, with an internet search you can find areas of interest for hikes, and you can print out pages to take on your trip, but those are not as comprehensive or complete as this guide book. I find there is no substitute for a book I can hold in my hands; one in which I can flip from one section to the next; one in which I can earmark pages (yes, I do that); or, one in which I can write notes (yes, I do that too. It's okay, write in this book). A travel book is one that can travel with you, wherever you go – it is a planning tool, a field reference, a source of entertainment over lunch, or by the fire in the evening. It requires no battery, no charging cord, and no power to keep you informed and on track.

Third, Hubbard's book provides a 'then' perspective of what it was like back in the 1880s and 1890s in northern Maine. The book is more than a travel guide; it is a significant historical reference. The author included many facts of the late 1800s that readers and researchers will find valuable. Thankfully, the sections of Maine that Hubbard describes are not all that different 140 years after his first issue.

Sure, there are more *roads* since the original publication, depending on your definition of a road. The main road addition being the east-west *Golden Road*; a mostly-private gravel road owned by the logging companies that can be traveled to gain somewhat close access to the remote ponds, lakes, streams, and trails.

Sure, some towns Hubbard mentions no longer exist, for reasons you will discover within. And, sure, to access these locations most are now within a day's drive from Bangor, Portland, or a long day from Boston. It no longer takes a three-day train, stage, steamer, paddle trip, concluding with a three-mile canoe carry before you can prepare camp for the night. But now, as then, once you are *'there,'* you will find limited services at these locations; fewer even than during Hubbard's time. The farms, supply depots, and lodging houses for 'gentlemen travelers' Hubbard makes mention of, are long gone. A notable few sporting camps still remain scattered about, or have been built since, but for the most part you must carry-in what you will need, and carry-out when you leave.

As in the 1890s you will not hear, or see, vehicle traffic from your camp by a remote stream. At night, the absence of light pollution will provide you with a view of the stars exactly the way Hubbard saw them. Overall, the northern Maine woods are more the same, than they are different from when the book was first published.

In this edition, to supplement the *'then'* we have added the *'now'* in the form of references and annotations. New photographs supplement some of the original illustrations that have been restored and included in this edition. The original book also included various advertisements from outfitters, hotels, and rail companies. A few examples of these ads have been included within the sections and in the appendix as readers may find them entertaining. (I admit, I got a chuckle from the 1890 lodging ad that specifies, *"Fresh milk constantly on hand."* Contrast that amenity to the expectations from travelers today.)

Lastly, as a frequent vacationer to the north woods, I know of no other book as comprehensive as this one on the area of Maine included in the scope. It is true that the tours do not cover one-hundred-percent of the waterways or mountains in the region, but a wicked big chunk of northern Maine is included. This book will provide you with a starting point for further explorations where new trails and access points now exist.

Within these pages one will find fewer Indian place names, of which Hubbard specified in **"Woods and Lakes and Lakes of Maine."** So, in this regard, one book is the companion of the other.

It must be stated that the current editors take no responsibility for any inaccuracies on trails or access through waterways in this book. The text was written in the 1880s when access was much less restricted in the north woods than it is currently. Additionally, due to the removal of old dams, and the construction of new ones, some of the water landscape along the routes is different than what it once was. Sections of

Hubbard's 1899 map have been included to aid the reader with comparisons to a current map.

Today's explorers are expected to research their trip before attempting to navigate the woods and to be familiar with current maps. Do not rely solely on the descriptions in this text, and certainly not a GPS to identify your exact location, or all the side roads in the Maine north woods.

Additionally, since Hubbard's time, the Appalachian Trail has been blazed (1937), Baxter State Park designated (1931), and the Appalachian Mountain Club and the North Maine Woods Organization regulate a good portion of the forest. It is advised that you check the most recent and up-to-date information on access and fees from the various land managers.

*The Maine Atlas and Gazetteer* depicts camping sites along many of the trails, ponds, and lakes, but again, check for permits, fees and access based on location, as it may change. Always respect private land owners, camping rules, and by all means, do not have a fire without proper permits and even then, check the weather conditions. While the Maine Forest Rangers post fire conditions daily on the web, it is likely you will not be able to access from a remote campsite, so common sense must prevail.

Hubbard was not only a canoe-man, he was a train, steamer, and stagecoach traveler, which were the primary means of transportation in his time. The notes he made on using the trains for travel remain in the text as historical context because at that time trains serviced a good portion of Maine. Although the passenger trains have long since ceased operation, you can still enjoy a steamer ride on the *Katahdin*, the last operating one of its kind. The ship departs from Greenville and tours Moosehead Lake during the summer season.

Even though Hubbard published the tours with expected durations, which even he stated would require aggressive travel plans and constant movement, the itineraries in this book could last the leisurely explorer a lifetime of vacations camping out under the stars. There are so many places to visit and be entertained by all that nature has to offer, and this book can provide you with inspiration for exploration.

Hubbard started many of the sections with travel from Boston by train, the departure hub for many Maine summer visitors in the late 1800s. This should not distract the reader since you can easily pick up the routes on today's roadways of northern Maine.

Within some sections images of Hubbard's 1899 Map provide the reader a bearing on location. The Hubbard map was well regarded by sportsmen and travelers as the definitive source for the northern Maine landscape well into the 1900s. In fact, Maine Forester, George S. Kephart, in his memoir, *"Campfires rekindled: A Forester Recalls Life in the Maine Woods of the Twenties,"* refers to the Hubbard map as the bible map of navigational aids of the time; the time being the 1920s.

For any of the tours north of the Maine border, and into Canada, we anticipate you will follow the required border crossing rules that did not exist at the original writing. Unauthorized travel, even by canoe, across the boundary will be frowned upon.

As was done in the ***2020 Annotated Edition of Woods and Lakes of Maine***, we have added footnotes with supplemental information. Additionally, we have included new material that is inset within the original body of the text. These insets provide details about a particular location, Maine feature, or changes since Hubbard wrote this book. I am grateful to Fred Wilcox who wrote the insets on modern gear, canoes, fish and game, and campfires. When I asked Forester Fred if he was interested in collaborating on this book, he didn't hesitate to reply. In his 81st year, he now has his name on the cover of two Maine classic books covering the great outdoors.

In many sections, I have added the *Maine Atlas and Gazetteer* map number. This is important, because Maine is so large, and has so many mountains, ponds, streams, and lakes that names have been used more than once. Take for example the case of Mud Pond; it has been used, by my unofficial count, close to a dozen times (it's probably many more than that). I have a hunch some outdoorsmen have named a pond or two 'Mud' to keep the prime fishing grounds to themselves. The same may be true for ponds named Mosquito, Blood, and Snake – all actual pond names in the region. In all seriousness, there are multiple places named Horserace, Grand Pitch, The Forks, Hurd Pond, Elephant Mountain, and so forth. It is highly recommended you verify which you are headed to, and chart your course appropriately or you may find yourself in the wrong county. The area of Maine's Aroostook County alone (over 6,800 square miles) is larger than the states of Connecticut and Rhode Island combined.

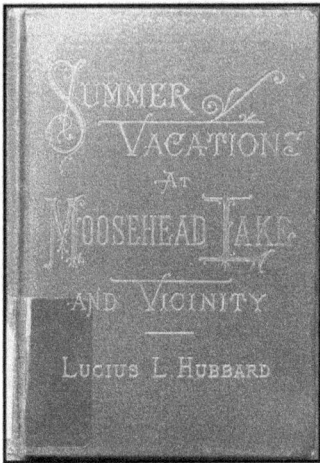

Cover of an 1889 original 4th edition.
Red hardcover with yellow inlaid lettering.

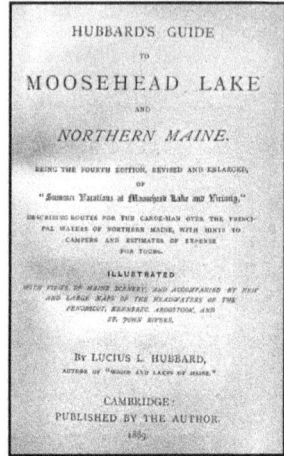

Title page within the cover to the left of the 1889 edition. Notice the difference in titles cover to interior.

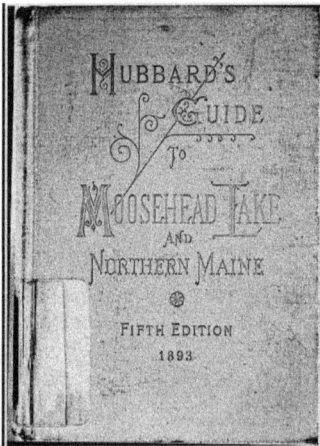

The 1893 fifth edition cover has been revised with the updated title.

*Photos courtesy of:*
*Special Collections Department - Raymond H. Fogler Library*
*University of Maine*

Hubbard issued five editions of this book. The first in 1879, a third in 1882, a fourth in 1889, and the fifth edition in 1893. The cover of the book up to the fourth edition, was titled, "Summer Vacations at Moosehead Lake and Vicinity." The final fifth edition was comprised of several smaller volumes, which were compiled into the final, *"Hubbard's Guide to Moosehead Lake and Northern Maine."*

In 1893 Hubbard included an Appendix of additional locations. I suspect this was added as an appendix due to the complications of type-setting in the 1880s to insert the new material into the interior of the book. These appendices have been incorporated where they fit in the tours for an improved reader experience in this 2020 edition. In a few situations, sections have been moved to a different chapter in an effort to improve the flow of the reading based on physical location of the tour.

While we have supplemented the book with notes and insets about the tours, we have also taken liberty to reorder the 'parts' of the volume. *"Part First"* and *"Part Third,"* which included Hubbard's tips for campers and game laws have been moved to the appendix. The reason being, much of the information no longer applies in the current day. However, within the appendix, notes have been included on modern gear, provisions, and game laws. This change moved *"Part Second,"* covering the tours, to the beginning of the book. As this part begins the journey through Greenville, which is the gateway to the north woods of Maine, this is appropriate.

Most all other items in the book remain the same, this includes spelling common to the 1800s. One term that may confuse modern readers is Hubbard's use of "logon." He uses this term frequently in this book, as well as in, *"Woods and Lakes of Maine."* He defines this word in his *Introduction* as, "a loggers' term, a derivative of 'lagoon.'" It is meant to mean a shallow arm of a stream or pond, typically where lilies and grasses grow.

Keep in mind, the tours do not provide a circular loop where you start out in Greenville, Maine and find yourself back in town. The tours, like the Penobscot, go east, west, north, and south; they branch out in all directions. Pick and choose your desired location in northern Maine and you will likely find a Hubbard tour described in this book to aid your planning.

This is not a guide book for those seeking popular trails, such as within Baxter State Park. There are plenty of references for that location available. Hubbard, while he covers some of the mountain peaks across northern Maine, and he certainly appreciated scenic views, his primary focus was on water travel. I imagine this is because back in his time, they were traveling almost exclusively as sportsmen, not hikers seeking a view from above. Blazed trails to mountain tops were also not as common as they are today in the quantity we are afforded. The reader can find more information online from Maine trail sites for trailhead and current parking locations in the vicinity of each tour. Keep in mind, *"vicinity,"* could be a carry location, or mean a base camp that is miles from a trailhead. Readers can find these locations online or with a current *Maine Atlas and Gazetteer*.

I trust this book will be of interest to those who visit the waters around Moosehead Lake, and maybe you discover a new place to explore. For those who have a desire to experience the backwoods, this book will assist you in your planning, with a caveat – these pages are merely a primer into further research required for access, roads, and services you will require for your trip. For some of you the book may simply serve as an entertaining account of northern Maine history of the late 1800s, and in that case you will find an abundance of spectacular places described within.

I think Hubbard would be proud of what the people of Maine have done to keep the large swath of the state where he once traveled, wild and undeveloped. I am honored to be publishing this classic book during Maine's Bicentennial year.


Tommy Carbone

Greenville, Maine
August, 2020

## About Lucius L. Hubbard

# 2020 Edition

Lucius Lee Hubbard
1849-1933

Lucius Lee Hubbard was born at Cincinnati, Ohio, August 7, 1849. He attended Phillip Exeter Academy for two years, and graduated from Harvard in 1872. Following college, he traveled abroad studying the German language, history, and international law at the University of Bonn.

On September 29, 1875, he married Frances J. Lambard of Augusta, Maine. Until 1883, he resided in Cambridge, Massachusetts. Outside practicing the law, his interests were varied. He was an avid collector of stamps and he owned one of the largest collections of early Americana, including original Robinson Crusoe books. Ultimately, his personal fireproof library became too small to house his stamp and book collection and many were sold. Hubbard spent many vacations in the Moosehead Region and the remote north woods of Maine.

In 1877, he published a small book, entitled, *"Summer Vacations at Moosehead Lake and Vicinity."* This became a starting point for a number of books about northern Maine, which he compiled and published as, *"Hubbard's Guide to Moosehead Lake and Northern Maine."*

In the fall of 1881, Hubbard, along with a personal friend and two Indian guides, embarked on a journey of over 160 miles in a birch-bark canoe; that trip is the subject of his book, *"Woods and Lakes of Maine. A Trip from Moosehead Lake to New Brunswick in a Birch-bark Canoe."*

Hubbard also published a "Map of Northern Maine – Specially adapted to the Uses of Lumberman and Sportsmen." The map was of significant detail for the period.

His interest in minerals brought him to Europe, where in 1883 he earned a Ph.D., with a mineralogical focus.

For a more in-depth summary about the interesting life of Dr. Hubbard, see the biographical sketch added in, *"Woods and Lakes of Maine – A Trip from Moosehead Lake to New Brunswick in a Birch-Bark Canoe. 2020 Annotated Edition.*

# Hubbard's Guide

## to

## Moosehead Lake

## and

## Northern Maine

### *1893 Fifth Edition*

## Explanation

The demand for a guide-book to a comparatively small, wild region is necessarily limited, and its sales are unremunerative. People are apt to be contented if they have but a map of the region. In the present case the author would point to the fact that this guide-book tries to offset the errors that must exist in a map.

The public will hardly expect a fifth edition of a book to be printed "just for the fun of the thing." Hence, without an apology for so doing, the publisher has felt obliged to raise the price of the present issue (in paper, *without* map) to one dollar a copy.

*2020 Edition Note: In the 1893 fifth edition, Hubbard included the above explanation (partially reproduced here) on why he published the book and justification for a price increase. The $1.00 a copy price equates to about $23 in 2020 dollars.*

**Mt. Kineo from Kineo Cove**

(Sketch from Original Text)

**2020 Edition** - Mt. Kineo from Rockwood Landing

Copyright, 1893,

By Lucius L. Hubbard.


Original Publisher:

University Press:

John Wilson and Son, Cambridge.


2020 Edition New Material

Copyright Burnt Jacket Publishing

HUBBARD'S GUIDE

TO

# MOOSEHEAD LAKE

AND

NORTHERN MAINE.

*BEING THE FOURTH EDITION, REVISED AND ENLARGED,*

OF

"Summer Vacations at Moosehead Lake and Vicinity,"

DESCRIBING ROUTES FOR THE CANOE-MAN OVER THE PRINCIPAL WATERS OF NORTHERN MAINE, WITH HINTS TO CAMPERS AND ESTIMATES OF EXPENSE FOR TOURS.

ILLUSTRATED

*WITH VIEWS OF MAINE SCENERY, AND ACCOMPANIED BY NEW AND LARGE MAPS OF THE HEADWATERS OF THE PENOBSCOT, KENNEBEC, AROOSTOOK, AND ST. JOHN RIVERS.*

By LUCIUS L HUBBARD,

AUTHOR OF **"WOODS AND LAKES OF MAINE."**

CAMBRIDGE:

PUBLISHED BY THE AUTHOR.

1893.

TO THE

Friends and Companions

Who Have Shared with Him the Pleasures of Camping Out in
The Woods of Maine,

The Author

Affectionately Dedicates This Little Volume,

In the Earnest Hope That, Even If It Should Contain Nothing
New to Them, It Will At Least Serve

To Recall Bright Memories of Days

That Are Past.

## 2020 Table of Contents

# Introduction

*

To the care-worn business man and overworked student, no relaxation from the constant wear of their respective callings is so grateful as that which comes while camping in the woods. "The accompaniments of life are removed, and selfishness, ambition, and care have here no place; a man is most truly thrown upon his own resources. To be alone with nature, without book, without work, without care, without the slightest hindrance to wandering at your own sweet will, with a heart which beats 'true to the kindred points of heaven and home,' and to be for this purpose in the very heart of the Moosehead forests, is more than all the trout fishing, and almost the rival of the matchless views which meet the eye."[1] In the wild woods life is regenerated, and even after two weeks of camping out and canoeing one issues forth with renewed strength for the work of the coming year. Rest and recreation are an absolute necessity. A celebrated jurist of this country, no longer living, used to say he could do a year's work in ten months, but not in twelve.[2]

It then becomes a practical question, how deep into the forests must one penetrate with his birch-canoe to find this seclusion and relaxation, and what are the means of attaining them?

---

[1] Rev. Julius H. Ward, in Harper's Magazine, August, 1875.
**2020:** pages 350-364. A wonderful article about Moosehead Lake.

[2] **2020:** American financier and banker, J.P. Morgan (1837-1913) was later credited with this quote, but he one-upped it by saying he could do a year's work in <u>nine months</u>, but not in twelve. Since Morgan did not die until 1913, Hubbard is quoting someone earlier.

The advantage to canoe-men of having some definite and tangible information concerning the different lakes and water courses over which their routes may take them, is too well known by those persons who have camped out in the woods of Maine to need proof. It often happens that the tourist comes to a part of a stream where the difficulty of further progress seems insurmountable. After successful efforts made to overcome the obstacles which first appeared, others take their place, and the chain seems unending. The luckless canoe-man in ignorance turns back disappointed, and seeks an easier route elsewhere, when, if he had but known it, smooth water and a picturesque and attractive course lay before him, within easy reach.

With a knowledge of this need, gained by experience, the writer has prepared the following pages for the benefit of habitues of Moosehead Lake, and of others who may have in view a visit to some of the wilder localities in its vicinity. The brevity necessarily required in a pocket guide-book has caused him to set forth facts without any attempt at embellishment, plain, statistical facts, whose only function is to be useful. The book, aside from its illustrations, is not meant to be entertaining, and they who seek in its pages any elaborate or detailed descriptions of scenery will be disappointed.[3]

That part of the work devoted to camping is also merely an epitome. Many topics touched upon had to be passed over briefly, and left perhaps incomplete, while others of scarcely

---

[3] **2020:** In this edition, photos have been added along with insets pertinent to the location being described. In today's internet world the reader will find this book a useful guide to supplement with online research for current trail maps and writings by others for various excursions.

less importance had to be omitted altogether. The information and advice actually given is, moreover, very much condensed, and, such as it is, the writer offers it to beginners in the art of camping, as a stepping-stone to a more extended knowledge, which can best be obtained by experience.

He who goes into the woods to camp for the first time will be at a loss to understand many of the phrases in vogue among older campers and guides, some few of which, on account of their brevity, have been used in the following pages. The word "pitch" refers either to the resinous mixture used on canoes, to a small waterfall, or to the height of a stream. After a hard rain one may say, "There is a good pitch of water." "Rips" is a word used of a stretch of water, which is not long enough nor rough enough to be called "rapids." To "drop" a canoe over a "pitch" is to let it float over it, the canoe-man guiding it from the shore with a setting-pole, and with the "painter," or leading-rope.

A "landing" is a term used by lumbermen to denote a place cleared of bushes and trees on the bank of a stream or pond, to which the logs cut in winter are hauled, in anticipation of the spring floods.

"Logon," probably a derivative of "lagoon," means a very shallow arm of a stream or pond, where lilies and grass grow profusely.

The term "navigation" as used in the following pages refers to canoes, and readers will also note the difference between the right and left *banks* of a stream, and the same terms without the word "bank."

In presenting to the public this new edition of his *"Guide to Moosehead Lake and Northern Maine,"* the author owes a word of explanation for the many changes that have been made in the text. Portions of the information contained in former editions were gathered from third parties, who, in the main correct, nevertheless made no pretensions to exactness in their estimates of distances. In cases where, by subsequent personal examination of the ground, the author has found discrepancies, he has aimed to correct them, and now feels that the descriptions of the different canoe trips can be relied upon as fairly accurate. Some new matter has been added, chiefly in the form of an appendix[4], while many corrections have been made to the map.

In view of the improvement of both book and map, the author hopes that they may meet with the same kind reception accorded previous editions, and that he may be encouraged, in future editions, to lay before the public additional facts concerning a region that is yearly growing in favor with tourists, sportsmen, and health-seekers generally.

Cambridge, 1893

---

[4] **2020**: The new matter referred to has been incorporated within the 2020 Annotated Edition text at the applicable sections. Hubbard likely had added as an Appendix due to the complexity of typesetting required in 1893 to incorporate nearer to where the new information rightly belonged within the tours.

## A Note on Indian Nomenclature

**2020 Edition** – *The following note was initially included in the section after the "Ascent of Mount Ktaadn." It has been moved here as there are several instances of Indian nomenclature prior, and the reader may benefit to review these terms earlier.*

A great deal of interest has been manifested of late upon the subject of the Indian nomenclature of falls and lakes which occur in the course of the Penobscot River, and of mountains which rise near its banks. In the first place, as to the relative position of a fall and "dead-water" of the same name, Thoreau says, "This is generally the order of names as you ascend the river. First, the lake, or, if there is no expansion, the dead-water; then the falls; then the stream emptying into the lake, or river above, all of the same name."[5] This rule, or rather fact, seems, from the testimony of many of the Penobscot Indians, to hold good as far as Aboljackarmegas Falls, although John Pennowit, one of the oldest hunters of the tribe, has told the writer that they had no distinctive names for most of the "dead-waters" referred to, and consequently they can have no order of designating them. Above Abol Falls the so-called rule, by the same testimony seems to fail, for Nesowadnehunk Stream empties into the river *below* the falls of the same name, while the "dead-water" of that name is *above* the falls.

"The biggest mountain" near the Penobscot is pronounced by the Indians as if written "Ktaadn" (from the inseparable adjectival *kette* or *k't*, "greatest," and the inseparable generic, adene, "mountain"), and this spelling has been adopted by the

---

[5] *The Maine Woods.*

best authorities as more nearly correct than the form "Katahdin." For "Sourdnahunk" the writer has substituted "Nesowadnehunk," as agreeing more nearly with the Indian pronunciation. The latter spelling is used by Thoreau, and as the word is said to mean "stream flowing between the mountains," one can detect the generic *adene* better in the latter form than in the other, which consideration alone might well determine one's choice.

One of the first forms, if not the very first published, of the Indian name for the West Branch of the Penobscot at Nickatow is given by Greenleaf as "Che-too-kook" or "Che-sun-kook." The form given the writer by John Pennowit is "Ket-tegwe-wick," from *kctte*, "greatest," *tegwe*, "stream" (Râle), and wick, a form of the locative, "at the greatest stream."

---

### 2020 Edition

The full title of Hubbard's memoir book is, *"Woods and Lakes of Maine. A Trip from Moosehead Lake to New Brunswick in a Birch-bark Canoe. To Which are Added Some Indian Place-Names and Their Meanings Now First Published."*

In that book, within the chapters and in a detailed appendix, you will find Hubbard documented the Native American names of mountains and lakes that in many cases are no longer found on the maps. He includes not only the meaning of the name, but the derivation from the language, many of which he compiled from first hand conversations and interviews.

# MOOSEHEAD LAKE AND IMMEDIATE VICINITY

\*

## *Boston to Bangor*

For a number of years past the quickest, and perhaps as comfortable a way as any of making the journey between Boston and Moosehead Lake has been to leave the former place in the evening, breakfast at the depot in Bangor, and proceed in the morning train from that city. Or one could leave Boston in the morning and pass the night in Bangor; but the uncertainty of finding good hotel accommodation, added to the inconvenience of thus breaking the journey, made people prefer the more direct way, albeit it was the more fatiguing. Improvements lately made in the train service of the several railroads along the route render it possible to reach Kineo in one day from Boston[6], either by way of Bangor, or by a short cut via Newport and Dexter, over a new railroad from Dexter to Dover. Full particulars are contained in a time-table at the commencement of this volume. By either route baggage is now checked through to Kineo[7], but it may be well for passengers to see that their trunks are put on board the steamer at West Cove (Greenville Junction).

---

[6] **2020**: Passenger trains no longer service the Moosehead area, or much of Maine at all. The best you can do currently is the Amtrak Downeaster from Boston and go as far as Brunswick, Maine by rail, which isn't much use if your destination is the north woods. The drive from Boston is about six hours, and from the Bangor airport about two hours.

[7] **2020**: Getting your 'trunk' to Kineo, if you still happen to travel with one, will do you as much good as a train ticket, since there is no longer a resort hotel to stay at on the peninsula.

The train of the Maine Central Railroad for Moosehead Lake is made up at and starts from the principal depot in Bangor, stopping for passengers at the Exchange St. depot, on the east side of the Kenduskeag river, a quarter of a mile beyond.

**Hubbard's Map of Moosehead Lake Area - 1893**

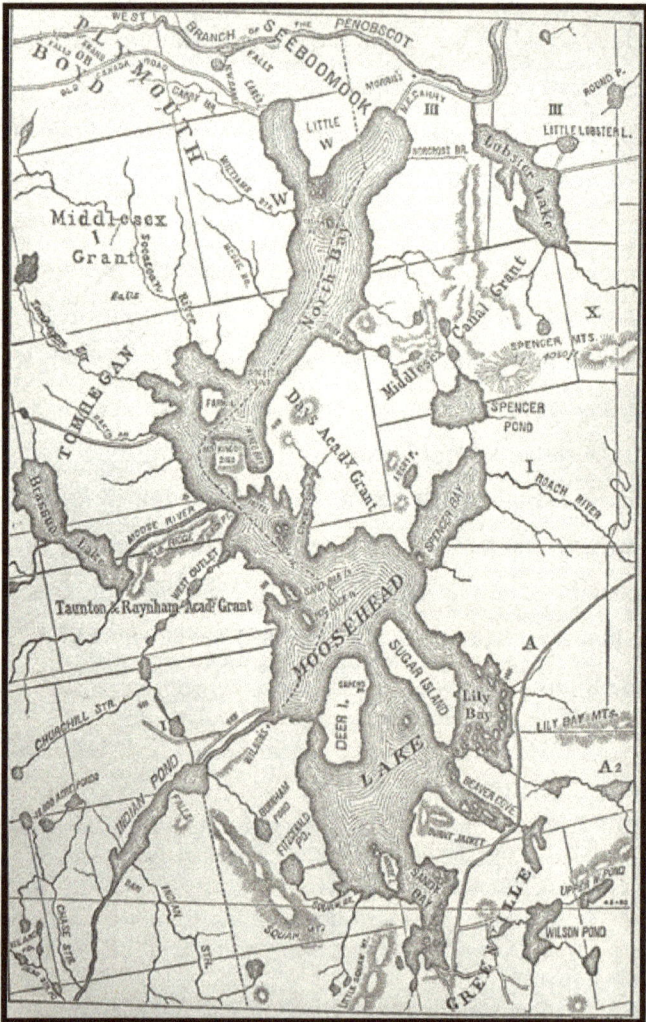

## *Bangor to the Lake*

Leaving Bangor at half past seven in the morning, the train carries one along the west bank of the Penobscot, over the European and North American Railway, which is now a part of the Maine Central system, twelve miles, to Oldtown, where it goes on to the tracks of the Bangor and Piscataquis Railroad. Here from the car window can soon be seen, across the water, the Indian island,[8] with its church and numerous dwelling houses, —an object of curiosity to all strangers.

In clear weather good views of Mt. Ktaadn can be had from South Lagrange and from Milo. At the latter station connection is made with a train for Katahdin Iron Works, and at Monson Station with one for Monson, twenty minutes' ride beyond, a town already famous for its slate quarries, for the picturesqueness of its situation, and for the bracing quality of its atmosphere.

The country through which the cars pass is pretty, although not specially interesting until they near the town of Blanchard, beyond Monson Station. Russell Mountain and other peaks then appear on the left, frowning down on the valley of the Piscataquis. The road-bed lies on the brow of a ridge east of the valley, and crosses several deep ravines over high trestle-work, affording many a picturesque view of the valley and of the mountains beyond.

At Shirley the cars leave the ridge along which they have been cautiously creeping, and from this point the route lies through flat and swampy land, and emerges finally at West

---

[8] **2020**: Indian Island is Penobscot Indian reservation land near Old Town on the Penobscot River.

Cove, at the foot of Moosehead Lake, at the junction of the International or Canadian Pacific Railroad. The last mile or two of road lies on the side of a "kame."[9]

**Foot of Moosehead Lake - (Approaching Greenville)**

\*

West Cove, or Greenville Junction, is as yet a small but growing settlement, which has sprung into existence since the completion of the Bangor and Piscataquis road to the lake, in July, 1885. The Moosehead Inn, a large and commodious hotel recently built, will be found convenient for transients. Hotel stages connect here for Greenville, a mile and a quarter to the east. Passengers for Kineo continue their journey up the lake by steamer.

---

[9] **2020:** Hubbard places *kame* in italics throughout the book. A kame is defined in geology as a steep-sided mound of sand and gravel, typically left by a melting sheet of glacial ice.

From West Cove Spencer Mountain (Sabōta´wan) is visible on the north, while the Squaw Mountains lie immediately on the west.[10]

**2020 Edition**
**A Note on the Maps Included in this Edition**
Dr. Hubbard was not only a distinguished geologist and author, he was also a map maker. His *"Map of Northern Maine – Specially Adapted to the Uses of Lumberman and Sportsmen,"* was updated and reissued several times.

The version referenced in this book is his 1899 edition. Hubbard's map is finely detailed and it is impossible to reproduce in a book format in full size. A version can be found on the internet where you can zoom in on specific locations. In this book, we have included sections of his map as relevant to the tour being described in his writing.

These map sections were not included in the original release of this book, but rather have been added to make it easier for the reader to gain a sense of location. While the Hubbard map is fairly accurate when it comes to water bodies, the editors encourage you to use more up to date maps when navigating the north woods. For the most part, names of mountains, lakes, and ponds are the same, but several have been renamed since Hubbard's time. Roads, depending on your definition of such, now traverse the area and canoe carries may or may not exist. A good gazetteer

[10] **2020:** Hubbard usually uses the mountain names as told to him by the native American Indians. See, ***"Woods and Lakes of Maine, 2020 Edition."***

will include current canoe and kayak launch locations for lake and river trips.

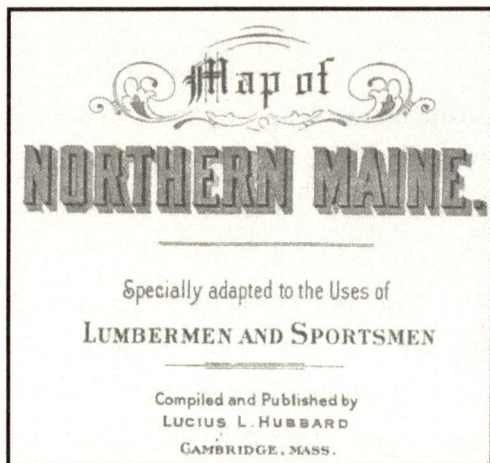

**Map of**

**NORTHERN MAINE.**

Specially adapted to the Uses of

LUMBERMEN AND SPORTSMEN

Compiled and Published by
LUCIUS L. HUBBARD
CAMBRIDGE, MASS.

**Hubbard Map Title, 1899**

In addition to including the Hubbard map references, this edition includes references to the map numbers of the, "Maine Atlas and Gazetteer." The Gazetteer, originally published by Delorme, is the de facto standard when it comes to an up to date navigational guide of Maine. Many editions have been published over the years. The map numbers in the book refer to the 22$^{nd}$ edition of the gazetteer.

Since maps are continuously updated, the reader is expected to refer to the latest information available. Luckily, lakes, ponds, and streams are terrific navigational markers and you will easily be able to orient to the location even on a different map.

The Hubbard map of Northern Maine is public domain, and as of this writing the file is available at DigitalMaine.com. The file may be reviewed online or downloaded to your computer.

*

**Greenville Junction, 2020**
The depot building is currently being restored through
donations and the work of volunteers.

*

## Greenville and Vicinity

Greenville, a small village with one church and about two hundred inhabitants, is at the southern end of Moosehead Lake, on the arm called the East Cove, and is the focus of the logging operations on the upper Kennebec and Penobscot waters. The advent of two railroads in recent years has stimulated business at Greenville, and all is bustle and activity where formerly existed the monotony of a quiet country resort.

Apart from its being a silent witness of this activity there is nothing, in summer or winter, specially to interest strangers in Greenville, more than in many other favorite country resorts. The view of the lake from the village is pretty, although circumscribed, but perhaps the mountaintops, and the snatches of water visible among the rocky and wooded islets near at hand, awaken a larger anticipation of the scenes and enjoyment still to come.

There are two hotels in Greenville, the Eveleth and Lake Houses, only the latter of which pretends, of late years, to cater to summer visitors. Guests can obtain teams at reasonable rates, with or without a driver, to make excursions to Wilson Pond or elsewhere in the neighborhood. Campers-out will find several good stores at Greenville, where they can get almost all the necessary articles of camp fare, or of camp equipage, including canoes.

---

### 2020 Edition

Greenville is different, and the same, as Hubbard described in 1893. There is more than one church now, and year-round residents numbered 1,646 as of the 2010 census. You can no longer take a passenger train to reach Greenville, but it still remains the gateway to the north woods. Currently there are a number of hotels that cater to sportsmen and tourists alike. Sporting camps and Maine Guides are available for the tourists who wish to experience a guided fishing, hunting, or moose tour trip.

At the time Hubbard was writing this book, one of best rod handlers in the north woods was Fly Rod Crosby. That was her nickname of course. Her real name was Cornilia Thurza Crosby. She was Maine's **first** registered guide (1897), she shot the last legally killed caribou in Maine (1898), and marketed the Maine outdoors at the New York Sportsman's Exposition in 1898 at Madison Square Garden.

Before Crosby became a legend of the Maine outdoors, she had careers in the telephone and banking industry. She was also a contributor to the papers with a syndicated column called, *Fly Rod's Notebook.*

It is interesting the way Hubbard noted, "there is nothing, in summer or winter, specially to interest strangers in Greenville, more than in many other favorite country resorts." Although we don't consider the region 'a resort' in the modern sense, and most visitors to the Maine north woods come for the wilderness experience, there are now two small golf courses, a few high-end inns, and several restaurants, a couple of which remain open all year long. For winter activities, along with snowmobiling and outdoor recreation, the ski center has once again been operating.

Greenville is now, as it was then, a quiet mountain and lake town with plenty to do for those who love the outdoors. This book provides the reader with tours around and beyond Greenville. The amenities in town will provide the visitor with a vacation to remember should you choose to remain close to the village, or to supply yourself with an outfit, or maybe a guide, to go deeper into the woods.

## Wilson Ponds

Near Greenville there are a number of ponds and streams in which trout abound, and which sportsmen frequently visit. The most noteworthy are the Wilson Ponds, the nearer of which is three miles distant, to the east. A good wagon road runs two miles of the way, to a farm where teams can be left and baited. The other mile may be walked, and the path leads over the farm, down a steep bank to the lower and larger pond. Fish are taken here almost exclusively with bait,[11] and it is said that when they bite here, they will not rise in the lake, and *vice versa*. Boats can be hired at fifty cents a day.

A boat-ride across the lower pond and a short walk over a good path take one to the upper pond, which lies very prettily ensconced among surrounding mountains. Gerrish Pond, west of Big Wilson, Eagle Stream, Coffee House Stream (so called from the fact that a tavern or "coffee-house" stood on its banks in former days when the road to Moosehead ran due north through the centre of Monson), and other tributaries of Wilson Stream contain many a trout-hole, while numerous waterfalls along their courses, high and picturesque, add to the pleasure of a day's ramble through the cool recesses of the surrounding forests.

Three miles up the Lily Bay Road a hotel for permanent boarders has been built by Mr. Victor McFarlane on the old Cameron farm. It affords a magnificent view of Squaw Mt., the lake, and the pretty islands below.[12] Other pleasant walks and drives may be had in different directions, and a variety of pretty excursions may be made on the lake by sail-boat or canoe. With all its varied attractions one can spend a few days in the neighborhood of Greenville very pleasantly and quietly.

### *Fitzgerald and Squaw Ponds * Squaw Mountain*

From the foot of the lake it is about six miles by water to Johnson's Landing, a mile west of North Squaw Brook, whence

---

[11] **2020**: Refer to current Maine Fishing Regulations.

[12] **2020**: Currently there are two inns at the crest of Blair Hill in this approximate location.

a logging road leads, half a mile, direct to Fitzgerald Pond. Squaw Pond can be reached from West Cove by a path two and a half miles long, or one can go the whole distance overland from Greenville, perhaps a mile further. A boat is usually kept at the pond.[13] Squaw Brooks are not navigable by canoes for more than a few rods.[14] Fishing is sometimes good at their mouths, and in the ponds of which they are the outlets.

The ascent of Squaw Mountain is made most easily over a path bushed out and cut anew in 1880. It leaves the north side of North Squaw Brook, and for two miles or more runs nearly west with a slight rise, being thus far an old logging road and wet in some places. It then turns to the left, crosses a gully, and rises abruptly, the entire distance to the summit being about six miles, and requiring somewhat less than four hours to accomplish it comfortably. Half a mile below the summit are a miniature pond, a brook of good water, and excellent campground well protected from the wind. A magnificent panorama opens out before one from the summit, the view taking in mountain, lake, and forest for miles, and including the Spencer Mts., Ktaadn, Joe Merry, White Cap, and other peaks near Katahdin Iron Works, Barren, Boarstone, Russell, Bigelow, Abraham, Miseree, and Bald, from the southeast, around to the west and northwest. Squaw Mt. is 2,267 feet above Moosehead Lake, or 3,262 feet above sea-level. The descent to the lake can be made in two hours.

---

[13] **2020:** The boat from 1893 is no longer there.
[14] **2020:** A rod is English measure of distance equal to 16.5 feet (5.029 meters).

**2020 Edition**

There are several name changes at this location since the initial publication of this book. Fitzgerald Pond is now known as Mountain View Pond. Additionally, in the early 2000s the Maine legislature removed the word 'squaw' from place names. North Squaw Brook is now Moose Brook, Squaw Pond is Moose Pond, Big Squaw Mountain is Big Moose Mountain, and Little Squaw is Little Moose Mountain.

The word squaw is retained in this book for historical accuracy to the text, the meaning of the word at the time, and the factual linguistic analysis. Interested readers may review the works written that have more fully explained the origin of the word to the Algonquian word "esqua," "squa," and "skwa," which refers to the totality of being female, or woman, and is a totally decent word. A fuller explanation is contained in a new appendix added to this edition as the word relates to the legend of Mt. Kineo and Squaw Mountains.

In 1905, the Forest Service erected the first fire tower in the United States at the top of Squaw Mountain. The tower was in operation until 1968 when air patrols replaced watchmen. The tower was relocated to the Greenville visitor center. A replica of the watchman's cabin has been added in recent years.

The summits of Big Moose and Little Moose provide some of the most fabulous views of Moosehead Lake. Parking locations for the trails are well marked on current maps of the area.

**Squaw Mountain Fire Tower**

**Replica of Squaw Mountain Watchman's Cabin**

*

## *Moosehead Lake*

Each renewed visit to Moosehead Lake attaches one more firmly to its magic presence and lovely views, every feature of which offers the returning traveler an indescribable welcome. Stretching here and there in irregular and broken confusion, its coves and bays grope about, as it were, like the arms of a cephalopod studded with islands numerous as the days of the year, from the tiny rocklet with its scanty, half-starved offspring of bushes, to the more extended area, covered with prodigal growths of fir and spruce; surrounded by mountains whose soft outlines and ever-varying tints are objects of untiring admiration; — these, and a thousand other beauties that steal unconsciously into the spirit, make up a combination that cannot fail to charm.

Moosehead Lake, nine hundred and ninety-five feet above sea-level, is about thirty-eight miles long, and varies in width from one to fourteen miles. Several hotels and taverns have sprung up, here and there, on its shores, and of late years the continuity of its dark green forests has been broken by the bright patches of farm lands, and white farm-houses peep up in many places, to indicate the thrift of their sturdy owners.

---

### 2020 Edition

Over 11,000 years ago, Moosehead Lake was formed by a melting glacier. The lake originally drained into the Penobscot River at the north end, near what is now named Seboomook Lake. About 8,000 years ago the land north of the lake, relieved of the prior weight of the glacier, rose. Following the land mass shift, the lake drainage moved to the East Outlet into the Kennebec River.

Interestingly, how Moosehead Lake came to be known by this name is a mystery. In, "Spragues Journal of Maine History," Vol. XIV, No. 2, from 1926 over two pages (p. 87 – 88) is devoted to researching the origin of the lake becoming named Moosehead, with no conclusion. The article title is, "History of the Chadwick Survey from Fort Pownal in the District of Maine to the Province of Quebec in Canada in 1764."

---

The piece is written by Mrs. Fannie Hardy Eckstorm. The Journal editor describes Mrs. Eckstorm as, "one of Maine's talented writers, herself a lover of Maine's ancient history and a historian and research worker, faithful and efficient."

Mrs. Eckstorm begins the discussion of the history of the naming of Moosehead Lake, fittingly with reference to Lucius L Hubbard's writing about the lake's name in, *Woods and Lakes of Maine,* from 1884.

Taking a summary from the journal article, the names given to the lake are as follows:

- 1761 – Moose-deer Lac or Lake Orignal – (Montrésor's Map)
- 1761 – Keseben (form of K'chi-sebem – the big lake)
- 1764 – Lake Sebem (Chadwick map)
- 1776 – Xsebem (contracted form of K'chi-sebem and often represented as K'sebem)
- 1786 – Moose Lake (Jay's Map)
- 1795 – Moose Pond (Sullivan)

Prior to 1884 and Hubbard's review of the Augusta Land Office plans, the lake is referred to as, Seboumook, Sebaumock, Seeboumock, and Seboumock.

In 1881 Hubbard includes the earlier Indian names as printed on his maps, but by this time, Moosehead Lake had become commonplace as the name of Maine's largest lake.

In 1926 Mrs. Eckstorm notes, "the English from Maine and Massachusetts continued to use K'sebem or simply, "The Lake," almost to present."

Mrs. Eckstorm concludes, ***"When the name of "Moosehead Lake" came in, I do not know; nor why."***

\*

Adding to this research, we know that in 1853, Thoreau traveled to Moosehead and asked his Indian guides why the name was called Moosehead. They pondered and discussed the native words of Sebamook and Sebemook. The Indians continued and said, "the whites called it Moosehead Lake, because Mount Kineo, which commands it, is shaped like a moose's head, and that Moose River was so called "because the mountain points right across the lake to its mouth."

Thus, we know as early as the mid-1800s the common name was already being used, at least by the non-native inhabitants.

I propose the following pictures for you to decide why sometime between 1795 and the mid-1800s the name "Moosehead Lake" became commonplace. The naming as attributed to the legend of Glusgehbeh is given in, "*Katahdin, Pamola, & Whiskey Jack – Stories from the Maine Woods,*" by Tommy Carbone.

From, Montrésor's Map, 1761

Lake is labeled as:

Moose-Deer

and

Lac or Lake Orignal

This map legend states, "*made, probably in 1761, by Colonel John Montresor, British Engineer.*"

| | |
|---|---|
|  | From, Chadwick's Map, 1764<br>Labeled as: Lake Sebem<br><br>*The Chadwick Map of 1764 from the original in The Colonial Office, London reduced to about one-fourth* |
| <br><br>Sebaim L. indicated Moosehead Lake. *(A small oval)*<br>Chenosbec indicated Chesuncook Lake. *(A larger depiction)* | From, A General Map of the Northern British Colonies, 1776 (Similar in 1783)<br>Labeled as: Sebem L.<br><br>*NORTHERN BRITISH COLONIES IN AMERICA. THE PROVINCE OF QUEBEC, THE GOVERNMENTS OF NEWFOUNDLAND, NOVA-SCOTIA, NEW-ENGLAND AND NEW-YORK* |
| <br><br>*Certainly not the actual shape.* | Osgood Carleton's 1795 map of the district of Maine. If this labeling is original, this would be the earliest notation. Why this map was not mentioned by Mrs. Eckstorm is unknown. |

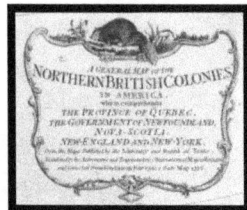

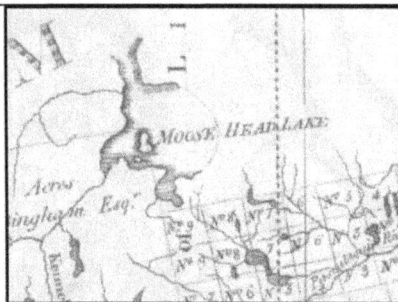

| | From, Colton Map of Maine, 1857<br><br>Labeled as: "Moosehead Lake."<br>The outline has taken shape. |
| --- | --- |
| | From, Hubbard's Map, 1899<br><br>Labeled as: "Moosehead Lake."<br>inc. Indian names of Sebamook and Xsebem. |

*Above images are only pertinent sections of the noted maps.*
*All maps are in the public domain and available online.*

Maybe the question is not *when*, Moosehead Lake became known as such, but *who* first drew the lake with some semblance of its most realistic shoreline. Sometime after 1800 maps began to indicate the true shape of the lake. On Colton's 1857 map of Maine, the shape of Moosehead Lake is closely realized. In 1874, John Way Jr. of Boston published a map with a fairly accurate depiction. The outline view likely led to the commonplace name being adopted.

At the foot of the lake will be found boats of all sizes and descriptions. Tourists go up the lake either in sailboats, which are to let by the day or week with the services of their owners, and as many more guides as may be necessary, or they take passage on one of the steamers which ply regularly between the foot of the lake and Kineo. The latter make two trips a day in the season between these places, and in the summer season run daily from Kineo to the head of the lake. Their captains are very obliging, and to accommodate parties often go out of their regular course to the East Outlet, Spencer Narrows, and other points less distant. At almost any time a steamer may be chartered for a day or excursion at reasonable rates.

## 2020 Edition

The first steamboat was built on the shores of Moosehead Lake in 1836. Many more would follow, being built by local shipbuilders, shipped in by train, and in one case pulled by 50 oxen uphill from south of Guilford. In the late 1800s and early 1900s it is estimated that between 25 and 50 steamers navigated Moosehead Lake.

Many of these steamers were the workhorses of the north woods. The steamers delivered lumbermen, supplies, cement to build the northern dams, and sometimes even train cars. The steamers also played a part in dragging booms of logs down the lake to the Kennebec River for log drives.

Once Moosehead became a tourist destination, the steams also ferried passengers to Rockwood, Kineo, Northeast Carry, and Seboomook.

Many of the steamboats were burned to their hulls and subsequently sunk. Recently, a documentary film has been made about the sunken steamboats of Moosehead Lake. If you paddle East Cove, or tour slow enough in a motorboat, you might just see the remains of one on the bottom of the lake.

The only surviving and operational steamboat on the lake today is the steel-hulled Katahdin II, which was built in 1914 at Bath Iron Works. The 102 foot long ship has since been retrofitted with a diesel engine and offers tours of the lake.

*

A telegraph line is now open at all seasons to Greenville, Wilson's at the East Outlet, and Mt. Kineo House.

Those who go up the lake from Greenville, instead of from West Cove, find themselves threading their way among a number of small islands, passing to the right and almost within touching distance of Mile Island with its white barrel-capped mast, then almost grazing on the other side Ledge Island, the most prominent mass of granite in the lake. West Cove, the point of land north of it, and the sloping sides of Moose Island glide by on the left successively, and the steamer is abreast of Burnt Jacket Cliff on the east in quite an open expanse of water, from which a fine prospect is had of Squaw Mt. Elephant Mt. is prominent on the right, and glimpses may be had of White Cap Mt. further east.

The steamer's course then lies past Birch Island, between Deer and Sugar Islands, which are so large as to be undistinguishable from the mainland. Emerging from her narrow channel she has now accomplished half of her journey (ten miles), and enters the widest part of the lake, where it is fourteen miles across from the Kennebec Dam to the head of

Spencer Bay. Beyond the latter the two Spencer Mountains, round Kokadjo, and long Sabohtawan, whose summits have been visible from West Cove and from time to time from the surface of the lake, now stand out in all their immensity, no foot-hills near to dwarf their proportions. East of them, on a clear day, Ktaadn's mightier but more distant mass discloses its rugged outlines and more varied contrasts of light and shadow, calling forth expressions at once of surprise and admiration.

North and west of the Spencers is Lobster Mt., to the left of it Little Kineo, Dry Mt., and Kineo, whose form, all but its very summit, long and flat, has hitherto been hidden from sight, while northwest and west the Blue Ridge, opposite Kineo, massive Bald Mt, and the forked peaks of Mts. Abraham and Bigelow can all be seen distinctly on a clear day.

### East Outlet * Indian Pond

West of Deer Island are the where the Kennebec resumes its course, previously interrupted by the lake at the mouth of Moose River. This is now a station of the International R. R., has a small hotel, and is a favorite fishing-ground in September. Black, Green, and Snake Islands[15] lie in the lake near the shore just above the outlet.

The Kennebec is very rapid immediately below the dam, and although a part of the distance between the dam and Indian Pond is easy to run, it is considered safer to be hauled across, five miles, over a good road. On the right bank of the river, about two miles below the dam, is a farm where a team can be secured to do the necessary hauling. A road runs from the same

---

[15] **2020:** One of at least two islands in the lake by such name.

farm to Churchill Stream. Indian Pond is divided into two parts, connected by a thoroughfare, and altogether is over three miles long. There is good fishing at the mouth of West Outlet Stream, in the thoroughfare and at the outlet of the pond. Below this point the river is wild and "ragged" for seven miles, and canoes seldom venture to brave the perils of its navigation.

### Roach Pond

Ten miles from the Kennebec Dam, on the opposite or east side of the lake, is Spencer Bay, which extends northeast four miles from narrows of the same name. Into its upper end empty Spencer Brook and Roach River. The latter stream flows some six or seven miles from Roach Pond.[16]

Roach Pond is rapid, rocky, and hard to navigate. A road lies on the right bank. The better way to reach the pond is by road from Lily Bay. A tavern stands on the shore of Lily Bay, near the mouth of North Brook.[17] From here to Roach Pond is seven miles, and to Greenville, thirteen. A buckboard can be procured at the Lily Bay House to haul one to Ray's, at the outlet of Roach Pond, where there is a substantial hotel with all the comforts which care and attention can provide in this isolated region. The ride is rather rough, and occupies about two hours and a half. At the dam in the river, near the hotel, and in pools

---

[16] **2020:** In 1913 the Maine legislature acted to rename the Roach River and the Roach Ponds to Kokadjo River and Kokadjo Ponds. In 1936, the United States Board on Geographical Names explicitly noted these bodies of water as, "*First Roach Pond* and (Not *Lower Roach Pond*, *Roach Pond* and *Kokadjo Lake*, nor *First Kokadjo Lake*." The Indian names are covered by Hubbard in, "Woods and Lake of Maine."

[17] **2020:** What a surprise a tavern in this location would be. South of here you will find Lily Bay State Park. The coves and tiny islands will provide a day of paddling exploration.

below the dam, and also at the upper end of the pond, good trout fishing is to be had. From the mouth of South Brook on the east side a good logging road leads two miles southerly to Big Lyford (sometimes called Little Pleasant) Pond, passing around its west side to the south where it branches, one fork leading down the West Branch of Pleasant River to the Gulf, and the other leading northerly to Big Lyford dam, thence Easterly two miles to the West Branch Ponds. These latter lie close under the main peak of White Cap, and the fisherman may be sure of good sport here. With an early start from Roach Pond one can visit these secluded ponds and return comfortably the same day, allowing three or four hours for rest and recreation. There are plenty of trout in Big Lyford Pond, although they are not very large, and report speaks well in this respect of the Little Lyford Ponds,[18] some five miles lower down the river.

The road from Roach Pond to Big Lyford runs in the opposite direction along Roach Pond, crosses North Brook a mile and a quarter from its mouth, and turning west follows the town line for nearly four miles until it joins the Lily Bay road just east of Ray's.

The "South Inlet" is for three-eighths of a mile a broad and sluggish stream, running through a bog where the trees have been killed by high water, an inviting locality for ducks and larger game. From this end of the pond Kokadjo and Sabohtawan, the latter, not now the rounded peak it seems to be from Moosehead Lake, but a long ridge running nearly east and

---

[18] **2020:** Much of the land in this region is public reserved land and some is managed by the Appalachian Mountain Club. See online information for trails, access, and fees.

west and terminating on the east in a precipitous bluff, are conspicuous on the north, and White Cap with its threefold summit bounds the line of sight on the south. From the "North Inlet," in addition to White Cap, may be seen Baker Mt. and many peaks of the Lily Bay group. This is, on the whole, the most attractive part of the pond, except for outdoor camping facilities, which are not of the best. A good log-camp, however, just above the mouth of the brook, is not altogether uninviting, and the brook itself, winding through a boggy meadow, is an acquisition which may outweigh other disadvantages of location. Up this brook for nearly a mile and a quarter the water is sluggish and fairly deep. Beyond that point it becomes more rapid and shallow, and canoe navigation for the remaining two miles is, in ordinary seasons, a matter of some difficulty. At high water, however, a canoe can be poled up to the Second Pond.

The brook between Second and Third Ponds is only two and a half miles long, and is rather easier to navigate than the other. From a small mountain back of Shaw Farm fine views can be had of Penobscot, Second, Third, and Fourth Roach Ponds,[19] and Trout Pond. Roach Pond is about five miles long.

### Spencer Pond * Lucky Pond

Spencer Pond empties through Spencer Brook, two miles, into the bay of the same name. In low water a canoe will have to be dragged up the brook, or carried over a good road, which lies to the west of it. At the western end of the pond, which is about a mile and a half in diameter and substantially round, is

---

[19] **2020:** Interestingly, in this chain of ponds there is a First, Second, Third, Fourth, Sixth, and Seventh Roach pond, but the fifth is absent.

a bog where cranberries grow in profusion. The usual camping ground is on the northeast side of the pond, diagonally across from the outlet, and about midway between the fishing grounds, two small streams which come into the pond, one on the north, and the other at the southeast corner. The north brook is sometimes hard to find. Its outlet is concealed by several small grassy islands. A mile up the brook is Little Spencer Pond. Spencer Mountains lie to the east of the pond; the nearer peak (Kokadjo, Kettle Mountain) rises abruptly almost from the shore, and is 3,035 feet high. Into Spencer Bay, on the west, empties a brook which comes from Lucky Pond.

This little sheet of water is rather narrow, and about three quarters of a mile long. It is a boggy place, and good ground for deer and caribou. A canoe can run up the brook some distance in "dead" water, and one then steps out into the road which runs up the right side of the stream to the dam, where it crosses and goes around the pond. It is only about fifty rods from the head of the "dead" water to the pond, and little more than a mile from the latter to the lake.

## On Moosehead Lake – East of Spencer Bay

Six miles from Capen's Landing on Deer Island the steamer passes Hog Back and Sand Bar Islands on the left, and as it approaches its goal the indistinct cluster of bright buildings at the foot of Mount Kineo is more easily separated into its component parts. Two miles from Sand Bar, Moody Islands are passed, on the right, and after two miles more the boat steams into the cove just east of the hotel, and is soon moored to its wharf.

## *Mount Kineo*

Mount Kineo, the most imposing mountain in the neighborhood, is midway up the lake, and, connected with its eastern shore by a narrow neck of land, forms quite a promontory. It is 763 feet above the level of the lake, or 1,758 feet above sea-level. A sheer precipice on the south and east sides, it falls away less abruptly towards the west, and slopes gradually to the north, affording at its base very good farming land. On this slope, at Hardscrabble (Point), is raised, each year, a considerable quantity of grain and hay, on which the Kineo House stock is fed.

The eastern cliff of the mountain hangs over Kineo Bay. Its perpendicular height above the water is over seven hundred feet, and the lake near its base is 231 feet deep.

From the cliff, skirting around northeast, runs a very pretty beach, divided, by a stretch of rocky, wooded shore, into two parts, — Cliff Beach, less than a mile from the hotel, and Pebble Beach, a mile and a half from it. From Table Rock off Cliff Beach, a few yards from shore, good fishing may be had late in the season. In fact, good fishing may be had, from canoes, all around Kineo Bay, and all the way around the mountain.

The south cliff is inaccessible except in one place near the western end, up a rift in the rock, where a flight of broad stairs offers a safe foothold for a steep climb. The descent of the mountain by this route, to the hotel, can be made in half an hour.

The ascent may also be made from the west corner of the mountain, — Kineo Point, — and necessitates a boat ride of less than a mile from the "Three Sisters," a group of pine-trees on the beach west of the hotel.

Two and a half or three hours are enough to accomplish the round trip comfortably, and the view one gets from the summit well repays the toil of climbing. A cool spring on the top furnishes refreshing drink to the thirsty.

From a point on the water, between Kineo Point and the Three Sisters, and some distance further from shore than on the direct line between them, may be seen a good profile, on the southeast comer of the mountain.

## Legend of Kineo

The legend of Kineo, as formerly given in these pages, is now omitted, because the writer has been unable to find any familiarity with or confirmation of it among the Maine Indians of today.[20] The word "Kineo" is said to mean "high bluff," and if this meaning is correct, the mountain can certainly never have been named by the Indians from one of their chieftains, but rather the reverse would be more likely. Kineo Mountain seems to have been connected early in the imagination of the Indian with the moose, for we find the lake spoken of as "Moose-parun" (sic), from a "remarkable mountain . . . Indians say it resembles a moose-deer stooping."[21] From the promontory south of Kineo the mountain certainly does look not unlike the outline of a stooping or reclining moose, facing towards the west.

---

[20] **2020:** The legend of Kinneho and his mother Maquaso has been re-added to this edition in the appendix.

[21] Hugh Finlay's Journal, published in 1867 at Brooklyn by F. H. Norton.

A more credible legend makes this part of Moosehead Lake the scene of a great hunting exploit. A mighty warrior, or medicine-man, is on his way through the forests, when he spies two moose. He throws off his pack (Sabohtawan, the more easterly of the two Spencer peaks) and gives chase. The smaller moose (Kineo Mountain) is finally killed. The hunter, after having cooked and eaten of its flesh, turns his kettle upside down (Kokadjo, the more westerly of the Spencer peaks) in order that it may not rust, and takes up the trail of the other moose.

The Abnaki name for Moosehead Lake is said to be "Sebaygook." The Penobscots called it "Xsebem."[22] Each of these words designates a large body of water (Sobagoo, Abnaki, "the ocean").

### The Mt. Kineo House

The first hotel at Kineo was built by Capt. Joshua Fogg in 1848. The property passed successively through the hands of Wm. C. and Henry T. Hildreth, brothers, and Homan Rowell, and was for many years, then and subsequently, under the management of H. G. O. Barrows. In the early part of 1856 the Kineo tract, including the mountain, came into the possession of the late W. W. Chenery, who held it until his death. On January 1, 1861, John R. Crocker succeeded Mr. Barrows as manager, and in this year some eight thousand dollars were spent in enlarging and improving the hotel. It was two stories and a half high, had forty bedrooms, a dining room to seat fifty-six people, a billiard-room, large office, and parlor. On the 1st

---

[22] **2020:** Hubbard also notes the use of Sebam'ook in, *"Woods and Lakes of Maine."*

of January, 1868, O. A. Dennen became manager for Mr. Chenery, and on the 17th of February following the house, which stood on the site of the present hotel, was burned to the ground.

In the spring of the same year the old bowling alley was made to serve as a hotel, on ground east of the site of the original house. It received additions in 1869, a tower in 1870, in 1871 a parlor extension on the east end and an additional story between this part and the tower. In 1872 the old bowling alley was removed and a new dining room built. In 1876 an annex and boathouse were added, and in 1880 and 1881 further additions were made to the main house. On October 29, 1882, the entire complex of buildings, save the barn, was destroyed by fire. The same autumn a small building, the winter hotel, was erected, followed, the next spring, by the guide-house and a saw-mill. During the summer the present annex was begun, and completed in five weeks, and in July work was commenced on the present hotel, which was opened on the 29th of July, 1884.

The present Mt. Kineo House is one of the finest country hotels in Maine. It is owned by a stock company, and is still under the management of Mr. Dennen, who has succeeded in giving it a foremost position among hotels of its kind. It is heated by steam, lighted with gas, has fire escapes, electric bells, bathrooms, and all the conveniences and equipments of a first-class hotel. A telegraph line connects Kineo with the outer world, and there is a daily mail to and from Greenville and points beyond.

Walking, boating, bowling, tennis, and billiards are the principal pastimes of its guests. Besides the walks to Cliff and Pebble Beaches, which lead partly through pasture lands and partly through woods, and the climb up the mountain, there is little walking to be done.

About three quarters of a mile from the Three Sisters, southwest, and off Birch Point, is a buoy, kept well baited in summer, where whitefish and "lakers" of considerable size are often caught. In nearly the same direction, a little more westerly, and a mile and a half from the Three Sisters, is the mouth of Moose River, properly the Kennebec. Up the river for a mile and a half the water is "dead," and offers a pretty morning or afternoon excursion.

\*

**Mount Kineo House – Moosehead Lake**

**Mt. Kineo and Table Rock**

*

The paddle or sail around the mountain — six miles — is somewhat more of an undertaking, but enjoyable. A small boat is usually to be found on Cliff Beach, which parties who walk over the neck can use, to row under the cliff, — perhaps a good substitute for a paddle around the mountain.

In the other direction, east, one can paddle a quarter of a mile to Little Gull Rock, a mile and a quarter to Big Gull Rock, and two miles and a half to Cowen's Cove. The latter is principally noted for the abundance of frogs which live in the grassy land at its head. In the same direction, on the shore beyond Little Gull Rock is a miniature pond, separated from the lake by a strip of land a few feet wide, and at its upper end is a cranberry-bog. This is the narrowest part of the neck.

Moody Islands, two miles south of the hotel, furnish at times good deep-water fishing, and are very attractive as picnic-grounds.

Guests of the Mount Kineo House, who go into camp for a few days, can have their rooms locked up during their absence, and are provided with provisions for the excursion. These include all the usual articles of camp fare, such as pork, potatoes, flour, baking powder, hard bread, butter, sugar, coffee, tea, salt, pepper, and the like, but no canned goods. No reduction is made on the bills of persons who go in this way. The alternative is to give up one's room, buy one's provisions, and trust to good fortune to secure a room on one's return.

Connected with the hotel at Kineo is a store, where all staple articles of food, and some luxuries, can be bought. The prices asked are just enough above retail prices at Greenville, or anywhere else, to cover the extra cost of transportation, and to leave a small margin for profit.

Fishing tackle of good quality can be bought or hired of the superintendent of the hotel.

It is to be hoped that the conservative spirit dominant thus far at Kineo, among its *habitues*, will still continue to shape its customs of plain dress and reasonable hours of rising and retiring. Gentlemen can live in woolen shirts, and appear in them at all times, without giving offence or appearing discourteous, while ladies are not obliged to make a change of toilet for each meal. It must be confessed, however, that Saratoga trunks and fine dresses, which in former years were conceded to be out of place here, are of late unfortunately on the increase.[23] Ladies that have little or no sympathy with camp life, and spend the summer at the hotel, may perhaps be pardoned this attempt to introduce fashion into the wilderness. It is fair to presume, however, that fashion's exactions will never succeed in putting an end to the long-established freedom of Kineo.

---

### 2020 Edition

The freedom of Kineo, in a sense anyway, could have come to an end if not for land conservation efforts 100 years after Hubbard wrote this book.

In 1840 the State of Maine sold the peninsula to J. Bradbury for $350. Subsequently, Bradbury began the development of the property for north woods tourism. Several Kineo Houses and additions were built over the next sixty years.

By 1914, thanks to the network of railways that transported tourists to the region, and the steamers that ran up and down the lake, the development of the Kineo House property along with the cottages, the golf course, bowling alley, and 400 seat dining room were a destination for the wealthy. It had become a resort of grand proportions.

With the advent of air travel and the personal automobile, the Kineo properties suffered a decline in visitors. Between the 1930s and until 1970, when the hotel permanently closed, the property operated in various states of service.

---

[23] **2020:** The round top Saratoga trunks were made popular in the late 1800s by those visiting the racetrack and spas around the Saratoga Springs area in upstate New York. It is interesting that Hubbard remarks their appearances, along with fine dresses, as *unfortunate*. I suspect this is in relation to a rough 'camp kit,' of his own choosing.

In 1990 *freedom* to Kineo was ensured when the state, through The Land for Maine's Future (a program established in 1987 when Maine citizens voted to fund a bond to purchase lands of statewide importance) purchased part of the Mt. Kineo peninsula property. The section of the penisula, including Mt. Kineo, that is open to public access is managed by the Maine Bureau of Parks and Lands.

*

Besides the short excursions by water, already noted, one can paddle, or go by steamer, about three miles south of the hotel, to the West Outlet.

### West Outlet

Much less water passes out of the lake here (West Outlet) than at the other outlet, and consequently the stream, which runs nine miles to Indian Pond, is rapid, shallow, and rocky, except where broken by ponds. Of these there are eight or nine. The first lies within twenty-five rods of the lake, and is hardly more than a "logon."[24] A like distance beyond the first is the second pond, which is a mile long and half as wide. The third is a small round pond, or perhaps more properly only a stretch of "dead" water[25] in the stream. Beyond it, half a mile from number two, is number four, twenty-five rods wide and half a mile long. Twenty rods more bring one into number five, which is half a mile long and nearly as wide. The sixth lies twenty rods

---

[24] **2020:** As noted in the Introduction, the term "logon" is a logger's term, likely a derivative of 'lagoon.' It is meant to mean a shallow arm of a stream or pond, typically where lilies and grasses grow.

[25] **2020:** Dead-water as a nautical term refers to fresh or brackish water on top of denser salt water. In the context here, the term indicates a place of water with little, to no, current flowing.

beyond, is round and deep, and has a rocky shore. The seventh is three quarters of a mile from number six, and is a mile long and about half as wide. At its foot used to be a dam, at Bodfish Falls. Canoes can be "dropped" over the ledges here, which together are about six feet high. The mouth of Churchill Stream is just below the falls, and one must paddle up it a mile and a half to the dam, where the best fishing is to be found.

A mile below Churchill Stream is a stretch of "dead" water, by some called the "Alder Ground," and by others Long Pond. It is a mile and a half long, and perhaps thirty rods wide. A short distance below it is Round Pond, the last of the series, and one of the largest, above which, on the left, at the mouth of a small brook, trout are to be found. It is a mile and a half or more from Round Pond into Indian Pond.

### Brassua Lake * Brassua Stream * Moose River

Brassua Lake lies to the west of Moosehead, and its lower end is due west of Kineo. One goes up Moose River for a mile and a half, through "dead" water, to a small island, opposite which non-working members of a party take to the path on the north side, while the canoes push up the stream two and a half miles, through rapid water, to the lake. The worst places are the dam, and Sam's Pitch, a few rods above it. At the former it is well for the inexperienced canoe-man to get out and draw his boat up by the "painter"; at the latter promptness of action only is needed.

Brassua Lake is six or seven miles long, and from one to two wide. At its southwest corner, opposite the outlet, is the mouth of Miseree Stream, once, and even now, a good fishing-ground. It is navigable for only a short distance. The favorite campgrounds have always been on the south shore of the Lake. Into its northeastern end empties Brassua Stream. The stream flows into Little Brassua Lake.

Brassua Stream is quite a pretty little river, and which, with the exception of a short stretch of rapids two miles from the mouth, is navigable for three or four miles. In a Leith Pond above the rapids, and in the stream beyond, are good feeding grounds for ducks. Just below the rapids are good trout holes and fair camping sites.

Midway up the lake, and flowing into it from the west, is Moose River again.

About two miles of smooth, deep water bring one to the mouth of Tom Fletcher Brook, a good fishing ground, named after a trapper who was drowned in the rapids up the river. Report says he was trapping in the woods with two companions, and, at the close of the season, returned alone to camp one day, took all the fur, and hurried downstream with it. The judgement of Heaven seems to have overtaken him, for his body was soon found some miles below camp, and was buried at the mouth of the brook.

A short distance above this spot the river widens and forms Little Brassua Pond. Here are a number of grass islands, which afford playground to muskrats and hiding places to ducks.

From this point it is a mile and a half — rapid water — to Rolling Dam Ledge, thence two miles to the mouth of Stony Brook, where there is a difficult pitch, and two miles more to the dam. Between the dam and a point half a mile below Stony Brook the stream is full of rapids and pitches, and usually one will do well to "carry" the entire distance (left bank). Between the dam and the outlet of Long Pond it is two miles. Several rips and some shallow places may give the canoe-man trouble. At Demo Rips, half a mile above the dam, the canoe can be hauled up or let down by the painter.

## Long Pond

Long Pond is some ten miles long, and of irregular shape. Its shores are attractive to the camper-out, and afford some very pleasing glimpses of landscape, with mountains in the background. Seven miles of a winding and substantially smooth water-course lie between Long Pond and Wood Pond, although it is only four miles by land from one to the other. Moose River Bridge is half a mile below the latter pond, and over it passes the Canada Road.[26]

---

### 2020 Edition

Here Hubbard has arrived in Jackman. The Canada Road noted by Hubbard is Main Street (Rt. 201 / 6). This is the last settlement before the Canadian Border. If you continue on this road into Canada it becomes, *Route du President Kennedy.*

At this location, you may access the 34-mile Moose River Bow Canoe trip that takes the paddler through the beautiful scenery of Attean Pond, Attean Falls, and Holeb Pond.

On Gazetteer map 39, west of Jackman you will find the three summit Burnt Jacket Mountain. (The smaller two summit mountain of this same name is along Moosehead's Sandy Bay.)

---

[26] The description of Moose River above Wood Pond will be found in another place.

## Moosehead Lake - Tomhegan River

Tomhegan River empties into a cove about six miles from Kineo, on the west side of Moosehead Lake. It is an interesting stream, and well repays a visit. About two miles from the mouth, or perhaps less, are some "rips," above which "dead" water reappears for a time, and open alder-land soon takes the place of dark, overhanging banks. A canoe will have to be carried around these "rips." Fishing can be had at the mouth, and in pools near it.

From the "rips" a good road runs, some seven miles, up the left bank of the stream to the pond, around whose shores great quantities of cranberries grow.

## Moosehead Lake – Socatean Stream

Four miles from Tomhegan, and about seven northwest from Kineo, in an extensive bay, is the mouth of the Socatean River (Stream).

The Socatean River is one of the prettiest streams that empty into the lake. Its water near the mouth is without perceptible current, black, and apparently deep, and its banks are sprinkled with graceful hackmatacks, and fringed with bright-hued grass, mingling, at the water's edge, with lily pads.

Four miles up the stream are the Falls and Pool, formerly a favorite resort for camping parties, but not so popular since the ravaging fire which ran through the forest there several years ago. Fishing is good at the mouth, and here and there up the stream, especially above the Pool and at the upper Falls, which are three miles from it. A good road runs up the east side of the stream.

## *Duck Cove*

Duck Cove, on the east shore of the lake, midway between Kineo and the Northeast Carry, and about ten miles from the former, lies under the shadow of Eagle Mountain, which is shaped very much like Kineo. At a distance it resembles it so much as to be called by some people "Little Kineo," a name applied by many of the old settlers exclusively to the larger mountain east of the Shaw farm. Back of it, and on an open road half a mile long, is a pond, where of late years fishing has been good. The road begins on the south side of the brook.

Baker Brook, in a deep cove just above the mouth of Moose River, Moose Brook, above Socatean Point, and Williams Stream (*now Williams Brook*), opposite Centre Island, all of them on the west side of the lake, afford more or less fishing, but the "catch" is apt to be small in size, if not in numbers.

The lake, after growing wider near Kineo, narrows again at Socatean Point, between which and Farm Island is a stretch of water known as the Devil's Blowhole. The wind is ever contrary here, causing "chop-waves" in profusion, and is consequently annoying to canoe-men.

---

**2020 Edition**

Hubbard is referring here to Big Duck Cove. There is also a Little Duck Cove just north of this location.

Williams Stream might now be noted on maps as Williams Brook. Socatean Point is labeled on the Gazetteer south of Mansell Brook. Toe of the Boot, not mentioned by Hubbard, is north of what is now named Socatean Point and the land that causes the narrows which Hubbard referred to as the *Devil's Blowhole*.

From this point, Bald Mt. looms up conspicuously on the west. On the east the Spencer peaks slowly rise into prominence from behind Little Kineo, while north of them are Lobster and Eagle Mountains. Looking south, Kineo slowly assumes a foreshortened appearance, — on its right being Blue Ridge and on its left the Squaw Mt. range. Mt. Bigelow's sharp peak rises far to the west of Blue Ridge. From opposite Duck Cove glimpses may be had of Soubungy and the Nesowadnehunk Mts., and from a point nearer the head of the lake, as well as from the west of Farm Island, Mt. Ktaadn comes into full view.

\*

## 2020 Edition

Hubbard's focus in his guide book was on the navigational waterways. This is mainly because during his time the purpose for going deep into the Maine woods was for hunting. The lakes, ponds, and streams were the highways to take the explorers where there were no roads.

There are many canoe trips in this region even today, although most people do not arrive by train, travel by steamer to Kineo, hire a guide and set out in a canoe. Roads provide access to launch sites closer to your desired starting location.

While Hubbard focused on waterway navigation, it does appear he took time for excursions to climb some of the peaks. Around the area already presented in this book there are hiking trails to be explored. Among them Big Moose and the Spencers, offering varying degrees of difficulty. Don't let the name fool you, Little Spencer is one of the more challenging hikes in the Moosehead area. The climb to the summit requires the use of ladders and scrambling over rock.

For hiking trails, difficulty, and access points, we refer you to one of the many hiking guide books, the Maine Trail Finder online, or Maine.gov Natural Heritage Hikes pages.

*

**Socatean Falls and Pool**

## TOURS BEYOND MOOSEHEAD LAKE
### *Penobscot Waters - Northeast Carry*

A small hotel stands on the shore of Moosehead Lake, at the end of the Northeast Carry, and affords comfortable accommodation and good fare to a limited number of guests. In the summer season, steamers in their rounds of the lake touch here regularly once a day, at other seasons twice a week.

Tourists can have canoes (luggage included) hauled over the carry, two miles, to the Penobscot, for a dollar and a half each. There are two teams to be had, one at the hotel, and the other from Luce's farm, at the other end of the carry. Each team can take four canoes and their luggage at a load. The road rises gradually towards the middle from each end, and is pretty level, but wet and muddy after a rain.

At the farther end of the Carry is a United States post office in charge of Mr. George C Luce, who has fitted up and refurnished his house for the comfortable entertainment of guests.

### *West Branch of the Penobscot - From Northeast Carry*

Recent measurements of the road from the N. E. Carry to Chesuncook Lake make the distance 21 miles and some rods, inclusive of the carry. From Luce's (the old Morris farm) the distance by road to Chesuncook is therefore about 19 miles, and as the road is more direct than the stream, the distance by the latter is greater than heretofore supposed. This stretch of river may be divided and characterized as follows:

## RÉSUMÉ

| | |
|---|---|
| N. E. Carry to Lobster Stream (dead water) . . . . . . | 2 ½ m. |
| Lobster Str. to Little Island (current and rips) . . . . | 2 ½ m. |
| Little Island to Moosehorn Str. (dead water) . . . . | 4 m. |
| Moosehorn to Sears's Clearing (on the right) . . . . | 2 m. |
| Sears's to Ragmuff Stream (on the left) . . . . . . . . | ¼ m. |
| Ragmuff to head of Big Island . . . . . . . . . . . . . . | 1 ½ m. |
| Big Island to Fox Hole . . . . . . . . . . . . . . . . . . . . | ¾ m. |
| Fox Hole to head of Rocky Rips . . . . . . . . . . . . . | 3 m. |
| Head of Rocky Rips to foot of Pine Stream Falls . | 2 ¼ m. |
| Foot of Pine Stream Falls to Chesuncook Lake . . | 2 ½ m. |
| | 21 ¼ m. |

Between Moosehorn Stream and the foot of Pine Stream Falls there is comparatively little still water. By the road, which is quite good and lies on the right bank, it is 3 ½ miles from the head of Big Island to Pine Stream, and from here to the head of Chesuncook Lake 2 ½ mile farther.

Go to the right of Big Island, at the head of which, for a few rods, the river is rather shallow, but, except in dry seasons, there is depth enough to carry at least a canoe and luggage safely through to Fox Hole. Here the channel turns sharply to the left, lying within two feet or less of the left bank, and soon deepens again.

From the head to the foot of Rocky Rips is, perhaps, a full mile. Looking back from below them, when the river is at its ordinary summer height, no water can be seen in it at all, so thickly is its bed sprinkled with rocks and boulders.

A short stretch of "dead" water, containing several small grass-islands, separates Rocky Rips from Pine Stream Falls, the worst place in this part of the river. There are three principal "pitches," or falls, followed by perhaps three quarters of a mile of strong rapids. The writer's experience has been that it is better to go over the first pitch in the middle of the stream, then to the left over both the second and third pitches, but the height of the water at different times may make it expedient to change this course. In very high water, an easy passage by all three pitches may be found close to the left bank.

Rounding a bend about a mile below the rapids, one comes upon a huge pier in the river, and at about the same time bursts upon one's sight the glorious Ktaadn group of mountains, twenty miles to the east.

Fair camping grounds may be found here and there along the river, a convenient one being just above Pine Stream Falls on the left bank, nearly opposite the mouth of Pine Stream.

Of all the tributaries of the West Branch, passed in these eighteen miles, Lobster Stream is the only one navigable for any considerable distance, the water in it being deep enough to admit of easy passage to Lobster Lake, two and a half miles away, even in times of drouth.[27]

There is little fishing to be had on this route, except at Fox Hole, in a small inlet on the left, where there are supposed to be cold springs, and on the right and left among some small grass-islands above Rocky Rips, where there is quite a gravel bar in the river.

---

[27] **2020:** The word drought had three common spellings. Drouth is still used, but less so than drought. The third, as 'drougth' is no longer in use.

It takes, ordinarily, a little more than two hours to go from N. E. Carry to Moosehorn, and from there to Chesuncook Lake from four to five hours more.

## *Lobster Lake*

Lobster Lake (Peske-begat, "branch of a dead-water") is connected with the Penobscot by a broad and sluggish stream whose current is often reversed, and fills the lake basin to the extent of six or eight feet. The lake is elbow-shaped, and the north and northwest shores of its lower arm are flat and marshy, while those of the upper or southern arm are, for the most part, high and rocky. On the east side many ledges, often steep and difficult, jut out into the water, now and then enclosing charming reaches of sandy beach. An exceedingly pretty camp-ground is on the point south of Little Lobster Brook opposite a small island. From it can be seen Mt. Ktaadn and the Spencer peaks, while near at hand, and beyond the placid waters of West Cove, Lobster Mt. fills the view. From the head of West Cove, when the water is not low, a canoe can find passageway into the main body of the lake, through a series of pretty little coves, where pink-hued water lilies grow in abundance. Across the south end of the lake extends a narrow strip of sand-beach on which blueberries thrive, while beyond it a low, flat tract of land extends almost to the foot of Spencer Mts.

The ascent of Sabōta'wan[28] can be made in one day, from the S. E. corner of the lake, part of the way by a road that leads up Duck Pond Brook.

---

[28] **2020:** Big Spencer. Hubbard seamlessly writes the Indian and the newer names in his writing. As noted, he covers the Indian meanings and cross-references in, *Woods and Lakes of Maine.*

**2020 Edition**

**Sabōta'wan (Big Spencer) and Lobster Mountain**

*

### Chesuncook Lake * Moose Brook * Caribou Lake

Chesuncook Lake, "the biggest lake," a "bulge" in the Penobscot, as it has been properly called, is eighteen miles long, and from one to two miles wide. It is without special attraction, save the glorious view it offers of old Ktaadn.

From five to six hours are usually consumed in paddling over it, which time is increased or diminished according to the direction of the prevailing wind. Meals and lodging are provided at Hilton's (now Smith's), at the head of the lake.

Within the past few years, the management of the Chesuncook House, at the head of the lake, has much improved. The little hotel now offers comfortable accommodation for eight or ten persons, with good, plain, unpretentious country fare, most of it the product of the adjoining farm. The view of Mt. Ktaadn from the hotel is fine, and, owing to its situation, this place is destined to become a rendezvous for fishermen and hunters, as it is nearer the centre of the game district than any other hotel in the region. At the store now kept in connection with the hotel can be had canned goods and many other articles for camp use. Mr. Hilton, the manager for the past seven years, has recently been succeeded by Mr. Ansel Smith, an old resident of the lake.

**Chesuncook Lake**

\*

**2020 Edition**

The Chesuncook Lake House was originally built in 1864. It was a key supply point for logging operations of the north woods. In recent years it had catered to sportsmen and outdoor enthusiasts. In 2018, after 150 years of serving the area, the house was destroyed by fire. The owners have since rebuilt and are once again providing lodging and services to those deep in the Maine woods.

Moose Brook flows from a pond of the same name about two-thirds of a mile from the lake. Its water is dead, and a canoe can be taken up through it into Moose Pond, and from there "waded" through quick water three miles to Cussabexis Lake.[29] Between Moose and Duck Ponds it is impossible for a canoe to go, other than by being carried three-quarters of a mile to the dam. This group of ponds is seldom visited by sportsmen, and little is known of their attractions in the way of fish and game, although by some said to be good.[30]

### Caribou Lake * Kelly Ponds * Bean Brook

Caribou Lake lies to the southwest of Chesuncook Lake, and is connected with it by a thoroughfare two miles long, at times partly rapid, and at its mouth covered with lily-pads, and makes a good feeding-ground for ducks. The lake is seven miles long. Its shores are in places high and not unattractive. Several streams empty into it, in which there is some fishing to be had early in the autumn.

At high water a canoe can pass through the thoroughfare from Chesuncook to Caribou Lake without difficulty, but at other times some wading is necessary during the last three-quarters of a mile.[31] The outlet of Caribou Lake is scarcely twenty feet wide. Here and near its southern end the lake is full of sunken rocks. On entering the lake, one sees several pretty islands directly opposite. Behind them rises a high hardwood ridge, which separates this body of water from Ragged Lake.

---

[29] **2020:** Often spelled Cuxabexis.

[30] **2020:** This commentary is prior to the flooding of the area from the Ripogenus Dam completed in 1920.

[31] **2020:** Since the modern Ripogenus Dam was constructed these two lakes are wholly connected. Compare Hubbard Map to current.

Ragged Brook is rocky and shallow for some distance above its mouth. A team to haul canoes into Ragged Lake can be hired at the Grant Farm.

From the mouth of Caribou Brook one can paddle up stream half a mile to a landing on the right. From here a good road runs into the Chesuncook-Roach Pond road, which, turning to the left, one follows to where it crosses the stream, two hundred rods above the landing. This part of the route may be somewhat shortened by leaving the main road about sixty rods above the landing, and following a path that diverges on the left, either to the main road again, or only for about forty rods. From this latter point a loaded canoe can generally be taken up the stream to where the road crosses it, a quarter of a mile. From the crossing a good path leads along the east side, a quarter of a mile, to the third or lowest dam.[32] From just above the dam the water is dead for about a mile. At the end of three-quarters of a mile, where the brook makes a sharp turn to the right, at the upper end of an open bog on the left, begins the carry, which runs at first through an alder swamp, but soon reaches high and dry ground. It passes an old clearing at the second dam, and continues to the first or upper dam, two hundred and seventy rods. From this point a spotted line runs up the opposite or left bank of the stream, one hundred and eighty rods, to Kelly Pond,[33] but loaded canoes can generally run up into the pond without difficulty. Kelly Pond is nearly half a mile long, and not quite as broad. The best camp ground is on the east side, but

---

[32] Sluice-dam, not rolling-dam.

[33] **2020:** Kelly, Little Kelly, Grassy, and the Bean Ponds are small ponds clustered between Caribou and Rainbow lakes.

firewood is plenty nowhere except at the southwest corner of the pond.

From a small cove on the east side of Kelly Pond a good carry runs eighty rods, to Bean Pond, a narrow body of water, three eighths of a mile long. The latter lies north of a spruce-covered mountain that is visible from Kelly Pond. From the lower end of this little pond Spencer Mountain can easily be seen in clear weather. From the right of the outlet a good carry leads one hundred rods down to Bean Bog, through which dead-water extends for about three-quarters of a mile to a dam. From this point down to within at least a mile of Nahmakanta Lake, about three miles, navigation of the brook is entirely out of the question. Half a mile down the right bank of the stream one may find a logging road used by Murphy in 1882, which, after a mile, crosses to the other side of the stream near the town line, runs past Murphy's old camp, and after crossing and re-crossing the brook again finally, forty rods below the junction with Pollywog Brook,[34] strikes across through an old clearing to Rainbow Stream, one hundred and thirty rods, and after two hundred and ten rods more comes out on Nahmakanta Lake just west of the mouth of Rainbow Stream.

From the dam at the foot of Bean Bog, on the right, a carry runs down the brook a few rods, crosses it at a pool, and runs southeasterly nearly to two little ponds, and then northeasterly up Murphy Brook to lower Murphy Pond, a mile and a half. Across the pond a quarter of a mile, and up the brook a mile or more, and one is within forty rods of the upper Murphy Pond.

---

[34] **2020:** Close to Pollywog Gorge, a deep mile-wide gorge with logging history. The Appalachian Trail passes here at Crescent Pond.

A high and steep ridge separates Murphy Brook from Rainbow Stream. From the top of this ridge, just above the lower pond, a spotted line runs to the foot of a small double pond on Rainbow Stream just below the lake, passing a second, smaller pond. The best way to reach this line would be by taking a southeast course from upper Murphy Pond. Possibly a better way to reach Rainbow Lake from this side would be from the head of upper Murphy Pond over the northern spur of the ridge, which does not seem to be very steep.

## Rainbow Lake * Chesuncook Pond

Rainbow Lake is about five miles long and a mile wide. It lies in a granite basin, and its water is so clear that one can see bottom at fifteen feet. It teems with small trout which can be caught only at nightfall or early in the morning. No grassy inlets vary the monotony of its shores, or afford a feeding ground to deer and moose. Its chief charms are its seclusion and the fine view of Mt. Ktaadn from the outlet. The lake is best reached from Ripogenus, from the lower end of which a good road, hardly a mile long, runs southwesterly over a ridge to Chesuncook Pond. This road leaves the carry that runs down the West Branch of the Penobscot about twenty rods from the shore of the lake.

Chesuncook Pond is a shallow, irregularly shaped body of water, full of islands and rocks, and apparently void of trout. From a cove on its south side a carry runs one and a half miles to the northwest arm of Rainbow Lake. The carry at first runs through a cedar swamp, and was in 1888 well corduroyed. After leaving the low land, the carry is dry and excellent. Chesuncook

Pond is about thirty feet higher than Rainbow Lake, and a hundred and twenty feet above Ripogenus Lake.

## Red Brook * Duck Pond * Mud Pond

A good carry leaves Chesuncook Lake about one hundred rods north of the brook, and leads to the dam. Above the latter for half a mile navigation is good, then come falls and wading for a mile, above which dead-water extends for two miles.

Duck Pond and Mud Pond[35] are accessible from Chesuncook Lake by good roads, that to the former being less than half a mile long, while that to Mud Pond runs from the mouth of the brook, on the right, a short mile to the dam.

The carry past the Chesuncook Dam and falls may be shortened somewhat when the water in the stream is not low, by taking the path on the north side of the dam, and putting in below the lower fall.

## Ripogenus Lake

At the lower end of Chesuncook Lake the river narrows again for half a mile, flows over a succession of falls, and again widens into Ripogenus Lake. At Chesuncook dam, and in pools below it, good trout are often taken, and occasionally a salmon.

The carry lies several rods south of the dam, and is a good solid road. Owing to the higher level of the water since the erection of the new Ripogenus Dam,[36] canoes may be put into the stream at the end of half a mile, whereas formerly one had to carry a quarter of a mile further, to the lake. From and at the head of Ripogenus Lake begins a series of views of Mount

---

[35] **2020:** At some point, I aim to count all the Mud Ponds within Maine. This one is east of Chesuncook near Weymouth Pt. Gazetteer map 50.

[36] **2020:** Much smaller predecessor to the current Ripogenus Dam.

Ktaadn and the Neesowadnehunk range, which fairly enchant the lover of nature. Ever shifting as one moves on, now hidden by forest or intervening ridge, now bursting suddenly forth again in greater majesty, old Ktaadn's silent and more vivid presence excites our awe and commands our admiration.

Ripogenus Lake is two miles long and a mile or more broad. It is a favorite camp-ground for tourists going down the river, and, aside from the picturesqueness of its situation, has quite an attraction in the wildness of the river at its foot.

There is a cold spring in a cove on the south shore, near the outlet.

**Ripogenus Falls – Looking East**

*

## Harrington Lake

Into the northwest corner of Ripogenus Lake flows a stream of the same name, whose bed in summer ordinarily contains too little water for successful navigation. At high water, however, a canoe can be poled and dragged up, four miles, to Brighton Dam, with a possible portage around Island Falls and some rough places just above and just below them, about two miles up the stream. The bed of the stream above Island Falls is very ledgy, and lies along the strike of the highly inclined slate formation, so that great care must be taken not to cut one's canoe.

An old road runs along the east, or left bank, of the stream. The road from Chesuncook Lake (four miles) strikes the stream below the dam, and one branch of it ends at the dam on the west side; the other continues up the east side to Harrington Lake. The carry around the dam and rapids below it, forty rods, can be made on either side, the left being the easier. Camp sites may be found near the dam, but firewood is scarce.

Brighton Deadwater, when the gates of the dam are down, forms a pond nearly two miles long, its lower end lined and choked with driftwood. Into its northwest side empty the waters of upper Ripogenus Stream.[37] On the northeast it receives the waters of Harrington Lake. For two-thirds of a mile the stream from the latter is rapid and, in places, ledgy; it then opens out into a shallow pond three-eighths of a mile in diameter; above the latter for a quarter of a mile, shallow, rocky, and running, it leads into Harrington Lake.

At high water one can go from Harrington Lake to Brighton Dam in less than an hour and a quarter, and from the end of the carry below the dam to the mouth of the stream in another hour.

---

[37] There is a discrepancy on the map, but the writer does not know which is wrong, the stream or the pond. (**2020:** This is a note from 1893. The Gazetteer has the stream and pond named the same.)

To come up the stream from its mouth poling and dragging a loaded canoe, may require a half day to the dam, and less than that from the dam to the lake.

Harrington Lake is about three miles long and one mile wide, and is almost surrounded by high land; the mountains at its east end lie within the Ktaadn granite area, and lend to the scenery a rugged picturesqueness. Mt. Ktaadn itself is not visible from the lake.

There is a good campground several rods back from the shore on Soper Brook. This stream joins the lake on the north, just east of a prominent ledge less than a mile from the outlet. A good road leaves the lake just west of the aforesaid ledge, and runs to the dam (1 5/8 miles) at the foot of the lowest dead-water which is three miles long. The road crosses here and runs up the east side of the stream, but, although generally traceable, it is in places hard to follow until after it has left the head of the dead-water. From that point for a mile and three-fifths it is good. The two upper dead-waters are short (1/4 to 1/8 m.), shallow, and narrow. In 1892 the writer went from the upper part of this stream, through the woods, to Neesowadnehunk Lake, but the route followed was four miles long and difficult.

The lowest dead-water on Soper Brook has a bog on its west side that extends to the base of Soubungy Mt. The summit of the latter, eight hundred feet above the dead-water can easily be reached from the latter. The precipitous cliff on the south side is six hundred feet above the bog, and reminds one of Mt, Kineo, the rock being also like that of Kineo, porphyritic.[38] The

---

[38] **2020:** The rocks that form the cliffs of Kineo, are now generally known as "Kineo rhyolite," a volcanic rock rich in silica. The high silica

ascent and descent may be made comfortably in two hours and a half. An interesting kame, beginning at the dam, runs along the dead-water cut through by the latter at the great bend opposite Soubungy.

## *West Branch of the Penobscot*

### Below Ripogenus Lake

The outlet of Ripogenus Lake is ordinarily a narrow and deep gorge, where the water foams and hisses in its rapid course between walls of rock. After freshets, the river flows over a broader channel to. the right, or south, of the entrance to the gorge, leaving quite a high and wooded island between the two. From this point, for a mile and a half, a good path runs along the river-bank, and enables one to get a fine view of perhaps the most wonderful, if not the most interesting, part of the Penobscot. Nearly the entire distance is a gorge with steep cliffs on either side, fifty or sixty feet high, in some places over hanging the stream, and with isolated masses of precipitous rock between them, whose tops are level with the banks on either side, and covered, like them, with ferns and blueberry bushes. The water seems to have worn away the rock and soil around these islands, giving them the shape of an old fashioned flat-iron, whence they derive the names of Big and Little Heater. The river pitches through this gorge in a succession of rapids, none very high, but together making a fall of two hundred feet or more.

---

content results in conchoidal fracturing, which makes the rock easier to shape. Source: Maine Geological Survey, 2018.

**The Big Heater**

**Ripogenus Gorge – Looking West**

The carry from Ripogenus begins at the lower end of the lake, to the right of the outlet. At the end of a mile one descends a short hill, and on the right Carry Pond can be seen from the road.

## Carry Pond

Carry Pond used to be famous for its trout. In the absence of canoes, a raft formerly served indifferently to bear people across the pond to the spring-hole where the fish lay. This pond has been so thoroughly fished of late years, that its supplies may not now always prove equal to the demand made upon them.

Half a mile from Carry Pond, on the road, is a large bowlder[39] on the brow of a steep descent. It lies in the middle of a small clearing, and from its top one gets a wide prospect over the valley below, and a fine view of Ktaadn.

At the foot of this steep descent, and beyond a small brook, a path turns off to the left and leads to the "putting-in place," two miles from Ripogenus Lake. Two-thirds of a mile more brings one to an old clearing forty-five rods above the "Arches," another difficult and dangerous impediment in the river. From the Arches it is one hundred and ten rods to Big Eddy, the end of the carry.

Canoes may take to the water again at the "putting-in place," but the stream below is dangerous, and there are three places where one has to lift over. Around one of them, the Arches, one must carry for thirty or forty rods on either bank. It is safer and more expeditious to carry over the whole three miles of road, than to attempt to run the river below the "putting-in place." A

---

[39] **2020:** Archaic spelling of boulder.

brook, the outlet of Carry Pond, empties into the river at the last-named point; the path to the latter crosses it twice after leaving the main road.

Once fairly embarked below the carry one glides easily downstream through rapid water, lifting over one rocky pitch, and at the end of two miles or less reaches Gulliver Pitch, or Ambajemackomus Falls.[40] The carry is about one hundred rods long, and begins at the foot of a steep descent in the river-bed, in a very rocky bend on the right.

Below Gulliver Pitch begins the dreaded "horse-race," which extends for a mile and a half, to within a third of a mile of dead-water. The river is impetuous, and its bed ledgy, refusing setting-pole hold. On all sides are dangerous rocks to be avoided, which call forth the canoe-man's skill, and put his nerve to the test. With care, however, one can run these rapids in safety, and will soon find himself in Neesowadnehunk Deadwater.

## Neesowadnehunk Deadwater

Neesowadnehunk Deadwater[41] a pretty little lake surrounded by growths of beech, birch, maple, and oak, with almost no fir nor spruce. It is a mile and a half long, and from its lower end one has a fine view of Ktaadn to the east, and a pretty but less pretentious picture to the west.

A good path follows the river on the right bank, to within fifty rods of the head of the dead-water, just above which its course lies along the top of a kame forty rods long and thirty

---

[40] **2020:** The spelling on the Gazetteer is Little and Big Ambejackmockamus Falls.

[41] **2020:** Now spelled, Nesowadnehunk.

feet high. There is a good spring on the right bank, at the foot of the "horse-race."

Leaving Nees-ow-ad-ne-hunk (corrupted to Sourdnahunk) Deadwater, a short run brings one to the carry of the same name, on the left. Care should be taken not to overlook and run past it, as the stream immediately beyond looks smooth, and a canoe once in the current might easily be swept along and over the falls (five feet), with serious consequences. Just below the carry, which is thirty-five rods long, over granite ledges, there is a good spring. Half a mile below the falls is the mouth of Neesowadnehunk Stream, below which for two miles one finds good canoeing, through "dead" water, to the mouths of Aboljackarmegas,[42] and Aboljackarmegassic, or Sandy Stream.[43] At this point parties usually camp who intend to make the ascent of Mount Ktaadn.

### Ascent of Mount Ktaadn

From a short distance up Sandy Stream — the more easterly brook — the path runs four or five miles over intervening ridges to the base of the mountain; the ascent thence continues up the slide on the southwest side of the mountain. It is perhaps less fatiguing to leave one's camp on the river bank early in the afternoon, with blankets, axe, and enough food for two days, (with) as light a load as possible, and camp that night at the foot of the slide, or at the brook about a mile from it. With an early start the next morning, one can in three hours climb up the slide

---

[42] **2020:** In *Woods and Lakes of Maine,* Hubbard notes this as, Āboljackarmé′gas, a branch of the Penobscot, at the foot of Mount Ktaadn.

[43] **2020:** This must now be Katahdin Stream.

(at an angle of nearly forty degrees) to the broad tableland, near the top of the mountain, — about three miles.

Here will be found, under and at the sides of several large rocks, springs or pools of water, cool, but of indifferent taste. There is said to be another and better spring part way up the slide, and to the east of it. As one ascends the mountain, vegetation becomes stunted, and disappears almost altogether just before the tableland is reached. A thick bed of dry moss covers the tableland, and a few dead and snarly roots scattered over it furnish scanty fuel to those who wish to make a cup of tea, or to warm themselves.[44] The summit of the mountain is about a mile east of the springs, and the ascent to it is gradual and easy. A flat surface of not more than twenty feet in diameter forms the western peak. To the west of it lies the tableland. On the east, perhaps a quarter of a mile, is another peak, said to be ten feet lower than the first. Between the two is a ridge so narrow, that *one step* towards the north would send one into eternity over a sheer precipice hundreds of feet high. On the south side, the mountain, although not so precipitous, is exceedingly steep, and a misstep might result in as certain, though not so quick, a death. When the wind blows with any considerable force, one can cross from peak to peak only by creeping. From the eastern peak a spur of the mountain runs northeast for some distance, and has apparently the same general characteristics as the ridge just described. It is known as Pamola, named after the dreaded Indian deity formerly supposed by the natives to dwell on the mountain. Surrounded

---

[44] **2020:** Do not kindle fires within the north woods, or Baxter State Park, except at permitted campsites and with permission.

by these walls and on the west by a continuation of the main body of the mountain which extends north from the tableland, is a deep basin which contains several small ponds, the water from one of which oozes through the granite boulders, for some distance out of sight, until it gushes forth as clear as crystal and as cold as ice. This pond for a long time was vulgarly supposed to be practically fathomless, but, like many other "good stories," its fabled depth has been reduced by actual measurement to its just proportions, 17 feet.[45] This Basin Pond is, according to Prof. Hamlin, 2,287 feet below the summit of West Peak, the altitude of which above sea-level is, according to Prof, Fernald, 5,248 feet, latitude 45° 53' 40", longitude 68° 54' 50".

On a clear day, it is said, one can see from the top of Ktaadn several hundred distinct and separate pieces of water. Millinokett Lake and Ktaadn Pond[46] are perhaps the prettiest bodies of water near at hand.

Parties who go up the mountain should be provided with extra warm clothing, as the change of temperature from below is apt to be very marked, and sometimes severe. At other times, however, the sun seems hotter on top than at the bottom of the

---

[45] See "Observations upon the Physical Geography and Geology of Mt. Ktaadn," &c., by C. E. Hamlin, Cambridge. Printed for the Museum, June, 1881. Also "Routes to Ktaadn," by same author in Appalachia for December, 1881.

[46] **2020:** Here Hubbard is likely noting, based on his direction of view, the Togue Ponds (Upper and Lower) which are northwest of Millinocket Lake and had been known as Katahdin Ponds. He is likely not referring to Katahdin Lake which is to the northeast of Pamola.

mountain, but this is very exceptional. Ladies have climbed Ktaadn, but only the strongest can do it.[47]

From the summit to the foot of the slide one can descend in an hour and a half, and from the latter point to the river in two hours and a half more. The Basin may be reached by way of the "saddle," north of the tableland.

---

### 2020 Edition

Katahdin is the tallest peak in what is now Baxter State Park. It is also the northern terminus of the Appalachian Trail.

The park was the vision of Percival P. Baxter (1876 – 1969). Baxter served as the 53rd Governor of Maine from 1921-1925.

In 1930 Baxter purchased 6,000 acres of land around Mt. Katahdin for $25,000 and he subsequently deeded the land to the State of Maine. The park was named in his honor. Additional purchases by the people of Maine and private donation, have expanded the park to over 209,000 acres. Additional history of the park can be read at *baxterstatepark.org*.

Katahdin's 5,267-foot summit is the highest peak in the park, and is among over forty other notable mountains within the park's boundaries. Visitation is regulated to keep the area as natural as possible. Information on camping and hiking in the area can be found at the website noted above.

\*

---

[47] **2020:** Please do not contact the editors, this book was written in 1893. Besides, we know more than a few men who have been turned back.

## *Mt. Ktaadn from the East*

If one is fonder of "tramping" through the woods than of gliding over lakes and down streams in a canoe, there is a route, other than that already described, by which the ascent of Mt. Ktaadn is frequently made.[48]

One goes by morning train on the European and North American Railway from Bangor to Mattawamkeag, where the cars connect with stage-coaches for Sherman Village, some twenty-four miles away to the north. It is seven miles from Mattawamkeag to Molunkus, where passengers stop to dine, and the entire drive to Sherman may be accomplished by five o'clock in the afternoon. The drive is pleasant and not tiresome. The stage fare is two dollars. At Sherman Village one can put up at the tavern, or, if early enough, push on by private conveyance, over a good road, four miles to Staceyville.

It is six miles over a very rough road from here to the East Branch of the Penobscot, to the old Hunt farm. Until recently this place was kept for some years by C. R. Patterson, who now occupies a farm a mile and a half above it. At Staceyville it may be well to hire a horse to carry one's load to Ktaadn Lake. At Patterson's a guide can usually be engaged, and, if one is going up the river, canoes as well.

The road, an old "tote-road" from here westward, crosses the river either at the Hunt farm, which is below the mouth of the Wassataquoik, or at Patterson's, above it, the former fork joining the latter on the north side of this stream, up whose left bank it runs for six miles. Re-crossing it, the road runs westerly four miles to Ktaadn Lake, from which a magnificent view is

---

[48] **2020:** Access is now within Baxter State Park.

had of Mt. Ktaadn in all its majesty. The best place to camp is at the head of the lake, a mile from the outlet, or at Reed's old lumber camp on Sandy Stream.

From the outlet of Ktaadn Lake it is over six miles to Reed's upper dam. The road runs part of the way along Sandy Stream, and crosses it at the dam, after which it is somewhat better than for several miles before, but soon becomes steep, and is lined with blocks of granite. From the dam to the Basin is nearly four miles, the latter being, according to Professor Hamlin,[49],[50] 1,700 ft. the higher, or 2,900 ft. above sea-level.

The wildest part of Ktaadn scenery is had from this neighborhood, and a better idea of its grandeur and impressiveness is obtained here than from any other point. Almost surrounded by perpendicular walls of rock, the tourist never ceases to wonder at what is before him.

Good fishing is found in Ktaadn Lake and Sandy Stream, or rather were found there before the habit became prevalent among guides and loggers of destroying trout in great numbers by the use of dynamite, — a flagrant outrage which cannot be condemned too severely.

### Abol. and Ktaadn Ponds

Descending the mountain, back to Katahdin Stream, Abol. and Ktaadn Ponds maybe reached in two ways; either by going up Abol. Stream to the pond of that name and carrying across into Ktaadn Pond (known as Togue Ponds, which are two ponds

---

[49] For a full and interesting description of this and other approaches to Ktaadn, see Routes to Ktaadn, by C E. Hamlin, in Appalachia, December, 1881.

[50] **2020:** Reference information on Baxter State Park for access and hiking Katahdin.

with a narrow neck of land between them), — or by carrying into the latter pond from Compass Pond, which is reached directly from the river. The ascent of Abol. Stream, although slow, is not difficult. From Ktaadn Pond a canoe can be taken down Sandy Stream into Milinokett Lake.

## Abol Falls * River and Compass Ponds

### Continuing down the Penobscot

Half a mile above the mouth of Abol Stream, on the opposite side, is an island (at low water probably not entirely surrounded by water). Behind it there is a small grassy pond. Five-eighths of a mile below this island and at the head of the *long* carry around Abol Rapids (to *Abol Falls*), just below the first rips on the right bank of the river and within a stone's throw of it, there is another small pond.

The carry past Abol Rapids and Falls is about one hundred and twenty-five rods long, on the right bank. When the river is not too high the *rapids* can be navigated safely. The carry around the *falls* is twenty-eight rods. There is cold water at the lower end of the carry.

From Abol Falls it is about a mile to the carry around Pockwockamus Falls, on the right bank. There are two rough places in the river here, — the upper one can be navigated when the water is not too high; the lower one is full of bowlders, and very rough. The entire carry is a hundred and twenty rods long, the part around the lower falls thirty-six rods. At its upper end the path is fairly good; the lower end is very rocky.

River and Compass Ponds are sometimes called Mud Ponds. The lower of the two is connected with Pockwockamus Deadwater by a stream nearly half a mile long, and this pond with the upper one by a crooked and shallow stream possibly a mile long. The brook above the upper pond is, at high water, navigable for about two miles, but ordinarily only for a short distance. From this brook a carry leads over to Ktaadn Pond (*Togue Ponds*).

### Hale Pond (Lower W. Br. Penobscot)

In Pockwockamus Deadwater half a mile below the mouth of River Pond Stream, is the head of a large island. On the west side of the latter, a quarter of a mile from its head, is the mouth of a small brook that flows out of Hale Pond. A canoe can ascend the brook for about forty rods, and there in a small meadow will be found a tote road that leads along the south side of the brook to the lower end of the pond, about ninety rods above. The pond is half a mile long, and boggy at its upper end. The road after having crossed the pond, runs up the north side of the inflowing brook, soon crosses it, and continues in a westerly by southerly direction to the lower end of the upper Hurd Pond, which it enters at a small cove north of the outlet, a mile and a quarter from Hale Pond.

### Hurd Ponds * Katepskonegan Ponds

At the northwest elbow of Katepskonegan (Debsconeag) Deadwater, in the very corner, is the lower Hurd Pond. A narrow point nearly separates the two bodies.[51] The pond is three-eighths of a mile long, grassy and covered with lily pads.

---

[51] **2020:** The Gazetteer does not note this "lower pond" as a distinct pond from the dead-water. Hurd Pond Stream flows into here from Hurd Pond. On the northwest end of Hurd Pond, the stream continues, crosses the Appalachian Trail and ends in Little Hurd Pond. Note: These Hurd Ponds are shown on Map 50, not to be confused with Hurd Pond and Little Hurd Pond on Map 55 near Caucomgomac Lake.

A clear brook flows into its upper end, probably navigable for half a mile. A road runs up the south side of the brook three-quarters of a mile to the upper pond (Little Hurd Pond), which is nearly a mile and a half long and a mile wide. On three sides the latter is surrounded by ridges; its shores are strewn with bowlders.

## Debsconeag Ponds

The lowest of the series of Katepskonegan Ponds empties into the dead-water of that name, a short distance below Hurd Pond, through a stream about half a mile long. This pond is two miles or more long, and is surrounded by high ridges. Its water is very clear.

The brook from the second pond is navigable for only a few rods. A road runs up its south side, about a mile, to the pond. The lower pond is celebrated for its togue and white fish.

## Pockwockamus Deadwater

Pockwockamus Deadwater is about three miles long. Immediately at its foot, on the right, begins the carry around Katepskonegan (corrupted to Debsconeak) Falls,[52] which is very good, and ninety-five rods long. Below it for half a mile the stream is narrow, and there are some rips in it. The dead-water then broadens out into the dimensions of a lake. This and Pockwockamus Deadwater are very attractive, not only in their own immediate charms of sand beaches, islands, and the varied and graceful vegetation of their shores, but in the fine views they afford of Ktaadn and the Neesowadnehunk Mts.[53]

---

[52] **2020:** Now spelled, Debsconeag.

[53] **2020:** Nesowadnehunk. Some of the mountains along Nesowadnehunk Stream are – Doubletop, OJI, and The Brothers.

Just above the outlet of Katepskonegan Deadwater[54] on the east side, is the carry around Passamagamock (Pescongamoc) (now *Passamagamet*) Falls, thirty-two rods long. Below the carry the river is rapid for a short distance. Pescongamoc Pond (now *Passamagamet Lake*), on the right, lies within twenty rods of the river.

### Ambajejus Falls * Ambajejus Lake

From here it is about a mile and a half to Ambajejus carry (on the left), just above which the river narrows. The carry is one hundred rods long, and steep at its lower end. The main channel in the river passes to the east around an island below the carry, over a short stretch of rapid water. Passamagamock Falls, and possibly Ambajejus Falls, may be navigated at low water. Ambajejus Lake, whose shores are covered with crumbling granite blocks and coarse sand derived from them, shows the effects of flowage, and is rather bleak and cheerless in comparison with the dead-waters higher up the stream.

At the lower end of Ambajejus Lake, on a point on the right, is the so-called Ambajejus House, used by river-drivers in the spring.

### Millinokett Lake

Millinokett Lake[55] is most easily reached from Ambajejus Lake, by a short carry which begins at the head of a grassy cove. The lake is very picturesque, and is studded with pretty islands, which, in combination with the glorious views of Ktaadn and surrounding mountains, make it a very attractive spot for artists.

---

[54] **2020:** Debsconeag on Map 50 to Passamagamet on Map 42.

[55] **2020:** Millinocket Lake (current spelling) can be explored as a side excursion off of Ambajejus Lake. It offers a fine view of Katahdin.

No trout are in its waters,[56] and the brook which is its outlet is about twelve miles long and unnavigable.[57]

**Millinokett Lake**

*

## *North Twin Lake*

About ten miles of paddling through Ambajejus, Pamedumcook, and North Twin Lake bring one to the dam at the foot of the latter, where the river is crossed by the Bangor and Aroostook Railroad. The carry around the dam is on the left. It is less than twenty rods long.

---

[56] **2020:** Landlocked salmon, lake trout, and brook trout can be fished at this time. Large perch are reported and are fiercely competing against the other fish for food.

[57] **2020:** The brook Hubbard references is Millinocket Stream, and now, due to the dam, provides Class I and Class II rapids for whitewater rafting to Shad Pond.

## *Quakish Lake*

Below the dam for a mile the river is rapid to Quakish Lake.[58] At the foot of this lake begins the upper end of the Fowler Carry.[59] Sixty rods below here is the principal western terminus of the carry. The river between is rapid, but navigable.

The carry is about two miles long, and at Powers's, at the eastern end of it, a team can be hired to haul canoes and luggage across to Milnokett Stream. A mile of easy canoeing down this stream takes one into Shad Pond, the last "bulge" of any consequence on the river.

By making the carry at Fowler's, one avoids twelve miles of very rapid water, and saves much time and labor. Grand Falls, on this part of the river, is about twelve or fifteen feet high, and can be visited most easily by paddling through Shad Pond and up the river for a mile and a half.

From Shad Pond, over twelve miles of rapid water, accomplished in three hours, bring one to the mouth of the East Branch,[60] whence it is twelve miles more to Mattawamkeag, where one takes the cars for Bangor.

To the lover of scenery, the tour down the West Branch offers perhaps more attractions than any other in that part of Maine. There are, to be sure, many carries to make, but the wildness of the river, the picturesqueness of the lakes within easy access of it, and the grandeur of Mount Ktaadn, which continually discovers some new feature, together form a combination of enjoyments seldom to be found.

---

[58] **2020:** Gazetteer map 43.

[59] **2020:** At what is now Ferguson Lake, Gazetteer map 43, at Millinocket.

[60] **2020:** At Medway.

## RÉSUMÉ

Chesuncook Lake to Dam . . . . . . . . . . . . . . . . . . . .   17 m.
Dam to Ripogenus Carry . . . . . . . . . . . . . . . . . . . .   2 ¾ m.
Ripogenus Carry . . . . . . . . . . . . . . . . . . . . . . . . . .   3 m.
Ripogenus Carry to Ambajemackomus Carry . . . . .   2 ½ m.
Ambajemackomus Carry to Abol Stream . . . . . . . .   6 ½ m.
Abol Stream to Ambajejus Falls . . . . . . . . . . . . . .   11 m.
Ambajejus Falls to North Twin Dam . . . . . . . . . . .   14 m.
North Twin Dam to Shad Pond . . . . . . . . . . . . . . .   5 m.
Shad Pond to Mattawamkeag . . . . . . . . . . . . . . . .   25 m.

*

## *Jo Merry Lakes * Nahmakanta Lake*

There are three lakes in this chain, — West, South, and Big Jo Merry. The first, or West Jo Merry, lies southwest of the others, and is over half a mile from South Jo Merry. Canoes have to be carried across from one to the other. Between South and Big Jo Merry there is a thoroughfare of forty rods or more in length. At times the water in it is substantially "dead," at others, quick.

---

### 2020 Edition

If rather than heading to Quakish Lake from Ambajejus, one goes west into Pamedumcook you can reach the Jo-Mary Lakes – as these lakes are now named (Gazetteer map 42).

Jo-Mary Lake is reached from Pemadumcook via Lower Jo-Mary Stream. A narrow pass connects to Middle Jo-Mary. At the southeast of this lake is Turkey Tall Lake.

From Turkey Tall Lake, Upper Jo-Mary Lake, the largest of the Jo-Mary lakes is reached through Upper Jo-Mary Stream.

---

> Alternatively, explorers can check-in at the Jo-Mary wilderness region using the Jo-Mary Checkpoint gate, which is easily accessible from Rt 11 driving south from Millinocket.

\*

From Big Jo Merry to Pamedomcook Lake is a mile and a half or more, by the stream, which is partly navigable by canoes. A good road runs from one lake to the other near the stream.

Nahmakanta Lake is most easily reached from Pamedomcook Lake. Nahmakanta Stream which connects the two is about seven or eight miles long, and for two or three miles is navigable. Canoes and luggage will have to be carried about four miles over the old carry-road, on the north side of the stream. The lake is a very attractive sheet of water some four miles long, and into its northern end flow two streams. The more easterly comes from Rainbow Lake.

### Rainbow Lake * Pollywog Pond * Wadleigh Pond

Rainbow Lake is four miles long, but, with the exception of several small ponds along its course, it has not enough water in ordinary seasons to make canoeing anything but a burden. A good road begins west of the mouth of the brook, soon crosses to the east side, and finally comes out at the foot of Rainbow Lake. It is better to "carry" over this road than to attempt to navigate the brook. If one follows up for two miles the other brook which empties into Nahmakanta Lake, one comes into Pollywog Pond, whence it is one-third of a mile to Wadleigh Pond, the connecting stream being very rapid. A road runs from

Nahmakanta Lake across the southern slope of Suntabunt Mt. to Wadleigh Pond.

---

**2020 Edition**

This area is covered on Gazetteer maps 42 and 50.

The mention of some ponds by Hubbard (such as Wadleigh), and not others, can only be explained by those ponds he chose to visit, or learned about through conversation. Wadleigh is no more a pond than others in its vicinity such as, Black, Female, Bear, Bean, Kelly, or the Fisher Ponds.

Suntabunt Mountain is now known as Nesuntabunt.

Pollywog Gorge, which lies near Pollywog Pond, is a mile-long gorge that was part of a logging highway. Old growth trees can be seen here. The Appalachian Trail runs along the rim of the trail. There are numerous side trails with views of the surrounding mountains.

---

\*

# CHESUNCOOK FARM AND TAVERN.

———◆———

Situated at the head of CHESUNCOOK LAKE, on its Western Shore. Magnificent Panorama of Mt. Katahdin and the Sourdnahunk Mountains.

Meals and lodging furnished at all times on short notice. Fresh milk constantly on hand.

Campers going down the *St. John*, or *Penobscot Rivers*, or up to *Caucomgomoc Lake*, supplied with Pork, Flour, and Potatoes.

# NORTHWEST COVE MOOSEHEAD LAKE

*

---

### 2020 Edition

Hubbard now returns to the north end of Moosehead Lake at Seboomook and Northwest Carry.

The Northwest Carry was a busy transportation hub for logging operations and those taking the trip down the West Branch and Allagash. A number of lodging establishments were once located here catering to sportsmen and tourists.

Prior to 1919 the only access this far north was by water. Thus, steamers were busy all season long transporting tourists and loggers.

The corresponding Gazetteer maps are 49 and 48.

---

*

## *Northwest Carry*

Carry Brook, a small stream in which abound sunken logs, stumps, and snags, empties into the northwest arm of Moosehead Lake, in its upper left-hand corner, and to the left of the N. W. Carry hotel. Paddling up this brook for nearly a mile, to the head of navigation, one comes to a landing on the left bank, from which one reaches, a few yards distant, the direct road from the lake to Seeboomook Meadows. This road runs northwest, and for some distance covers the same ground as the Old Canada Road, which leads from Moosehead to Canada Falls, and beyond to Canada.

From the landing to the meadows is a long mile and a half, the road being good, except after a rain, when the walking is soft. Someone promptly appears at the landing with a horse and sled, if previously asked to do so, and hauls canoe and luggage across the carry, charging from a dollar and a half to two dollars per load.

Seeboomook Meadows consist of a small tract of ground lying near the West Branch, and the pond which covers a part of it, from a quarter to three eighths of a mile in diameter, is connected with the river by a shallow and narrow stream flowing northeasterly for a quarter of a mile from its east side.

## West Branch of The Penobscot * Seeboomook Falls

This part of the river is pretty difficult of navigation, and parties find it easier and shorter to be hauled across the Northeast and Northwest Carries, and to paddle over the lake between them, than to attempt to accomplish the same distance on the river. A visit, however, to Seeboomook Falls is quite worthwhile, if one has the time.

---

### 2020 Edition

Hubbard was traveling this section of the river before the modern dam was built at Seboomook Lake. The first 18-foot timber dam was built in 1893. A larger timber dam was built in 1912. The Great Northern Paper Company built the existing concrete dam in 1936. It is used today to control the flow of water to the river.

On the image from Hubbard's 1899 map, notice the absence of Seboomook Lake, which was created by the building of the 1912 dam. The river section Hubbard describes would have been very different than today's West Branch canoe-trip. This, of course, is prior to the construction of The Golden Road.

---

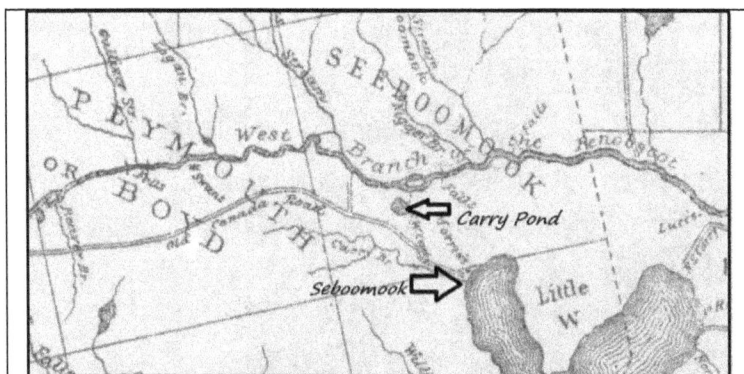

**Hubbard's Map – 1899**
**Northwest Carry and the West Branch**

The early dams were significant to control the flow of water for logging operations. The dam here was used to drive logs close to Carry Pond. From there, steam-power was used to pull logs by chain high enough to be dropped into a sluice that ran into Carry Pond. The logs were then floated down Carry Brook into Moosehead Lake. From there, the logs were boomed to the East Outlet for the trip down the Kennebec to the mills.

*

Just below the foot of Seeboomook Island are the first falls, past which, on the left, one must carry for a fifth of a mile. One mile and a half of good canoeing follow, — good except in one place, the Dam Pitch, where one must lift one's craft over. Then come the long falls. At high water one must carry at least three-quarters of a mile, in low water nearly double that distance, the path being on the right. Some three miles below the rapids is the mouth of Russell Stream, and from there to the Northeast Carry, or Luce farm, is two miles more. Seeboomook Falls is a wild and dangerous place, and the dread of log-drivers on the Upper Penobscot.

### Russell Stream * Elm Stream

Russell Stream is rather small, and for five miles out of six and a half to the pond, rapid; but a canoe can be worked up its channel slowly, or one can be hauled in to the pond by a team from Luce's. Russell Pond used to be good moose and caribou ground.[61]

Elm Stream can be reached by a road from the N. W. Carry, that terminates at a deep "logon" above and opposite its mouth. For nine miles the stream is usually navigable, partly through an alder-ground. The three miles next below the pond are very difficult, but a road on the left bank is good.

### West Branch of the Penobscot, Going up from Northwest Carry

Opposite the mouth of Seeboomook Stream, on Seeboomook Island, is a good campground. The river here is black and deep, a character it maintains for some eight miles above, as far as Swan's farm, and is in places very picturesque.

A half-mile brings one to the head of the island, above which the river widens, and after two miles and a half more the upper, or artificial, mouth of Nelhudus Stream is reached; the natural mouth is some rods below, and is generally impassable. Good fishing is to be had, late in the summer, in pools here and there among its windings.

---

[61] **2020:** Farther up Russell Stream is Cassidy Deadwater.

From the opposite or right bank of the river, just below Nelhudus, a good tote-road leads into the Old Canada Road,[62] — it being about six miles from the river to Moosehead.

From Nelhudus four and a half miles, past the ruins of Camp Pocahontas and around several sharp bends in the river, bring one to Swan's farm, on the left. On the high bank, along which at the west end of the clearing leads the path to Swan's "shanty," is a convenient camping ground, without, however, a very bountiful supply of good fire-wood.

Above Swan's the river for half a mile is shallow and the current strong, rendering it necessary, in low water, to wade and to drag canoes. At the end of this half-mile is the first or lowest pitch of Gulliver Falls, between which and the next pitch — a few rods — Gulliver Stream[63] empties into the river on the right. The second pitch is at the foot of a small island, going to the left of which one soon passes up over the third pitch, — the head of the rapids. In moderately high water two men can take a loaded canoe up over these rapids without much difficulty; but in low water resort must be had to the dragging process.

About three miles of deep "dead" water intervene between the head of Gulliver Falls and the foot of Big Island, passing up the right side of which, three-fourths of a mile, to the head, one comes to open land, and to more shallow and in some places "strong" water. The passage around the left of the island is narrower, and a quarter of a mile longer.

---

[62] **2020:** Now Seboomook Road which leads to Pittston Farm.

[63] **2020:** Gulliver Brook. Branches into East and West. The West leads to Third St. John Pond. Gazetteer map 48.

On the left, a few rods above the island, is the mouth of a "logon," pushing up which for forty rods a pool will be found encircled by lily-pads, where small trout are abundant.

From Big Island a mile of paddling brings one to King's High Landing, where from ledges on the left there is also good fishing. From this point it is less than a mile to Cunningham's farm, at the forks of the North and South Branches, where a team can generally be had to haul canoes around Canada Falls.

### RÉSUMÉ

| | |
|---|---|
| N. W. Carry (Moosehead L.) to mouth Seeboomook Brook. | 3 m. |
| Mouth of Seeboomook Brook to Nelhudus Stream . . . | 3 ½ m. |
| Nelhudus Stream to Swan's . . . . . . . . . . . . . . . . . . . . | 4 ½ m. |
| Swan's to head of Gulliver Falls . . . . . . . . . . . . . . . . | 1 ½ m. |
| Gulliver Falls to head of Big Island . . . . . . . . . . . . . | 3 ¾ m. |
| Big Island to the Forks . . . . . . . . . . . . . . . . . . . . . . . | 2 m. |

*

It takes from five to six hours to go from Moosehead across the carry and up the river as far as Swan's, and from four to five hours from Swan's to the Forks. In low-water it may take the better part of a day to accomplish the latter distance. Green Mt. is visible from Seeboomook Meadows.

## South Branch of the Penobscot

Leaving the forks,[64] and ascending the South Branch (much narrower than the main river), a mile and a half of swift water over a bed of rocks, in places so thickly strewn as to render the passage of a canoe almost impossible, brings one to the foot of Canada Falls. More or less wading will be found unavoidable over this stretch, except in high water, the worst part being immediately below the falls. The river here makes a very marked bend, having flowed for two miles and a half in almost a semicircle northwards, and then sweeping off at a sharp angle towards the east. Canada Falls consists of a succession of deep, narrow gorges, down and through which the water froths and roars. This part of the river is well worth seeing; but to take through it a loaded canoe, by alternate dragging and carrying, will require the better part of a long day. It takes much less time to make the long carry — a mile and a half— over the Old Canada Road, which leaves the foot of the falls, runs up the steep bank, then southwest by south, and at the end of three eighths of a mile turns sharply to the right. A mile and a half over a good road, hard and dry except in one place, is a pleasant substitute for an all-day's journey along and through the river. Put in at a dam at the head of the falls, and after a long half-mile through a very rocky stream, and past one "pitch" where the "painter," or leading-rope, will be needed, another dam marks the place where smooth and deep water finally becomes a reality.

---

[64] **2020:** Hubbard is referring to the North and South Branch Forks; not to be confused with the more popular use of "The Forks" on the Kennebec, west of Lake Moxie.

On the left bank just above the foot of the falls, and again just above the head of the falls, cold-water brooks will be found.

From the upper and larger dam, it is half a mile to Bog Brook. Until well away from the dam, lookout for large rocks just under water.

Passing by Bog Brook, which seems to be the sluggish outlet of a small bog about a quarter of a mile from the river, one paddles two miles, the latter of which is around an oxbow, and bending sharply to the west, comes to the mouth of Alder Brook. Up the river, about a mile from here, is the mouth of Hale Brook, opposite which is a flat ledge projecting halfway across the stream, and below the ledge a deep pool, where trout of medium size abound. A good campground lies just over this ledge. It affords plenty of hard wood and good water, and the hunting-grounds of Alder Brook are conveniently near it. A "logon" a few rods up the river on the same side, is a favorite feeding-ground for ducks. A logging-camp back of the "logon" will afford dingy shelter to parties not provided with a tent, and cool brook-water is near at hand. A good road runs back from this camp to the Old Canada Road, which it joins about a mile from the river.

A few rods above Hale Brook the character of the river banks changes, from a densely wooded to an open grassy elm-land, which character they maintain for a mile and a half. The sportsman's course is generally west; and two miles from Hale Brook, the water begins to be shallow in places, over which wading and dragging may be necessary. A mile and a quarter of this sort of navigation gives place to a mile of shallow, rock-strewn, "dead" water separated into two stretches by a short interval of quick water, and then for two miles more follow a succession of pools alternating with gravel and sandbars, when the mouth of Penobscot Brook is reached. This small stream, about five feet wide, flows out of Penobscot Lake, several miles through swampy ground, is choked up with fallen trees, and is entirely unnavigable. Its volume of water is about one fourth that of Bald Brook, which properly is the Penobscot, and should so be called.

Above this point canoeing is out of the question, excepting, perhaps, immediately after a very heavy rain, when, by dint of energetic poling, a canoe might ascend this boulder-strewn stream to apiece of "dead" water and alder ground, a mile or more above the junction of the two brooks. A tote-road, however, follows the stream, on its right bank, beginning three miles or more below Penobscot Brook, and becomes quite good a short distance above it. It crosses several ridges, and passes three decayed logging-camps, until, bearing off to the south, to the west of Bald Mountain, it finally joins the Canada Road in Sandy Bay township.

Penobscot Lake is best reached by taking to the Old Canada Road, and carrying canoe and load over it, from some point on the river near the road. The road, be it said, above the old camp near Hale Brook, has not been much used of late years, and is therefore "grown up" in places.

**RÉSUMÉ**

Forks of North and South Branches to
Canada Falls . . . . . . . . . . . . . . . . . . . . . . . . . . . . . .    1 ½ m.

Foot of Canada Falls to Upper Dam c. . . . . . . . . . . .    2 m.

Upper Dam to Penobscot Brook . . . . . . . . . . . . . . .    10 m.

\*

It takes about five hours to go from the Forks to the upper dam, and from six to seven hours more to the mouth of Penobscot Brook.

## *Alder Brook*

Alder Brook, twenty years ago a favorite feeding-ground for moose, runs through a stretch of country for the most part open and flat, and affording the best opportunity in the neighborhood for "still-hunting." Long grass covers its banks, with plenty of alder-bushes and some scrubby willows interspersed. For about two miles a canoe can run up the stream with ease, the general direction being south, and, beyond that point, west. The writer, on his only visit to this brook, in 1878, found a new beaver dam about two miles from its mouth, which so raised the water as to render the passage very good for nearly a mile and a half further. The water above the dam was so deep, however, that he does not hesitate to express an opinion that very little difficulty in ascending the stream would be met by the canoe-man, even in the absence of such a dam. A good camping ground will be found on the right, just below a short piece of shallow water, over which the canoe must be carried. Above these "rips" the stream is deep again for a mile, followed by a mile of shallow and deep places alternating. An old "landing" is at the foot of the quick water, which now appears in earnest, and here the canoe must stop, unless the brook should be high.

The bed of the stream above this point is very rocky, and continues so for a mile and a half to an old dam. On the right a road leads up the stream, at the landing blindly to be sure, but above the dam it opens out and affords good walking up to, and beyond, a ridge which runs north to the pond. The brook above the dam appears to be dead for about two miles and a half, its course being nearly east. It comes from the pond southerly, three quarters of a mile, to the point where the road crosses it; the latter goes a quarter of a mile further before it reaches the ridge spoken of above. Along the top of this ridge is a good path. The water of the pond is not cold, and the locality seems to promise little, either for fish or for game. Bald Mountain lies four or five miles southwest.[65]

This excursion, from the mouth of the brook to the pond and back, can be made comfortably in one day.

*

---

### 2020 Edition

Alder Brook no longer exists. On Hubbard's 1899 map it was a branch off what was the South Branch of the Penobscot. Notice how the South Branch meanders off to the northwest and eventually terminated at Penobscot Lake.

Today, the Gazetteer map 48 and 47 shows the South Branch passing through Canada Falls Lake (in the area of Alder Brook on the Hubbard map) and meandering towards the Canadian Border to disappear north of Sandy Bay Mountain; 12 miles southwest of Penobscot Lake.

---

[65] **2020:** Boundary Bald Mountain. Gazetteer map 47.

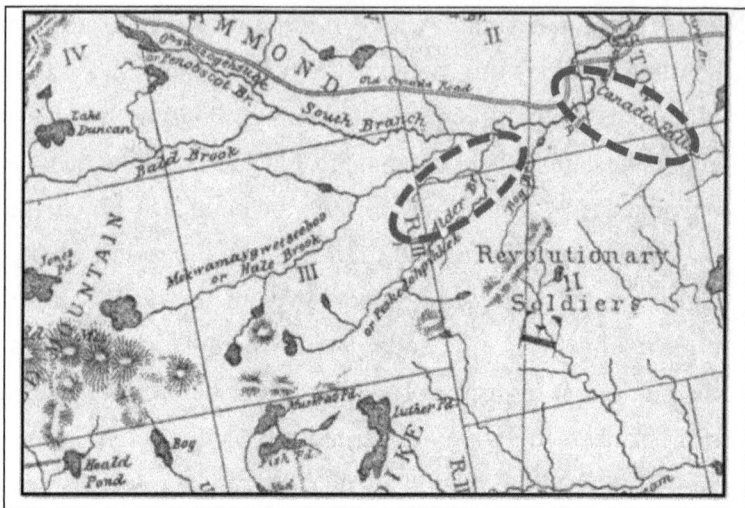

# GROCERIES

AND

## SUPPLIES.

---

### J. H. EVELETH & CO.,

Opposite the EVELETH HOUSE, and connected
with the POST-OFFICE.

GREENVILLE, MAINE.

---

*Constantly on hand a general assortment of
Staple Provisions, Dry Goods, Crockery, and
Glassware, Drugs, Hardware, Lumbermen's
Supplies, Fishing Tackle, and Ammunition.*

## SPORTSMEN'S AND CAMPERS' OUTFITS

*Carefully put up, and put on board the Steamer,
while passengers are at dinner.*

## NORTH BRANCH OF THE PENOBSCOT

The ascent of the North Branch of the Penobscot, is difficult and slow, at and from its very junction with the South Branch. Wide and shallow, it flows over bars of gravel and sand, which lie a few rods apart and separate stretches of deceptively smooth water. Large rocks strewn thickly over the bottom make it difficult to find a channel for even a lightly laden canoe.

From the forks to Big Lane Brook,[66] on the left, is about a mile and a half; thence three quarters of a mile to Leadbetter Brook on the same side; thence three quarters of a mile to an old camp (Spencer's) on the right, and from there to Leadbetter Falls, about three quarters of a mile further, or nearly four miles in all.

Leadbetter Falls consists of several short pitches, over which a canoe can be pulled up or let down by the "painter" without much trouble, except, perhaps, in high water, when they can be run, coming down, on the paddle. The carry is only a few rods long, and lies on the right, going up. The tote-road follows the river here, and as far up as High Landing, two miles above, where one branch leaves it and runs north and northeast, until it again nears it within three miles of the foot of Abacotnetic Bog.

---

### 2020 Edition

Abacotnetic Bog on the Gazetteer is noted as Little Bog on Map 48, A3. The North Branch on Hubbard's map, noted as the N.E. Branch, appears to terminate here at the bog. To the east of the bog, is St. John Pond, now Fifth St. John Pond.

---

[66] **2020:** Lane Brook. Little Lane Brook is on the right (north side).

This pond is significant because in 1939 the Great Northern Paper Company dug a 2-mile long canal from the pond to the North Branch of the Penobscot. This allowed water from the Baker Branch of the St. John to flow into the North Branch. With this greater flowage logs were then sluiced through the corridor to Millinocket. The canal on the Gazetteer map is given no name. The canal appears to be close to what was an old tote road (see arrow added).

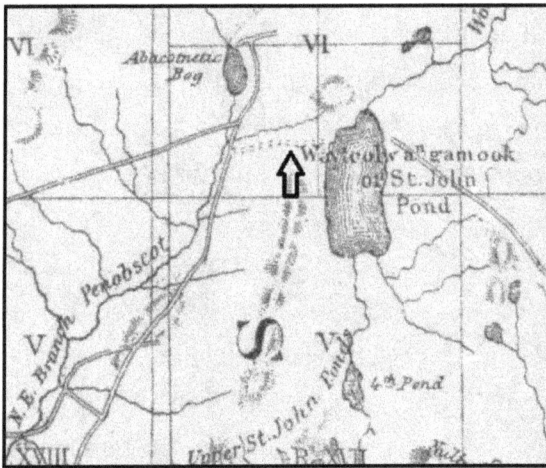

The other branch (of the North Branch of the Penobscot) follows the stream up to the mouth of Dole Brook, but is no longer very distinct.

The river immediately above Leadbetter Falls is somewhat deeper, and navigation a trifle easier. Four miles from the falls one comes opposite West Green Mt. (The *eastern* peak is from time to time visible from the lower parts of the stream.) There are now more stretches of dead-water and the stream grows perceptibly narrower. Up to this point it has seemed shut in, as it were, and its banks have been lined for the most part with soft-wood ridges. Now, however, the country grows more open, and hard wood predominates, while the rocky character of the river-bed changes for several miles to that of sand and gravel.

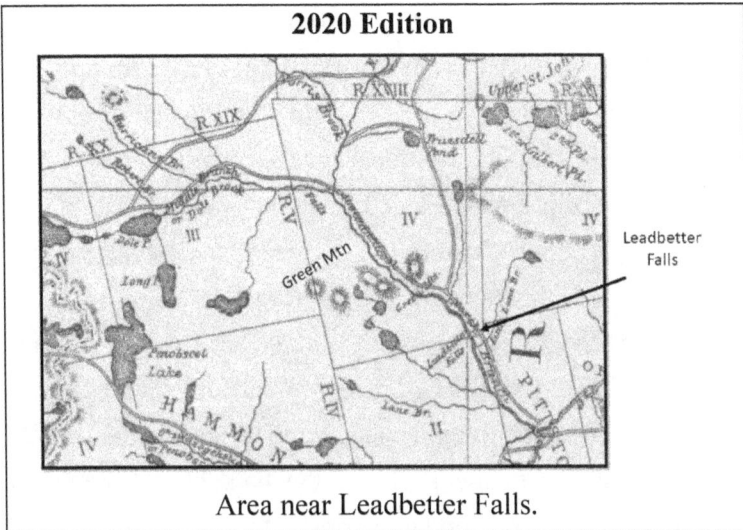

**2020 Edition**

Area near Leadbetter Falls.

A few minutes' walk brings one in sight of East Green Mountain, a half-mile higher up the stream, which at its base winds abruptly from the west, and the canoe-man's course tends more northwesterly. Following, for a mile, a ridge which descends from the western mountain northerly, one comes to an island half a mile long; the better channel, formerly on the west side, is now on the east. From the island it is a mile to Dole Brook.

For sixty rods above this point (on the North Branch) navigation is irksome; then it improves. Truesdell's Landing is about two miles above Dole Brook, and less than a mile below Norris Brook. Just below and just above the latter the North Branch is difficult for about a mile. In Tp. V, R. XVIII,[67] on the

---

[67] **2020**: Tp. V, R. XVIII is the notation for Maine Township T5 R18 WELS. Most all of Maine's unorganized territories are named in this

stream, is the clearing of L. C. Moore, two miles above the south line of the township.

One mile above this clearing the Alder Ground begins, and extends some eight miles to Abacotnetic "Lake," a narrow body of water surrounded by an extensive bog. From Moore's up to St. John Pond carry, some seven miles, navigation is ordinarily not very difficult; the worst part of the route is between Norris Brook and the Forks. Indeed, it is only after a hard rain, or during a wet season, that the ascent of the North Branch is practicable with any degree of comfort.

In the absence of high water, wading, and dragging of canoes will be the order of the day, with scarcely any intermission, — a process tiresome to the voyager, and ruinous to the canoe.

The road from the Forks to the bog, after leaving High Landing, runs a mile and a quarter to Spencer's camp of 1878-9; thence five and a half miles to Truesdell and Hildreth's camp (1878-9), which stood at the east end of Truesdell Pond. From this point to the north line of the township is a mile and three-eighths; the road crosses a brook just a mile above Truesdell's old camp. From the north line of this township it is a mile and a half to where a branch road leads west, one mile, to Moore's clearing. From Moore's it is seven miles by road to St. John Pond carry, thence two miles to Abacotnetic Bog, the latter road being more or less grown to bushes. The North Branch road from the Forks is quite good to a point where it descends from

---

way. WELS stands for West of the Easterly Line of the State. The R is the range number counted from the easterly line to the west. A map of the regions can be found at: www.maine.gov/mdot/maps/

a ridge, four hundred feet above the stream, in Tp. V, R. XVII; then it is apt to be wet.[68]

## RÉSUMÉ

| | |
|---|---|
| Forks to Leadbetter Falls | 4 m. |
| Falls to Dole Brook | 6 m. |
| Dole Brook to Norris Brook | 3 m. |
| Norris Brook to Alder Ground | 4 m. |
| Alder Ground to Head of Bog | 8 m. |

*

Ordinarily it will take two days to go from the Forks to Dole Brook. Beyond that point it is impossible to give an estimate of tune. It might take a day to reach the bog, or it might take several days.

### St John Pond * Baker Lake

St John Pond is reached from the North Branch of the Penobscot by a boggy road nearly two and a half miles long, that leaves a "landing" below the mouth of a small brook, whose course the road follows almost to the pond.[69] The latter is a hundred and fifteen feet above the level of the North Branch at the carry. St. John Pond is between two and three miles long and a mile or less broad. Into its upper end flow two brooks, the more westerly of which is the outlet of several small ponds, the streams between which are for the most part quite unnavigable. The lowest pond of the series, five and a half miles up, might be reached without much difficulty, in seasons of high water, but at other times for nearly half of the distance canoes must be carried.

---

[68] **2020:** Currently travelers use the Golden Road to North Branch Access Road.

[69] **2020:** See Hubbard map in prior section describing the canal at St. John Pond.

From Abacotnetic Bog, Baker Lake may be reached by two routes. The shorter route leads from a point a few rods up the brook which flows into the bog at its upper end. The carry, having been seldom used of late years, may be hard to follow. Two miles of rather soft walking bring one to Baker Brook, down which a canoe can be propelled without much difficulty to Baker Bog,[70] two miles and a half of the way being "dead" water. Between this bog-pond and Baker Lake, however, navigation is more difficult, and the water in the brook for nearly three miles "tumbles down hill," as the guides say, in a way that is discouraging.

The other route is by way of (Fifth) St. John Pond, whose outlet, the Woboostook or Baker Stream flows eighteen miles, in an almost semicircular course, to Baker Lake. For six miles canoeing is said to be pretty good, then come about eight miles of carrying and dragging, between which and the lake are four miles of "dead" water.

The first of these routes is always preferable, because even in low water there is about one third as much carrying and dragging to be done over it as there is in the second, while in the latter some parts of the stream are choked by logs and driftwood; and when there is an abundance of water and good canoeing in one stream, there is also enough for as good canoeing in the other.

Baker Lake has a good reputation for fish and game, which certainly ought to be abundant there, owing to the difficulty of reaching the place.

---

[70] **2020:** Gazetteer map 54, now Sweeney Bog.

From Baker Lake there is "strong" water, but plenty of it, to Seven Islands, some sixty or seventy miles distant, from which place parties can be hauled across to Long Lake, on the Allagash, and come back to Moosehead by way of Chamberlain Lake and Mud Pond, or else descend the Allagash into the St. John again, thus avoiding the dangers of Black River Rapids.

---

### 2020 Edition

Seven Islands (Gazetteer map 61) was possibly the largest settlement on the upper St. John River in the mid-1800s. My version of the map doesn't even have so much as a map dot to signify the history. To find Seven Islands, locate the intersection of 17 Mile Road. and Thibodeau Road. West of this there are several islands in the river. This is the location of Seven Islands. During the boom of logging operations, much of the land on these islands was farmed. The crops provided the food for the lumbermen who worked the woods through the winter. As the winter logging season approached, there would have been 200 – 400 men at Seven Islands.

South of Seven Islands, is Nine-Mile Bridge. In the early 1900s this Maine outpost required a year-round game warden. In her Memoir, *Nine Mile Bridge*, Helen Hamlin describes her years living in the Maine woods near this location.

Nine Mile Bridge is so named because the bridge is nine miles from the Canadian border at Lac Frontiere. This bridge was built in 1927 by Canadian lumber baron Edouard "King" Lacroix. Lacroix built a road from Lac Frontiere, all the way to Churchhill Depot, coincidently the location of Helen Hamlin's first teaching job. Lacroix needed the bridge and roads to supply his lumber operations in the Allagash. Lacroix also built dams and railways through the north woods in order to move the lumber required for his operations to feed the mills in Maine.

*

One day is enough in which to go from Abacotnetic Bog to Baker Lake, or two days from St. John Pond to the lake, and from that point Seven Islands may be reached in less than two days.

### Dole Brook * Dole Pond

Dole Brook or Middle Branch, will be found generally impracticable of navigation, and, aside from the falls, of little interest, either by way of scenery or promise of game. The main fall is about a mile and a half from the mouth of the brook. The water here trickles down the rock about ten or twelve feet. An eighth of a mile above, there is quite a long ledge, which slopes from the left bank to the centre of the stream, and forms its bed in times of freshets. It is worn into all sorts of basins and fissures and odd shapes, by the action of the water.

At high water, that part of the stream above the falls will not present many obstacles to the canoe-man, and is chiefly used, at such seasons, either by lumbermen or smugglers.[71] A tote-road runs from the mouth of the brook, on the northside, to Canada. It is as a whole quite good, lying through groves of soft wood, "burnt-slash," and over hardwood ridges. It runs pretty near the brook as far as the falls, then halfway over the "slash" nears it again, soon leaves it a second time, however, and,

---

[71] **2020:** During Hubbard's time, smugglers in the Maine woods dealt in timber, furs, and alcohol.

veering to the north, meets an old road (Lee's) from Dole Pond to the upper North Branch. Here it turns at a sharp angle, leads southwest and west, and again comes out to the stream just below Dole Pond. Plunging again into the woods, and crossing Robert Brook, one soon comes out at an old clearing. The old storehouse, the skeleton of which still remains standing on the bank of the pond, was built years ago, when lumbering was good in this region. Supplies were brought here from Canada, and grain and hay raised on the clearing during the summer, and distributed in winter to the neighboring lumbermen.

Dole Pond about a mile and a half long, and one mile broad in its widest part, is shallow and uninteresting, as is also Frost Pond, its counterpart, two and a half miles beyond. Between the two is an extensive "logon" frequented by caribou. No thoroughfare connects this "logon" with Dole Pond, the stream in summer disappearing almost wholly in one place, in or beneath a bog.[72] There seem to be no fish in these ponds and streams.[73]

## Long Pond

To the south of and emptying into Dole Pond by a small stream navigable in high water, and about two miles in length, lies Long Pond, a charming little sheet of water between two and three miles long, and varying in breadth from a half-mile to a mile. It is shut in by high wooded hills on every side, and

---

[72] **2020:** Hubbard must be referring to Frost Pond Flowage and Frost Pond. Gazetteer map 47.

[73] **2020:** Hubbard seems to have visited many ponds without fish. As of the latest Maine.gov survey of Dole Pond, there were squaretail brook trout noted in sufficient quantity to not require stocking.

seems to be quite deep. There is said to be good fishing in its waters.

### RÉSUMÉ

| | |
|---|---|
| Mouth of Dole Brook to Falls ................ | 1 ½ m. |
| Falls to Burnt Land ....................... | ¾ m. |
| Burnt Land ............................... | 2 m. |
| Burnt Land to Dam ....................... | 4 ¼ m. |
| Dam to Storehouse ....................... | ¾ m. |
| Storehouse to Frost Pond .................... | 3 ¼ m. |

\*

## D. T. SANDERS,

# Canoes and Campers' Supplies,

### GREENVILLE, MAINE.

———•———

*Hardware, Glassware, Crockery, Dry Goods, and Groceries of all kinds and descriptions; Canned Goods, Tea, Coffee, and Baking-Powder; Fishing Lines and Trout-Flies in great variety; Paddles and Setting-Poles.*

———

## Wants of Campers carefully attended to.

———

*Canoes to let by the week or month, at reasonable rates.*

# TOURS SOUTH OF ALLAGASH LAKE

## *Caucomgomoc Lake * Black Pond*

---

### 2020 Edition

Hubbard arrives at Caucomgomoc Lake in his tour by way of Chesuncook. Access to this lake by road can be made through the Caucomgomoc Checkpoint Gate.

Paddling from Chesuncook, the newer dam provides smooth water up through Caucomgomoc Stream, and through Black Pond.

Gazetteer map 55 shows Caucomgomoc Stream exiting Black Pond again with, "The Horserace," just below the Caucomgomoc dam.

Caucomgomoc is Indian for 'big-gull lake,' (in Hubbard's, *Woods and Lakes of Maine*.)

---

\*

Caucomgomoc Lake empties its waters through a stream of the same name, about twelve miles long, into Chesuncook Lake. With the exception of the upper three miles of the stream and two short falls, the water is smooth and navigation unrestricted. Until within a few years this region has been little visited, but from its accessibility and picturesqueness it is fast becoming a popular resort.

Leaving Chesuncook Lake, paddling about a mile, past the mouth of the Umbazooksus and over a small "rip," brings one to a miniature pond, at the northeast corner of which, to the left of the falls, is the end of a thirty-rod carry. There are two main pitches to these falls, some three and four feet high respectively. Putting in either at the head of the upper pitch, or further up the stream, around a bend at the foot of a very steep bank, about two miles intervene before the second fall is reached, — a single pitch of seven feet. Brandy Brook, between these two falls, furnishes good fishing after the first of September.

From the upper falls to Black Pond is a mile and a half, and across the pond a mile and a quarter more. Thus far the water is deep and black, and the river banks pretty wide a part. Beyond Black Pond the banks converge, the water is clearer, and a current is appreciable. For three and a half miles, past Little Scott Brook, no obstructions exist. At its mouth, and in the river above, trout may be taken in a number of places. About a mile above this brook are the Oxbow Rips, two or three rods long, and here passengers will have to walk, and, in low water, carry canoes and baggage. At the foot of the bank, around the bend, is another good trout hole.

Half a mile more brings one to the foot of the "horse-race," a mile and a quarter long, up which a canoe with a light load may be poled or dragged, without great difficulty unless the water is very high or very low. Around Horserace Falls, nearly three-quarters of a mile above dead-water one may have to carry.

A good road runs from the head of Chesuncook Lake up Caucomgomoc Stream, touching the latter at the second falls, and again about two miles from Caucomgomoc Lake. The last two hundred rods of this road are apt to be wet and miry; the rest of it above Oxbow Rips is on high ground, and dry.

It takes about a day to go from Chesuncook Lake to Caucomgomoc Lake. The carry around the "horse-race" can easily be made, canoe and baggage, in three hours.

The lake is one of the prettiest spots in Maine. It is about seven miles long, and three miles broad at its widest part, is of irregular shape, and has several small islands at its upper end. A charming camping ground will be found on either side of a small point of land, which juts out from the west shore, some five miles from the outlet. On the north and south sides of the point are long stretches of sand beach, back of which is good level camping ground and plenty of wood, and on the north an icy cold brook. From the south side the view is fine, taking in a wide expanse of blue water. On the north, the lake narrows considerably and the view is much more limited, being broken by pretty islands, and overshadowed, as it were, by forest-clad mountains on the west, — a decided contrast with the other view.

The shores of the lake are in many places rocky and covered with cedars, and, excepting at the upper end, offer few good camping-places.

\*

---

**2020 Edition**

The point Hubbard describes has since been named, Hubbard Point (Gazetteer map 55). I've indicated the approximate location on Hubbard's map with an arrow. It is less than a mile southeast of the Caucomgomoc Checkpoint.

Notice the different waterway between Chesuncook and Caucomgomoc lakes on Hubbard's map and a map of today. The modern dams have provided greater access between these bodies of water.

---

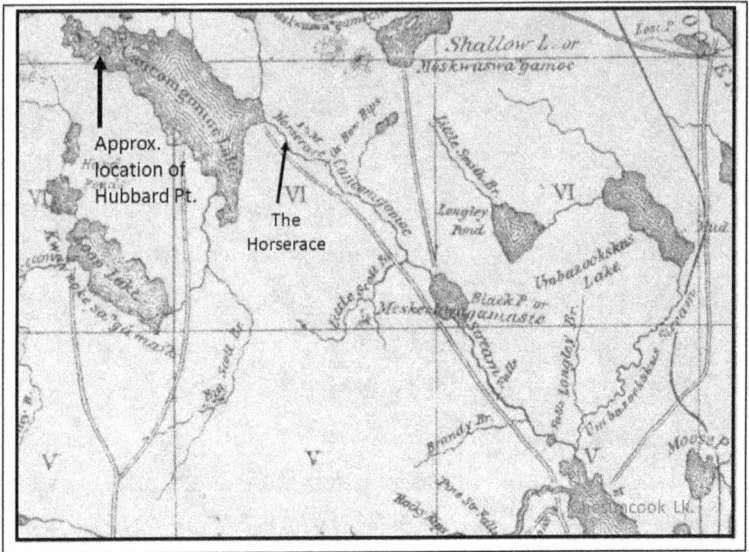

*

## *Avery Brook * Loon Stream*

Avery Brook empties into the head of Caucomgomoc Lake, to the west of a broad piece of meadow-land and "logon." It comes from a small pond of the same name about a mile and a quarter distant, and varies in width from ten to thirty feet. For half a mile it is deep enough for a canoe, but for the rest of the way quite shallow, and will give abundant opportunity to wade, and perhaps to make two or three short carries over its bed. The pond is quite small and almost completely overgrown with sedge-grass and lilies, but contains an inexhaustible supply of small trout, which rise freely in the morning and evening. Good fishing may also be had at the mouth of Avery Brook.

From the south end of Caucomgomoc Lake, Loon Stream is dead for three-quarters of a mile; then, for a mile and a half, it is rocky and shallow, but, except in dry seasons, a lightly laden canoe may be dragged and poled up or down the latter part in less than two hours. A good road runs along the south side of the stream, opposite the rapids and shallows. From the foot of the upper dead-water to the mouth of Big Scott Brook is half a mile; thence three-eighths of a mile to the carry, on the left, or north, bank. The upper part of this dead-water is rocky.

### Big Scott Brook * Little Loon Stream

Big Scott Brook is navigable for three-fourths of a mile. Above that, for perhaps a mile, the brook is shallow; beyond this part an alder-ground extends several miles, above an old dam, the carry from Loon Stream into Loon Lake.

This brook, Little Loon Stream, is dead for half a mile or more from its mouth. It then becomes very narrow and rocky for another mile, to a point where a brook joins it from the north. Formerly a dam on this brook, three-eighths of a mile above, formed a small pond, but the dam is now rotten, and Nature has resumed her sway. Nothing but a bog remains. Above the junction Loon Stream soon widens out into a bog, and, at the end of another mile, into a pond. Both this stream and Withey Brook have more or less dead-water and bog above here.

### Loon Lake

Loon Lake[74] is sixty rods long and even prettier than its neighbor, but much more difficult of access. It is quite deep, and some three miles long by from one to two miles broad. Its outlet into Caucomgomoc Lake is in places shallow and rocky, but not very hard to navigate. From the mouth of Loon Stream

---

[74] **2020:** To the south of Caucomgomoc, map 49

one can ordinarily take a loaded canoe to Loon Lake in three hours.

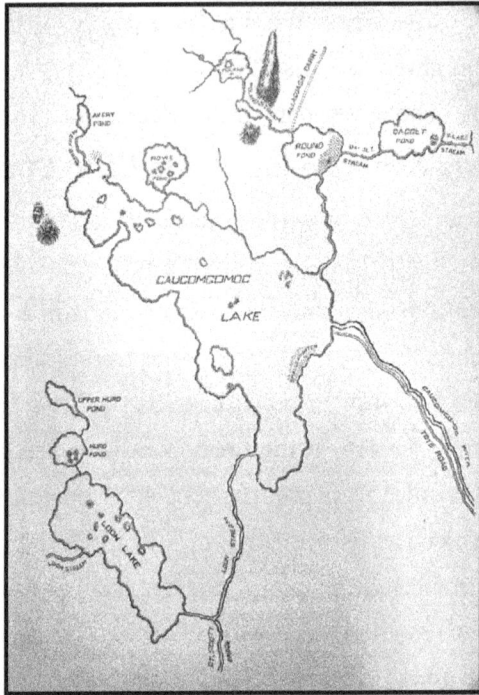

**Caucomgomoc Lake**

\*

Of Loon Lake itself not much is to be added, except that it contains much vegetable growth, and its water is, therefore, not very palatable. The writer knows of no good camp-grounds to recommend. There is one that is indifferent, opposite the mouth of the inflowing, or Little Loon Stream.

A good road runs along the south bank, beginning at the head of the dead-water (a half-mile from the mouth of the stream). It soon passes an old logging camp, crosses the brook three-quarters of a mile above it, and runs direct to the lower end of the lake, some two miles further.

## Hurd Ponds * Round Pond

Hurd Ponds are connected with Loon Lake by narrow and unnavigable brooks a few rods long. The lower Hurd Pond is not more than thirty rods from Loon Lake, over a good carry. The pond is quite pretty and must contain trout. A long, high ridge lies north of it, less than two miles away. The inlet from the upper pond enters the lower pond on the east side.[75] This second one is shallow, and its shores dreary and uninviting.

On the other side of Caucomgomoc Lake, and connected with it by a deep stream four miles long, and rocky only at its mouth, is Round Pond (called the "Sis," abbreviated from Caucomgomocsis[76] or Little Caucomgomoc), a body of water a mile and a half long by one mile wide. A good camping ground will be found on the northwest side of the pond at the foot of a hard-wood ridge, or on the northeast side. Good fishing may be had in a spring hole near the mouth of a small brook on this latter side, or at the mouth of, and in, Poland Brook.

## Daggett Pond * Shallow Lake

Daggett Pond is connected with Round Pond by a small stream a mile and a half long, through which at high water a canoe can easily be paddled. A beaver dam at the mouth of this stream for several years kept back enough water to answer all the purposes of the canoe-man going to Daggett Pond. This sheet of water, about a mile and a half in diameter, offers no

---

[75] **2020:** The lower pond is noted on map Gazetteer 55 as Big Hurd Pond. Little Hurd Pond, which Hubbard refers as the upper pond, is not all that different in physical size. **Not to be confused** with the two ponds of the same name located in the Debsconeag Lakes Wilderness Area near Abol Falls. These ponds were covered earlier.

[76] **2020:** Gazetteer map 55 noted as *Cis Stream*.

special attractions except, perhaps, in the way of cranberries, which grow in profusion on its northwest and southwest sides.

A mile and a half intervene between Daggett Pond and Shallow Lake, the connecting stream being too small for a canoe, but furnishing good walking in its bed for three quarters of a mile, past a miniature fall, to an old dam. Above this dam a canoe can be led and carried to a second dam, and from there paddled among sharp rocks to Shallow Lake.

Shallow Lake whose shores on nearly all its sides are swampy and covered with grass and hackmatack growth.

The lake is about two miles long and a mile and a quarter broad, and with the exception of a part, about a mile in diameter, towards its eastern end, is only from six inches to a foot deep, and covered with lily pads and sedge-grass. The bottom is mud unadulterated, and the waves and ripples made by the progress of a canoe will bring bubbles of gas in great quantities to the surface of the water, on all sides, even ahead of the canoe.

The lake lies diagonally north and south, and has two small islands at its west central end. A good road leads from its eastern extremity to Chamberlain Lake.

Black ducks are found here in great quantities, and cranberries are plenty. At the northwest end of the lake, near the outlet, there runs along the shore a natural ridge about four feet high, a sort of embankment, behind which the land falls two or three feet again.[77] There are no trout in Shallow Lake, but some have been taken at the mouth of Shallow Lake brook

---

[77] Probably formed by ice-pressure. See Dawson's Acadian Geology, 1st edition, p. 40.

in Daggett Pond. The boggy shores of both ponds are cut up with caribou tracks.

## Poland Brook * Poland Pond

Returning through Daggett and Round Pond, Poland Brook is for a quarter of a mile from its mouth deep. This character then giving place for another quarter-mile to a succession of "rips" and shallow places, through which some wading must be done. A miniature fall of three feet marks the reappearance of smooth water, which extends up to Poland Pond. Above the falls the stream widens considerably, and on either side are hackmatack bogs covered with grass and low bushes. Lily-pads cover the water except in the middle of the stream. These features predominate for two miles.

The stream then resumes its old appearance, narrows a good deal, and exchanges a muddy for a sandy and rocky bottom. One mile more brings one to Poland Pond.

Poland Pond a pleasing little sheet of water about three quarters of a mile long and half a mile broad. There is some swampy ground at its western end, which makes islands of two pieces of high land jutting out into the pond. A narrow channel which runs through this swamp leads over a succession of beaver dams, to quite an extensive beaver pond.

Wadleigh Brook,[78] which empties into the northern end of the pond, is clear and cold, and at times affords good fishing.

---

[78] **2020:** Gazetteer map 55. Wadleigh Stream originates at Wadleigh Pond and runs along Wadleigh Trail Rd.

## RÉSUMÉ

Chesuncook Lake to Caucomgomoc Lake . . . . . . .   12 m.
Caucomgomoc Lake, length . . . . . . . . . . . . . . . .   7 m.
Caucomgomoc Lake to Loon Lake . . . . . . . . . . . .   4 m.
Caucomgomoc Lake to Round Pond . . . . . . . . . .   3 m.
Caucomgomoc Lake to Avery Pond . . . . . . . . . . .   1 ¼ m.
Round Pond to Poland Pond . . . . . . . . . . . . . . . .   3 ½ m.
Round Pond to Shallow Lake . . . . . . . . . . . . . . . .   4 ½ m.

Parties who wish to visit and explore this region can best do so by camping on Round Pond, and taking one day for Poland Pond, and one for Shallow Lake and Daggett Pond. A light load, consisting of provisions for two days, an axe, kettle, frying pan, and blankets, can be taken from there with canoe to Allagash Lake, and a very pleasant and easy excursion made.

### Allagash Lake

At the head of the dead-water near the mouth of Poland Brook begins the carry which leads to Allagash Lake. The path runs along a ridge of low mountains, perhaps half or one third of the way up their sides, and is three miles long and quite dry and open. From the end of the carry it is about three miles around to the mouth of Allagash Stream, a quiet, cold, narrow, and deep brook, with a sandy and rocky bottom, and navigable for several miles with comparative ease.

There are no rapids, and but few "rips," for some distance from its mouth, but the current is quite strong. The stream, not having been "driven" of late years, is, higher up, somewhat choked with logs and drift wood. At and near its mouth there is good fishing.

The northeast shore of the lake is low and sandy, that on the west is rocky, and often precipitous to a height of fifty or seventy-five feet. West of the lake several mountains, the Toulbah range, appear quite strikingly; the country on the other sides, however, is flat and uninteresting.

---

**2020 Edition**

The Toulbah range, according to Hubbard in, *"The Woods and Lakes of Maine,"* lies between Caucomgomoc and Allagash Lake. Toulbah meaning "turtle," and the mountains are so called because of their low, flat shape. The term Toulbah did not appear on Hubbard's 1899 map.

The mountains all of which are not very high are now named individually as, Poland Mt. (East 1,820 ft., West 1,853 ft.), and Allagash Mt. (1,760 ft.).

The Allagash region is some of the most pristine wilderness in Maine. In 1966 the voters of Maine voted to protect the wilderness and subsequently the National Wild and Scenic Rivers Act of 1968 (WSRA) designated the Allagash as a 'wild river.' The designation ensured the Allagash River would be "generally inaccessible except by trail, with watersheds or shorelines essentially primitive."

Some of the lakes, ponds, and of course, the Allagash River, of the waterway are covered by Hubbard. The interested readers and explorers of this region are encouraged to research about the 92-mile-long connection of lakes, ponds, rivers, and streams in the Allagash Wilderness Waterway. Today, with road access to the waterway limited, parking is permitted within carry distance of Allagash Lake.

---

\*

Several small brooks empty into Allagash Lake, none of which are navigable. Good camping ground may be found on the west side of the lake about a mile from the inflowing Allagash, beneath a precipitous wall of rock.

Parties sometimes ascend Allagash Stream to Mud and Crescent Ponds, and carrying across, from the mouth of the inflowing brook, two or three miles (two different roads) to Chemquasabamticook Lake, and then go down the difficult stream of that name into Long Lake.

---

**2020 Edition**

This route passes through Clayton Lake to double back to the Allagash River. This is not part of the current official Allagash Wilderness Waterway Trail. As Hubbard notes, traveling Chemquasabamticook Stream would be a much more difficult paddle than the trail described next.

---

\*

Chamberlain Lake may be reached by going down the Allagash. The stream is quite rapid for two miles and a half from the lake, and flows with considerable current for another mile to Allagash Pond. At the outlet of the pond is a pretty fall, fifteen feet high, and between it and the head of dead-water two miles and a half, there are rapids, and three "pitches" over which canoes must be lifted. From the head of dead-water it is a mile and a half to Chamberlain Lake, the banks of the stream being lined with the trunks and roots of dead trees. When the water is fairly high the ascent of the stream takes but a few hours.

\*

---

**2020 Edition**

Hubbard has Allagash Pond (not labeled on his map) between Allagash Lake and Chamberlain Lake. Gazetteer map 55 labels this pond as Little Round Pond. The Gazetteer labels an Allagash Pond on this map at C1, as the source of Allagash Stream. This small pond does not appear on Hubbard's map.

\*

# M. G. SHAW & SONS,

# Groceries and Hardware.

**Steamboat Wharf, adjoining Lake House.**

———•———

Flour, Sugar, Canned Vegetables and Fruits,
Shoes, Moccasons, Woollen Shirts,
Socks, Bakers, Frying-pans,
Pails and Tin-ware, Drugs,
and Lumbermen's
Supplies, all at
Reasonable
Prices.

———•———

## CANOES FOR SALE AND TO LET.

*Greenville, Maine.*

# DOWN THE ST. JOHN RIVER[79]

*

The first part of this route Down the St. John River has already been described in the section, "West Branch Of The Penobscot - Going Down From Northeast Carry."

### *Umbazookskus Stream * Umbazookskus Lake*

From the head of Chesuncook Lake, and mouth of Caucomgomoc Stream, it is but a fraction of a mile to the mouth of the Umbazookskus, a stream which for four or five miles winds sluggishly, but with provoking pertinacity, through low meadow-lands which yield a yearly abundance of hay to the Chesuncook farmers. There is a cold spring on the right about a mile from the mouth of the stream. Above this stretch of "dead" water there is quick and shallow water for some two miles, or more, through which a canoe may be poled, or led, without much difficulty, except for perhaps a quarter of a mile, where carrying may become necessary. A good road runs on the right up to Umbazookskus Lake, and during the summer season, a team and "jumper" are constantly on hand to haul canoes and luggage over to Mud Pond, at an expense of from three and a half to five dollars.

---

**2020 Edition**

Here is a case where there are two Mud Ponds within striking distance of one another. One is to the east of Chesuncook, near Weymouth Point (Gazetteer map 50). The

---

[79] **2020:** At this point, Hubbard is still a long way from the St. John. Here he begins his trip through what we now refer to as, "The Allagash Waterway." The water highway will eventually meet the St. John.

other, the one Hubbard is referring to, is south of Chamberlain Lake (Gazetteer map 56).

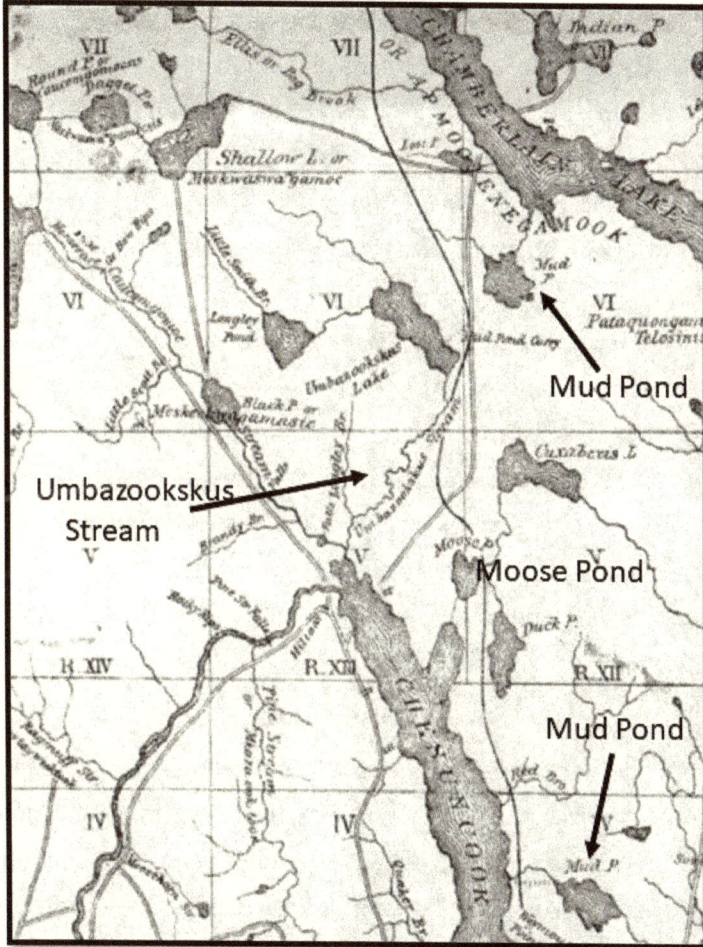

The Umbazookskus Stream on Hubbard's 1899 map, is a meandering little thoroughfare. Currently, most of the Umbazookskus is the size of a good pond following the construction of the Ripogenus Dam.

In the text Hubbard references the pains of this carry. The carry over to Mud Pond is no less easy today, than in the 1890s.

Paddlers crossing the carry have noted:

*"Most of this carry is either standing or flowing water several inches deep."*

*"We carried over thick mud."*

*"I counted over a dozen trees down that we had to portage over."*

*"Near the end, there was mud up to our knees."*

*"Not one map could agree on the distance. They ranged from 1.5 to 1.8 to 2.0 miles. It felt more like twenty!"*

*"We had to make three trips to carry our boat and gear. After six hours of trekking, I would have gone home, but then remembered it was back across that carry."*

*"Bring your mukluks."*

\*

## Mud Pond

Paddling a mile across the southeast corner of Umbazookskus Lake, one comes to the beginning of the famous Mud Pond Carry, the dread of guides, and abomination of sportsmen. This carry is two miles long, and although improved of late years, in many places has the appearance of the bed of a brook, with water and mud enough almost to float a canoe. Except in very dry seasons the traveller here sinks in mire up to his ankles, and without a pair of rubber boots is indeed "at sea." This hardship once over, by no means onerous if one has no heavy load to carry, the rest of the St. John trip is so comparatively easy and pleasant, that the remembrance of one's toil is soon lost, for the time, in keen enjoyment.

Mud Pond whose name carries with it its chief characteristic, is nearly round, and about a mile wide. Lifting over a dam at its outlet, wading may again become necessary for about three-eighths of a mile down the brook, which for half a mile near its mouth broadens into a sort of "logon," where ducks congregate.

### Chamberlain Lake * Eagle Lake

A good carry leaves the dam, on the left, and leads to the head of the dead-water three-eighths of a mile. Passing with difficulty through a confused mass of submerged stumps and floating tree-trunks, a run of two miles across Chamberlain Lake, or Apmoojenegamook, "at the great cross-lake," brings one to Chamberlain farm, where the most necessary articles of camp fare are usually to be had — at a good round price.

The shores of this lake are not very attractive. Some years ago a large dam was built at its natural outlet, and the water forced back and through an artificial "cut" or canal between Telos and Webster Lakes. This enables the lumberman to take his logs down the East Branch of the Penobscot River to a home market, instead of having to go into New Brunswick. The consequent rise of water in the lake flooded its shores and killed the trees on them for several yards back. Nearly all of the withered trunks which then lined the lake have fallen, and the shores look more as Nature made them, save the drift-wood which here and there in unsightly masses helps to make impenetrable any campground within. The tourist gladly passes on to the dam and lock, some three miles from the farm. Two short carries must be made past these obstacles, on the right, and after running through some quick water and a pleasing little lakelet, one emerges into Eagle Lake (Indian name of Pongokwahemook).

Eagle Lake is a pretty and irregular sheet of water, with attractive shores, and contains two or three good-sized islands. Several brooks empty into it, which are partially navigable, and through some of which access may be had to ponds beyond. The meaning of its Indian name is said to be "Woodpecker place."

### Smith Brook * Haymock Lake

Smith Brook, the outlet of Haymock Lake, empties into Eagle Lake on the east nearly opposite Pillsbury Island. It is dead-water for nearly two miles and a half from its mouth, to the head of an island, at which and above which the brook is shallow and its bed rocky. For the next half mile, the water is fairly deep until within a few steps of the foot of the "carry," when it again becomes shallow. The "carry" is a good one, lies on the left, and is three-quarters of a mile long. Near its upper end there is a small waterfall. For the next half mile, the canoe-man may find several old beaver dams, over which his canoe will have to be lifted, but beyond them the stream winds sluggishly through a bog for two miles and a half, from within a quarter of a mile of Haymock Lake, when wading becomes necessary.

An old path runs from the head of the bog, on the left bank, up to the lake. Fair camping grounds may be found near either end of the bog. Haymock Lake is about two and a half miles long and from a mile to a mile and a half wide, and surrounded by forests of mingled hard and soft wood. Its name is probably the latter part of the Indian word for Eagle Lake, Pongokwahemook, which by some accident or through the fancy of some ignorant white man was transferred to the tributary lake. The excursion from Eagle Lake to Haymock Lake and back can be made comfortably in one day.

### Russell, Soper, Snare, and Thoroughfare Brook

Russell, Soper, Snare, and Thoroughfare Brooks[80] are navigable for some distance, and afford good fishing in places, one of which is off a sandy point at the head of a small "bulge" in Snare Brook. The mouth of Soper Brook, for nearly a mile, is shallow, but above the dam the stream is deep, with one exception, for more than three miles, and is bordered by much the same country as that on upper Smith Brook. From Chamberlain Dam it is about three miles to Pillsbury Island, another mile to the mouth of Smith Brook, three miles and a half more to the Narrows, thence nearly two miles to the Thoroughfare, and two miles and a half through it to the mouth of Thoroughfare Brook, which is but a few rods from Churchill Lake.

### Churchill Lake * Spider Lake

Churchill Lake, or "Allagaskwigamook," "at the bark-wigwam lake," is about six miles long, and three miles broad in its widest part. Into it empty, on the southwest and only a few rods apart, the Twin Brooks, the more northern of which is the outlet of Spider Lake. From the beach midway between the brooks an old and difficult "carry" leads through a stretch of "burnt land," or "second growth," up the left bank of North

---

[80] **2020:** These brooks all connect from Eagle Lake.

Twin, a mile and a quarter, to a small sedge-grown and marshy pond. In seasons of high water, the canoe-man can take his loaded canoe up the stream from its mouth. At other times his luggage, at least, and perhaps his canoe too, must be carried as far as the pond, across which (a quarter mile) passage is almost always sure, even if slow. Above this point the stream will generally float a loaded canoe up to the dam at its head. An old and obscure path runs to the dam (one mile) along the left bank of the brook, leaving the latter just above Marsh Pond.[81]

Spider Lake (Allagaskwigamooksis) a cove-indented pond, is about two miles long and a mile wide. Its water is black and deep, and teems with togue. This is the first of the chain of lakes and ponds which leads to Munsungan Lakes and the Aroostook River, over a route used for many years by hunters and fur-dealers. Some old cedar trees on the "carries" still bear names and dates written as long ago as '49 (1849).

### Pleasant Lake * Harrow Lake * Musquacook Lakes

At the head of a small cove at the northeast end of Spider Lake, which lies opposite a small island, begins the "carry" into Pleasant Lake. Until the autumn of 1881 this path was but a "spotted line," used almost exclusively, in the winter, by hunters. In October of that year, however, the writer went by this route over Pleasant, Harrow, and Musquacook Lakes, down Musquacook Stream into the Allagash and St. John Rivers, and his guides "bushed out" the old tote roads where there were any, and cut new roads where none had before

---

[81] **2020:** Noted on Gazetteer map 56 as Grass Pond.

existed.[82] The "carry" first above mentioned runs northeast about a mile and a half, over level and dry ground and comes out on Pleasant Lake.

The carry enters just east of a small point or promontory which juts out from the south shore midway of the lake. Into this body of water, which is two miles long (less rather than more), and about a mile wide, only one brook of importance empties, — at its northeast end. This brook is said to flow through a small beaver pond, about a mile above its mouth. Several small and picturesque islands near South Point and a group of mountains ("Peaked" Mt. and others[83]) northeast of the pond make the landscape pretty enough to warrant the name Pleasant Lake.

Crossing towards the northwest, one enters Mud Cove, whose waters unfortunately emit a very disagreeable odor, which during unfavorable winds may prove a great annoyance to campers in the vicinity. Camping grounds, good in other respects, will be found at the head of the cove on the end of the "carry" to Harrow Lake, a few rods west of which is a brook of delicious spring-water.

The carry into Harrow Lake is a mile long, and, soon after leaving Mud Cove, runs over a very wet bog, its northern terminus being at the head of a deep bog-bound cove. On the left of the cove rises Pleasant Mt., a ridge which extends westerly for half a mile or more, and is very conspicuous from Churchill, Spider, and Pleasant Lakes. This "carry" appears to

---

[82] **2020:** The trip Hubbard refers to is covered in his memoir, ***Woods and Lakes of Maine.*** See 2020 Annotated Edition.

[83] **2020:** Pleasant, Mule Brook, Little Ragged, and Ragged Mountains.

be an old tote-road, the main branch of which skirts along the eastern shore of Harrow Lake, runs up Bog Brook and around to Clear and Mud Lakes of the Musquacook group.

Harrow Lake is about two miles long and half a mile wide, except at the east end, where two opposite coves increase its width to a mile or more. Its water has a dirty yellowish appearance, and seems to contain no fish, save some large specimens of the tadpole order. At the lower end of the pond the country is flat and boggy, and filled with forests of dead trees, many of which, having fallen, choke the outflowing stream. Good camping ground may be found on the eastern and northeastern shores of the lake. Paddling half a mile up the northeast cove, which soon narrows into the proportions of a brook, the canoe-man will find on the right the road heretofore mentioned, which runs towards Musquacook waters along Bog Brook.

### Bog Brook * Mud Lake

The lower part of Bog Brook is wet and swampy, but it soon rises on to higher ground, and at the end of a mile runs past an extensive bog which branches off northerly, while the road continues easterly along the course of the brook. At the end of another three-quarters of a mile the lower end of a more extensive bog is reached, through which the brook flows sluggishly for nearly a mile. The "carry" from here to Fourth Lake leaves the northeastern side of the bog a few rods above its lower end, runs northeasterly, soon skirting easterly along the south edge of a wide and open bog, or "barren," then northerly again, until it reaches Fourth (Musquacook) Lake a mile below its head.

Should the tourist prefer to continue up Bog Brook, he will find near its head, on the east side, a good road which will lead him forty rods to a tiny beaver pond, beyond which it is about half a mile over a bad road to Clear Lake, the source of the Musquacook, and a very pretty body of water. Northwest of it lies Round Mt., conspicuous from many points of the surrounding country. From the outlet of Clear Lake the old road runs along the stream past a small beaver pond, about a mile and a half, to Mud Lake.[84]

Mud Lake is all that its name implies, — a thin coating of water over a volume of yellow mud, which in many places seriously impedes the passage of a canoe. It is otherwise quite an attractive spot, and commands a fine view of Round Mt. on the west, and the Peaked Mt. group on the south, while Triple Mt. is visible on the northeast. A small and pretty island is quite conspicuous off the eastern shore of the lake, opposite an extensive bog where cranberries grow in profusion. The Lake is crescent shaped and somewhat over two miles long from "horn" to "horn." The stream which is its outlet is about a quarter of a mile long, and, excepting a short stretch near its mouth, will generally be found deep enough to float a canoe.

### Fourth Lake * Third Lake

Fourth Lake the next in the chain, is nearly if not quite three miles long and half a mile wide, lying northwest and southeast. Besides the stream from Mud Lake, three insignificant brooks empty into it, and the sameness of its shores and absence of variety in the surrounding scenery impress one unfavorably.

---

[84] **2020:** On Hubbard's 1899 map Mud Lake is also 5th Musquacook Lake.

The outlet into Third Lake (or Donald's Lake) is a small brook which flows from the northeast end of the lake. It is about a mile long, and usually shallow enough throughout its entire length to make wading expedient, if not necessary. Donald's "Lake" lies east and west, is a mile and a quarter long and five-eighths of a mile wide, and on its western shore is the resting place of "Dirty Donald," who for many years lived and hunted on Eagle Lake and Allagash waters. He was left at this pond, by a sturdy companion, in a feeble condition, and with only two days' provisions, and when found three weeks later he lay on his back on the floor of his little log camp, his face looking upwards through the open chimney place, and partly covered with a tin basin to protect it from the falling snow. Near him pieces of round-wood were found with the bark gnawed off, — sure signs of an awful death from starvation.

Paddling across from the southwest to the northwest corner of this pond, one enters the brook which leads to Second Lake. It is somewhat deeper than the last one, and about the same length, or a trifle longer.

### Second Lake * First Lake

Second Lake is a mile and a half, or more, long, and less than half as wide. At its foot is a very good log cabin, large enough for three or four persons. Near it fishing is said to be good, probably in deep water, for togue. A brook flowing in from the west affords good feeding ground for large game. A short thoroughfare leads into First Lake.

First Lake is the longest and narrowest of the chain. It is by some persons said to be four miles in length, but if measured would probably be found to fall short of three. At its foot are the ruins of an old dam, over which canoe and luggage must be lifted. From the left side of the dam a good road leads down the stream a short distance, and soon turns westward between two ridges, running thence ten miles to Depot Farm.[85] A logging-camp lies further down the stream, on the same bank, some little distance from the water.

---

**2020 Edition**

It was in this area on Hubbard's trip in 1881 when the weather had turned sharply colder with the temperature dropping to 20°F, they were low on food, and Hubbard and "The Captain" remained at Musquacook while their two guides went in search of supplies at Depot Farm. Two days passed before Hubbard and the Captain, their food reserves critically low, packed up camp and set off on their own. See: *"Woods and Lakes of Maine."*

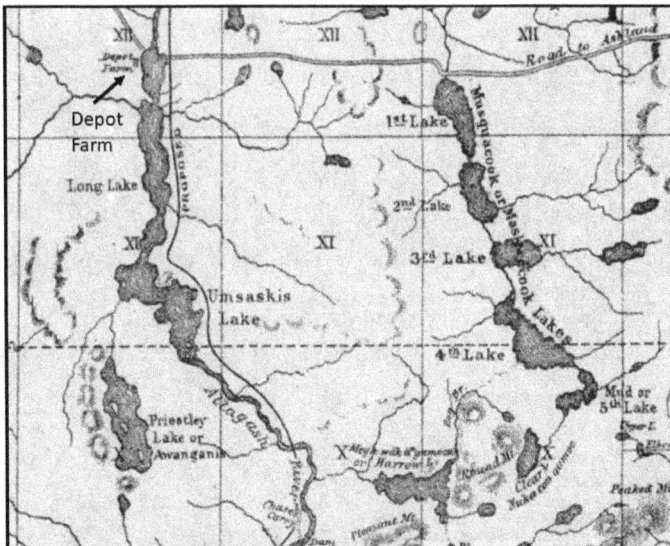

---

[85] **2020:** An 1800s supply point at the north end of Long Lake on the Allagash River.

## *Musquacook Stream*

For a mile and a quarter below the dam the bed of the brook is a mass of boulders, without pretense of having any channel, and bears the name of "horse-race."[86] The canoe-man, unless his bark be "shod," must "carry" past this obstruction, and will probably find that the road on the left bank will be useful for the greater part if not for the whole of the distance. A mile and a quarter below the "horse-race" a good-sized brook, sometimes called the "Little Musquacook," empties into the stream from the west, and a mile below it one comes to an alder-ground and deeper, smoother water. This continues for half a mile, when the water shoals again and for two miles runs over a wider bed. Another stretch of smoother water, along which is good camping ground, extends three quarters of a mile, after which for nearly six miles down to its mouth the stream is shallow and rapid, but ordinarily deep enough to float a loaded canoe. Robin's Brook empties into the stream from the east, about seven miles from its mouth. But few good camping grounds offer themselves along the twelve-mile course of the stream, fires having run through the forests, in 1881, on both banks, from below the alder ground nearly to the junction with the Allagash.

"Musquacook" is from *maskwemoosi*, "birch-tree" (Râle), and *auke*, "place," — "birch-tree place."[87]

---

[86] **2020:** Now Horse Race Rapids. Not, "The Horserace" at Caucomgomoc Lake.

[87] **2020:** Hubbard gives very few Indian names, and fewer derivations, in this book. For broader coverage, see, ***Woods and Lakes of Maine***.

## RÉSUMÉ

| | | |
|---|---|---|
| Allagaskwigamooksis Lake to Pleasant Lake | 1 ½ m. | 1 |
| Across Pleasant Lake to Harrow Lake Carry | 1 ½ m. | day |
| Pleasant Lake to Harrow Lake . . . . . . . . . . | 1 m. | ½ |
| Across Harrow Lake to Mouth of Bog Brook | 1 ¼ m. | day |
| Harrow Lake to Fourth Lake . . . . . . . . . . | 3 ¼ m. | 1 ½ days |
| End of Carry to Outlet of First Lake . . . . . . | 10½m. | 1 day |
| First Lake to Mouth of Musquacook Stream | 12 m. | 2 days |
| | 31 m. | 6 days |

**❧TURNER HOUSE❧**

*Water Street, Skowhegan, Maine.*

F. B. HESELTON, Proprietor.

*This Hotel, pleasantly situated near the Falls of the Kennebec, and within easy reach of the Railroad Depot, contains a hundred bed-rooms, besides Billiard-Room and elegant Dance-Hall.*

*Summer Boarders can have GOOD ROOMS and board, at from $1.00 to $2.00 per day.*

*Good Livery-Stable connected with the Hotel, where teams can always be had at reasonable rates.*

*Stages leave the house every morning (Sundays excepted) for Solon, Bingham, and the Forks of the Kennebec.*

## DOWN THE AROOSTOOK

At the upper end of Spider Lake, behind the largest island in the lake, is the mouth of the principal brook.[88] Fifty or sixty rods up this black and dismal stream, on the left bank, is the end of a "carry," which begins in a cedar swamp, but soon rising on to higher and firmer ground, continues a mile and strikes the brook again just below the outlet of a small "logon." Paddling across the latter three-eighths of a mile, and sixty rods more up the brook beyond, another "carry" begins, on the left bank. The path is good, although wet, and brings one in about five minutes to a small oblong pond, half a mile in its greatest diameter, and partly surrounded by bogs and cedar swamps. Here are the headwaters of Spider Lake and a "carry" of a mile and a half, which runs over uneven and, in some places, steep ground, connects them with Echo Lake,[89] the headwaters of the Aroostook.

### *Echo Lake*

Echo Lake is a little pond, about three-quarters of a mile long and three-eighths of a mile wide, lies between several high hills, whose forest sides take up and send back the sounds made on its bosom, until oft-repeated they die away in the distance. Deep, and fed by cold brooks and springs, it would seem to be a good place for trout. Just east of the end of the "carry," in 1879, there was a comfortable hunters' cabin.

---

[88] **2020:** The principal brook flows through the Portage Ponds. Hubbard is about 18 – 20 miles from the official Aroostook River start.

[89] **2020:** Echo Lake at 115 acres and the headwaters of the Aroostook River, is not much larger than Upper Portage Pond (96 acres). Note, there are several Echo Lakes in Maine. This one is T9 R11 WELS Gazetteer map 56, Piscataquis County, Maine.

At the eastern end of the pond, on the right of the small stream which is its outlet, a path runs through a cedar swamp, about sixty rods, to a pond eighty rods long. Three-quarters of a mile beyond and southeast of this pond is another pond, or, more properly, a "bulge" in the brook, three-eighths of a mile long. Into its upper end flows another small brook, and just below its outlet is an old dam. Good dry campgrounds can be found from time to time along the course of this stream, the forests being not so swampy as on Spider Lake waters.

From the dam just mentioned it is a mile and a half to Upper or First Munsungan Lake. An old and overgrown road runs along the right bank of the stream, in some places hardly distinguishable from the surrounding forests, and the canoe-man's only resource when the water is low, if haply this resource be left him, is to cut away a beaver dam just above the outlet of Bulge Pond and "sluice" himself downstream on the attendant flood. The brook is quite pretty, and runs over a rocky bottom, rapid and shallow almost all the way, beneath overhanging forests of both hard and soft woods.

## Munsungan Lakes * Munsungan Stream

The first of the three lakes of this name is three-quarters of a mile wide and a little less than two miles long. Emerging into its open area from the confined and forest-pent streams over which one has been laboring, the change is very acceptable. Along the southern shore of the lake runs a high ridge, from which doubtless one could get fine views of the three lakes and surrounding country.

A brook of quick and shallow water, a quarter of a mile long, connects First Lake with Second Lake. The latter is the largest of the three, and is three miles and a half long by nearly a mile wide.

---

**2020 Edition**

The lake here now runs together as Chase Lake, Munsungan Lake, and Little Munsungun Lake. Between Chase and Munsungan the stream is known as The Thoroughfare.

The land on either side of the lake has been identified, through archeological investigation, as being occupied between the Paleoindian Period (9,500-13,000? Years Ago) and the Ceramic Period (500-3,000? Years Ago). The rock found here was used by the inhabitants for the manufacture of stone tools.

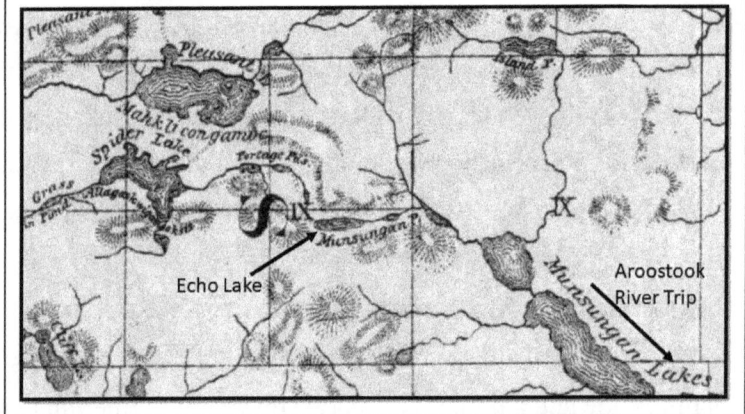

Echo Lake

Aroostook River Trip

---

\*

A thoroughfare of shallow and dead-water, about twenty rods long, leads into the lower or Third Lake,[90] which in turn is of about the same dimensions as First Lake. Togue abound in these waters, and an occasional moose may still be found roaming through the forests which border on them.

---

[90] **2020:** The Aroostook River trip typically begins in this area.

For about a mile below the lower lake the water of Munsungan Stream is "dead." It then tumbles over a few broken ledges, past which canoes must be lifted, for some two rods. From here to its junction with the Milnokett branch, about eight miles, the brook flows over a smooth bottom, and with the exception of a mile and a half its water is "quick," and navigation easy.

## Aroostook River

On the main Aroostook River there are some few rapids, but no bad places of any consequence. It is six miles from the Munsungan-Milnokett Forks to the mouth of the Mooseleuk, a stream whose upper waters abound in long reaches of dead-water and sequestered ponds, and up which, ordinarily, the canoe-man's course will not be very difficult.

Ten miles below the mouth of Mooseleuk one comes to Painter's, the first farm on this route, where potatoes, flour, butter, and milk can be bought. Two miles below, at Botting's farm, connection may be made with the stage which runs between Oxbow Plantation and Mattawamkeag, via Patten. From this point it takes ordinarily about four days to paddle to Caribou. When the river is high the same distance may be made in a day and a half or two days.

Of all the river routes for the canoe-man in Northern Maine this is the least interesting. Its chief hardships occur between Churchill and Munsungan Lakes, where a succession of "carries" and swamp-girt ponds have few redeeming features of landscape to break their monotony, while nowhere do wild gorges or picturesque waterfalls, as on the Penobscot River, reward the tourist's patient toil. On the main river, too, or on its upper waters at least, the farms are generally hidden from sight, and do not dot the forest reaches with their fresh green cultivation, as on the River St. John.

At Presque Isle or Caribou one takes cars for Woodstock, thence for Vanceboro and Bangor.

Stages leave Ashland, for Patten on Tuesdays; for Presque Isle, Mondays, Wednesdays, and Fridays.

\*

## RÉSUMÉ

| | | |
|---|---|---|
| Allagaskwigamook to Allagaskwigamooksis ... | 2 ¾ m. | 1 day |
| Allagaskwigamooksis to Echo Lake .......... | 4 m. | 1 ½ days |
| Echo Lake to Third Munsungan Lake ........ | 3 m. | 1 ½ days |
| Across Third Lake ...................... | 2 m. | |
| Thoroughfare between Second and Third Lakes . | ½ m. | |
| Across Second Lake ..................... | 4 m. | |
| Thoroughfare between First and Second Lakes .. | 20 rods | 1 day |
| Across First Lake ...................... | ¾ m. | |
| First Lake to Milnokett Stream .............. | 9 m. | |
| Milnokett Stream to Mooseleuk Stream ....... | 6 m. | |
| Mooseleuk Stream to Lapompeag Stream ...... | 2 m. | |
| Lapompeag Stream to Hayden Brook (First farm) ............................... | 8 m. | 1 day |
| Hayden Brook to Umcoleus Stream .......... | 3 m | |
| Umcoleus Stream to Otter Brook ............ | 1 m. | |
| Otter Brook to the Oxbow ................. | 1 m. | |
| Oxbow to Trout Brook .................... | 2 m. | |
| Trout Brook to Houlton Brook .............. | 5 m. | |
| Houlton Brook to St. Croix Stream .......... | 6 m. | 1 |
| St. Croix Stream to Scapan Stream .......... | 5 m. | day |
| Scapan Stream to Big Machias Stream (deadwater) ................................ | 7 m. | |

Big Machias Stream to Little Machias Stream . .  2 m.
Little Machias Stream to Gardner Brook . . . . . . .  10 m.
Gardner Brook to Salmon Brook  . . . . . . . . . . . .  6 m.
Salmon Brook to Presque Isle Stream  . . . . . . . .  12 m.
Presque Isle Stream to Caribou . . . . . . . . . . . . .  13 m.      2
Caribou to Little Madawaska Stream . . . . . . . . . .  5 m.      days
Little Madawaska Stream to Fort Fairfield . . . . .  7 m.
Fort Fairfield to Aroostook Falls  . . . . . . . . . . . .  4 m.
Aroostook Falls to St. John River  . . . . . . . . . . .  3 m.
                                                       127 ½    Total
                                                       m.        miles

THE STEAMER

# FAIRY OF THE LAKE,

Remodelled, and thoroughly overhauled, is ready to run
regular trips to MT. KINEO, or the *Head of the Lake;* will
also run, when desired, to SPENCER BAY, LILY BAY,
EAST OUTLET, or any other point on

## MOOSEHEAD LAKE.

Reasonable terms offered to Excursionists, by the day,
or for a longer time. *Address,* —

### J. H. EVELETH,
GREENVILLE, MAINE.

# ALLAGASH AND ST. JOHN RIVERS

*

---

**2020 Edition**

Hubbard returns us to Churchill Lake to continue the trip down the Allagash to the St. John. In *"Woods and Lakes of Maine,"* Hubbard traveled the Musquacook Stream to reach the Allagash River. See map in section on Musquacook Lakes.

This is the route typical of the Allagash Wilderness Waterway canoe trip north of Churchill Lake. Searching on www.maine.gov for the Allagash Wilderness Waterway map will provide a document showing points of interests and campsite locations.

---

*

From the head of Churchill Lake (Allagaskwigamook) it is about six miles to the remains of Chase Dam which are just below a bit of quick-water at the foot of the lake. This dam was built some years ago, in order to raise the water high enough to take logs up through the Locks into Chamberlain Lake, and thence down the East Branch of the Penobscot. Such a step was rendered necessary by the action of the Province of New Brunswick, which, although bound by the treaty of 1842 to regard all logs which should come down the St John as if they were the product of the Province, discriminated against the Yankees by levying a duty on *all* logs coming down the river, and the crown then paid a corresponding bounty on logs cut from the crown lands. During the same season, or a later one, John Glazier and an associate, from the Province of New Brunswick, were driving logs on the lower Allagash and St.

John Rivers. The overflow from Chase Dam was not sufficient to carry out their timber, and it was feared the "drive" would be "hung up." At this juncture, the story goes, a party of Glazier's men went up the river secretly, captured one of the two men in charge of the dam, and cut away the latter. The other man in charge escaped, and before he reached his party at Chamberlain Lake nearly succumbed to fatigue and hunger. It is needless to add that Glazier had all the water he wanted to carry his "drive" successfully down the river. The dam was subsequently burnt.

At the dam begins, on the left, Chase Carry, over which it is expedient for such persons at least as are novices in the management of a canoe to carry both their canoe and luggage. They thus avoid what is considered the worst place on the River, where the stream is filled with huge boulders, between which the water madly dashes and foams, making a tortuous channel for the navigator, if channel it may be called, dangerous and difficult of passage at all times, and only to be attempted when the water is neither very high nor very low. A part of this "horse-race" has received the pet name of the "Devil's Elbow," a term applied sometimes also to a spot nearly half a mile further down the stream, where the river narrows and where in the midst of rocks and foaming water a canoe must shoot across from one side of the stream to the other, or swamp.

The carry is about three-quarters of a mile long, and pretty well filled up with fallen trees and growing bushes. Immediately below it the water is quite rough for some little distance, and one must be constantly on the alert to avoid shipwreck. This over, however, a canoe glides smoothly down the river past meadowland and grassy islands into Umsaskis Lake, — some eight or nine miles in all.

## Umsaskis Lake * Long Lake * Round Pond

Umsaskis Lake is about four miles long, and two miles wide in its broadest part. It is really but a part of Long Lake, its name (more correctly Uem-sas-kek) denoting a place where opposing points of land run out to meet each other, or more graphically described by "tied together like sausages." Among the islands near its head is good feeding ground for game, and until within a few years past moose could usually be found there. From the foot of Umsaskis it is about six miles to the lower end of Long Lake.

Long Lake is chiefly noted for its Depot Farm. This farm was long kept by one Priestly, and later by one Johnson and his Amazonian wife, as a supply-centre for the Allagash loggers. Here one can get flour and potatoes at the modest prices, respectively, of ten cents per pound and twenty-five cents per peck. The present proprietor is named Harvey. Through his place runs the road from Seven Islands on the main St. John River, which continues eastward past the foot of Musquacook Lakes to Ashland.[91] From Depot Farm it is eight miles down the river to Round Pond.

The water in Round Pond (or Pataquongamis) is quite rapid in places, but easy of navigation. "Square Lake," as this body of water has often been called, is a misnomer, the adjectival part of its Indian name meaning "round." From its inlet to its outlet

---

[91] **2020:** Current roads can be found on Gazetteer map 62. An access road still passes through to Ashland.

is about two miles, the lake extending to the right from the inlet, thus making its total length somewhat greater.

## Allagash River * Allagash Falls

Three miles more of paddling, partly through dead-water bring one to the mouth of Musquacook Stream (a tributary to the Allagash River). High ridges on either bank, looking down on the widening expanse of placid water, give a new and pleasant sensation to the voyageur, and the stream so lately struggling against rocky barriers seems at last to have overcome them all, and to be indeed a deep majestic river. Destructive forest fires ran through this section of Maine in the summer of 1881, and have left very few green oases on the riverbanks. When the charred remains of the noble forest trees shall begin to fall, the scene will be desolate enough!

From the mouth of Musquacook Stream a mile and a half of dead-water bring one to some rapids, and nearly a mile more (of dead-water and current) to a rude clearing on the left, where the river narrows to half its former width. After three-quarters of a mile more of strong current, one passes, on the right, Five Finger Brook, so called from the various channels into which it separates near its mouth.[92]

Passing a small island just below the brook, four miles of strong current and "rips," with three or more "shallow" bars, bring one to other islands and a stretch of less rapid current another mile and a half of current and "rips," to Ben Glazier Brook on the left. Then follow a mile and a quarter of similar navigation past an island which lies near the right bank, to

---

[92] **2020:** The Fingers are nearly eight miles from the intersection with the Allagash over barely navigable waters.

Ramsay's farm on the opposite side. The river makes a wide sweep to the left around this clearing, and after about two miles and a half of uneventful paddling Finley McLennan's farm is passed, on the left bank below some rapids. Here or at Moir's, a mile below on the other side, one can get provisions and plenty of good butter and delicious milk.

One of the earliest settlers on this part of the river was one Monroe, whose name a brook and island bear. Finley McLennan has succeeded to the ownership of the Monroe farm, and his name is often given to Monroe's Island, the first of a group of nine which lie between here and Allagash Falls. The channel lies on the left of Finley's or Monroe's Island, past the mouth of McLennan's Brook. It is three miles to Allagash Falls. Several farms lie on either side of the river, owned by sons-in-law of Thomas Moir, a thrifty farmer from the Restigouche country, at whose house travellers are always sure of a cordial welcome. From Moir's it is two miles to Allagash Falls.

The river flows with considerable current until just before the falls are reached, when it grows rapid. Canoes can safely run the rapids, past the upper, to the lower carry, which lies on the right and is but a few rods long. The falls are quite pretty, and consist of one broken, ragged pitch, twenty-seven feet high by actual measurement. The water as it passes over the ledge of clay-slate is dashed into foam almost as white as milk, but it soon regains its former semblance, and flows on in tranquility, unruffled by other impediments than an occasional gravel bar.

Canoes can usually be put into the water immediately below, but out of sight of, the falls. The water breaks over a small ledge just below here, easy of passage save where the river is quite high.

The distances on the St. John, below the mouth of the Allagash, have been measured on the ice, while those on the Allagash (both above and below the falls), as given by the settlers on its banks, are by them said to be computed on the town lines. Hence when the canoe-man is told by a "native" that it is twelve and a half miles from Allagash Falls to the mouth of the river, he may expect the distance to lengthen out to at least fourteen miles, just as the distance from Musquacook Stream to McLennan's is twelve and a half miles instead of ten.

From the falls half an hour's paddle brings one to a small island and Kobscus or Keeobscus ("near the falls") Brook on the right. Most of the shallow parts of the river will now have been passed, and a continuous current, with occasional rapids, is to be expected. Twin Brook Rapids, the worst on the river, are about seven miles below the falls, and lie between two small streams, which flow into the river from its opposite banks.

There are no farms on the Allagash below the falls, until within a mile or more of its mouth, when the river makes two sweeping bends down a perceptible incline, and mingles its waters with those of the St. John. A goodly mountain looks down upon the now broad expanse of water, and high and pretty ridges extend along either bank for some distance.

## *St. John River (or Woolastook)*

Less than a mile below the junction of the two rivers are "Negroe" Brook Rapids, a dangerous place for inexperienced boatmen. "Negroe" Brook takes its name from the circumstance that a number of negroes first cut logs on it.[93] From here it is three miles to Cross Rock and rapids of the same name; one mile more to Golen (?) Rapids; three or three and a half miles more to Rankin Rapids, and nearly two miles more to Michu Rapids. The latter are less than two miles from the mouth of the St. Francis River, which joins the St. John from the north, and with its lakes forms the boundary line between Maine on the west and Quebec and New Brunswick on the east, for a distance of thirty miles, to the foot of Boundary Lake (Pohenagamook).[94]

## *Up the St. Francis River*[95]

From the mouth of the St. Francis it is five miles northwest to Glaziers' Lake, three miles across the latter, three miles more to Cross Lake, eighty rods over it, and three and a half miles further to "Beau" Lake. The latter is a mile wide and five miles long, and at its head is Morrison's farm, from which it is about fifteen miles to Boundary Lake. Here there is a settlement, from which it is twenty miles, over a good road, to railway connection. This route is quite a pretty one, and does not usually present many difficulties to the canoe-man.

---

[93] **2020:** This is now Pelletier Brook. See the explanation in, *Woods and Lakes of Maine – 2020 Annotated Edition*, for information on when Maine renamed locations.

[94] **2020:** Boundary Lake is the source of the St. Francis. It is in Quebec immediately north of the International Boundary (Aroostook County). This corner (literally) of Maine is as far north as you can get in the state. The northern most Maine town, however, is Madawaska.

[95] **2020:** Hubbard now travels northwest along the Canadian border towards Boundary Lake.

## *St. John River to Fort Kent*

From the Allagash to the mouth of the St. Francis it is twelve miles, and if at the latter point, the canoe-man should prefer a good bed indoors to a hard one under his tent, he will find it at the neat and attractive little white house of Martin Savage, which stands some distance back from the river, on the right or Maine bank of the St. John. Robert Connor, a successful lumberman, whose large and imposing house stands on the New Brunswick bank of the river, three miles below Savage's, is also very courteous towards tourists, and would no doubt gladly extend the hospitality of his house to tired or belated canoe-men.[96] After leaving the Allagash one will find that good camping ground and firewood grow more rare the further one proceeds downstream. Hence the foregoing bit of information.

After having passed the mouth of the St. Francis, the canoe-man will have New Brunswick on his left and Maine on his right, until he shall have passed Van Buren, and come within two and a half or three miles of Grand Falls, beyond which the St. John becomes wholly provincial.[97]

Below Savage's, one mile, the first "rips" or rapids in the river are at Toban Bar. Five and a half or six miles more bring one to Savage's Island, then a mile and a half to Harford's Rocks, and two miles more to Winding Ledges, just above which on the left bank is the first church the tourist will see. At low water the river at Winding Ledges is quite smooth. At high water however, its boils over the three sharp ledges which jut

---

[96] The roadbed of the Temiscouata Railway is now completed and open to this point.

[97] **2020:** At Hamlin, Maine. This is 70+ miles from where the St. John and St. Francis merge.

out into the stream (one from the left bank, the other two flanking it from the right bank), and to pass successfully a canoe must keep well to the left, until just above the break at the second ledge, then shoot across deftly to the other bank, follow it down and re-cross just above where the water breaks over the third ledge. Six miles more beyond Winding Ledges, or sixteen miles in all from Savage's, bring one to Fort Kent, where good meals and lodging can be had, or a supply of camp-stores purchased at reasonable rates. An old block house at the lower end of the town, near the junction of the St. John with Fish River, is well worth a visit.

## 2020 Edition – Map from Savage's to Fort Kent

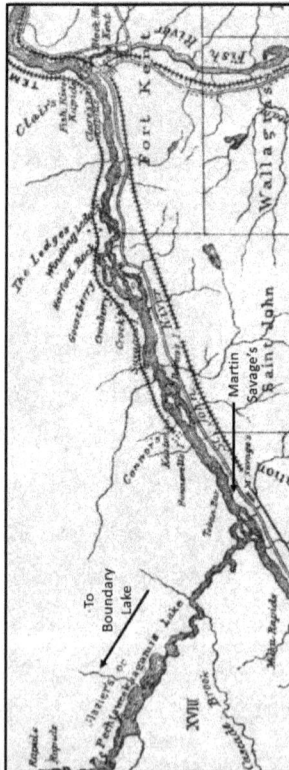

## *Fort Kent to Edmundston*

Fort Kent To Edmundston it is nineteen miles. The first rapids are just above and opposite the mouth of Fish River, at Clare's Bar, Fish River Rapids being a short mile further down the river. Six miles below Fort Kent, Baker River flows into the St. John from the north, and several islands lie opposite and near its mouth. Three miles below it and ten miles from Edmundston is Chatacoin, where prominently on the right bank stand a large gray church and group of school-buildings. On the opposite bank is a white church with unfinished steeple. It is safe to say that all of the churches on the upper St. John are Romish.

From Chatacoin it is about three miles to Michaud's Island and Rapids, and Frenchville, from which point a road runs about four miles to the shores of Long Lake, the head of one branch of Fish River waters. At Michaud's Island the river sweeps to the left, making one of those peculiar unruffled descents over an inclined plane, often noticed by the canoe-man on the Allagash and St. John, and for several miles flows almost due north. Settlements become more numerous on its banks, and the increased number of churches, mills, and well-kept dwellings, with now and then a ferry in use, indicate activity and prosperity among the French inhabitants. The only remaining quick-water to pass is at Rice's Rapids, about half a mile above Edmundston.

Edmundston lies on both sides of the Madawaska River (Matda-was-kek, "hedge-hog place"), at its junction with the St. John. It was formerly called Little Falls, and takes its present name from Governor Sir Edmund Head, during whose administration it is said to have been incorporated as a town. It has two hotels, and is at present the terminus of the New Brunswick Railway, and as such the busy centre of the local trade. The most interesting feature of the place is the crumbling foundation of an old block-house, which picturesquely stands on an outcropping ledge of slate in a grove of young spruce trees.

---

### 2020 Edition

Interestingly, Hubbard notes here, in his writings of 1893, that, "Edmundston lies on *both* sides of the Madawaska River."

Until what became known as "The Aroostook War" the inhabitants of the region certainly operated as if they were one single community; the border was inconsequential, unless lumber was concerned. The war, in which no military battle was fought, was the result over a boundary dispute amongst lumbermen.

The Boundary Commission settled the matter with the 1842 Webster-Ashburton Treaty. A line was drawn down the center of the St. John and Edmundston was effectively split in two.

Madawaska was first incorporated as a town (covering millions of acres) on March 15, 1831. The boundary agreement resulted in Madawaska being the northern most town in Maine and wholly south of the St. John River.

---

\*

From here it is thirty-six miles to Grand Falls, twenty-two more to the mouth of Tobique River, a mile above Andover, where the New Brunswick Railway crosses the St. John, and fifty more to Woodstock. The tourist, however, will probably be ready at Edmundston to leave the river, which continues to have the same general characteristics as during the previous twenty or thirty miles, and go by cars to Grand Falls, and thence to Woodstock.

## RÉSUMÉ

| | |
|---|---|
| Across Allagaskwigamook Lake | 5 m. |
| Chase Carry | ¾ m. |
| Chase Carry to Umsaskis Lake | 8 m. |
| Across Umsaskis Lake | 4 m. |
| Umsaskis Lake to Foot of Long Lake | 6 m. |
| Long Lake to Pataquongamis | 8 m. |
| Across Pataquongamis | 2 m. |
| Pataquongamis to Mouth of Musquacook Stream | 3 m. |
| Musquacook Stream to Allagash Falls | 15 ½ m. |
| Allagash Falls to Mouth of Allagash River | 14 m. |
| Mouth of Allagash to St. Francis River | 12 m. |
| St. Francis River to Fort Kent | 16 m. |
| Fort Kent to Edmundston | 19 m. |
| Edmundston to Grand Falls (by rail) | 36 m. |
| | 149 ¼m |

# EAST OUTLET HOUSE,

## KENNEBEC DAM, MOOSEHEAD LAKE.

HENRY I. WILSON, *Proprietor.*

### Favorite Resort for Fishermen.

The many pools in the river, close at hand, furnish exciting sport to the lovers of fly-fishing, while the near vicinity of *Churchill Stream, West Outlet,* and *Indian Pond,* serves materially to increase the attractions of the place. Mr. Wilson's knowledge of, and familiarity with the best hunting and fishing-grounds in the neighborhood, makes him a valuable adjunct to parties in quest of pleasure.

# A TOUR IN CANADA
## *Temiscouata Lake * Grand Falls*

At Edmundston, tourists who wish to visit the Temiscouata Lake region leave the St. John River and paddle up the Madawaska for twenty-three miles, through a succession of pools and easy rapids, the worst part of the river being that which one can see from the bridge at Edmundston. A good road follows the right bank of the stream seventy-nine miles to Riviere du Loup,[98] and, if one prefers, canoes can be hauled up the river to any point desired. Temiscouata Lake is of irregular form, twenty-seven miles long, and averages a mile and a half to two miles in width. A few scattered farms lie on its shores, which are still covered with a generous growth of forest trees, while high ridges greet the eye in many places, and give the landscape a pleasing variety.

Fifteen miles above Edmundston, or three miles above the boundary between Quebec and New Brunswick, opposite Griffin's, a logging-road of indifferent excellence leads four miles northeasterly into Little Mud Lake. This is the headwaters of one branch of the Touladi River, which flows in a roundabout course into Temiscouata Lake, sixteen miles from its outlet. A series of lakes and sluggish streams, it is but little higher than Temiscouata Lake, and its descent is very gradual and easy, thus offering to the canoe-man a plain course and rapid sailing.

Three-quarters of a mile across Little Mud Lake, and one enters Beardsley Brook, which flows eight miles into Squatook

---

[98] **2020:** A city on the St. Lawrence in Quebec named after the nearby river.

Stream, and thence two miles into Squatook Lake.[99] Ten miles over this lake, and ten miles of thoroughfare, bring one to Little Squatook Lake, which is six miles long and divided into two parts, and near which rise Squatook Peak and Sugar Loaf Mt. One mile of thoroughfare leads into Little Lake, across which it is rather more than a mile. Then follow a mile and a half of dead-water to the junction of Squatook Stream, with the Grande Fourche, or main Touladi, and the west branch of the same. From this point it is eight miles to Touladi Lake, six miles across it, and four miles down the stream to Touladi Falls, a stretch of water almost entirely free from rapids. Canoes must be carried around the falls, and some rapid water will be found below them, in the mile which intervenes between them and Temiscouata Lake.

If one prefers, one can send one's canoe by team to Cloutier's on Temiscouata Lake opposite the mouth of the Touladi, and go up that stream to the Forks, whence "poling" must be resorted to, in order to ascend either the West Branch, or the Grande Fourche.

Trout and whitefish are said to be very abundant in this region, and large game is frequently seen there. Birch canoes can be bought at Edmundston for ten dollars, and guides, white or Indian, can be hired at reasonable rates. The round trip from Edmundston and return can be made comfortably in a week, or, under favorable circumstances, in less time than that. Camping outfits should be procured at Edmundston.

---

[99] **2020:** Grand Lake Squatec.

## *Grand Falls*

Grand Falls,[100] an attractive little town on the St. John, two and a half or three miles east of the boundary line between New Brunswick and Maine, is fast becoming a favorite stopping place for summer travellers through the Provinces, and already has a large hotel and the other accompaniments of a growing place of resort. The chief feature of the town is, of course, the falls, where the river pitches in three successive leaps over a ledge some seventy feet or more high, and boils and hisses in its onward course down a gorge lined with precipitous walls. At the foot of the fall the water has worn away the rock to such an extent that logs fifty feet long passing over the fall disappear from sight, it is said, for several seconds, and shoot up into view again with tremendous impetus, often crushed and broken. A pretty suspension bridge spans the chasm just below the falls, and gives access to the country beyond, through which run many attractive roads.

From Grand Falls one goes by rail to Aroostook Junction in an hour and a quarter, passing in sight of Aroostook Falls, at the mouth of the river. If obliged to wait overnight for connection to Woodstock, holders of through-tickets can ride free on the cars up the Aroostook to Fort Fairfield, where there is a good hotel, and leave there the next morning for Woodstock via Aroostook Junction. (See Railroad time-tables among advertisements.)[101]

---

[100] **2020:** Hubbard continues his coverage of Canada here in Grand Falls, southeast of Van Buren, Maine.

[101] **2020:** These have been reproduced and are included in the appendix.

# EAST BRANCH OF THE PENOBSCOT

*

---

**2020 Edition**

Here, Hubbard brings us back from Canada to the woods east of Moosehead Lake. This tour will wind its way from Chamberlain Lake to the East Branch of the Penobscot River.

---

## *Telos Lake * Webster Lake*

The route from Moosehead Lake to Apmoojenegamook, or Chamberlain Lake, has been previously described.

At the southwest end of Apmoojenegamook Lake, at the "heel of the boot," is the natural mouth of a stream which now flows back into Telosmis Lake (Pataquongamis). This stream, virtually a thoroughfare, is rather wide and nearly half a mile long. Its shores and those of Telos and Telosmis Lakes are lined with the trunks and roots of dead trees. Telosmis is a mile or more wide, and somewhat longer than it is wide, and flows into Telos Lake, from which it is separated by only a narrow strip of dead trees. A fine view of Ktaadn, the Trout Brook, and other mountains is had from these lakes.

---

**2020 Edition**

Telosmis Lake is now noted as Round Pond on Gazetteer map 50. The thoroughfare is the current location of Chamberlain Bridge on the Telos Road. Round Pond (Telosmis) runs more freely into Telos Lake due to the more modern Telos dam.

---

*

Three miles and a half, or more, take one past and around a prominent point of land, where the lake begins to narrow, to the cut which was made some years ago to connect Telos with Webster Lake. What now seems to be the cut proper is a straight canal, only thirty or forty rods long and twenty feet or more wide, and at its lower end is the dam, which confines and regulates the water of the Chamberlain-Telos system. When this cut was first completed, and the water allowed to go through it, the latter soon washed away the soil from the bottom of the ravine which leads down to Webster Lake, and its course now resembles that of any natural brook, being broad and rocky. Springer, in his *Forest Life and Forest Trees*, says, "Originally the canal was three hundred rods long by four wide, and four feet deep; but the strong current of water flowing through, at the rate of one mile in twenty minutes, has changed the regularity of the channel to a more natural and stream-like appearance." According to the theories of geologists, the course of the waters of Telos and Apmoojenegamook (Chamberlain)

Lakes, was through this ravine before our continent was submerged, and those lakes were then very small, or did not exist at all. The ocean currents, however, deposited so much detritus at the foot of Telos Lake, that when the country rose again, the waters were turned back, formed the two lakes just mentioned, and flowed over into Pongokwahemook, or Eagle, and Allagaskwigamook, or Churchill, Lake basins, and thence down the Allagash River into the St. John. (Perhaps due rather to glacial action.)

A canoe without load can run from the dam down to Webster Lake at almost any time in summer, but usually not without difficulty. The water is rapid and the channel tortuous.[102] The road, a good one in the main, but soft here and there, runs on the right of the brook through the old Dwinel farm, thence along the south shore of Webster Lake past the dam, and down the stream to Trout Brook Farm and the outlet of Matangamook Lake.

Webster Lake is a very narrow body of water, two and a half miles long, and its shores are no better than those of the lakes above, the north shore being a series of burnt ledges, while all are lined with a confused mass of driftwood. An abundance of small trout can usually be taken at the dam.

### Webster Brook

Webster Brook is a turbulent stream, and on its course of eight or nine miles there are a great many "pitches" and much shallow water, and in ordinary summer seasons more or less wading will have to be done and hard work undergone to

---

[102] **2020:** Canoe outfitters run this trip regularly. The Telos Dam regulates the flow of the river.

accomplish its passage. Grand Falls, less than a mile from its mouth, if not the highest, is by all odds the finest waterfall on the entire East Branch. The main "pitch," without the rapids immediately above it, is twelve feet high, and from below one has a striking view of the foil and some high rock ledges beyond it. A succession of pretty cascades lie below the principal fall, and are worth seeing.

"Indian Carry" leads from Grand Falls one hundred and eighty rods over to the main East Branch, a stream much smaller than Webster Brook, and comes out on its bank about an eighth of a mile above the junction of the two streams. A good run of a little over a mile takes one past some good duck ground into Matangamooksis, or Second Lake.

---

### 2020 Edition

Webster Lake straddles the north-western border of Baxter State Park. Grand Falls on Webster Brook is labeled, Grand Pitch, on Gazetteer map 56.

Matangamooksis, or Second Lake, and Matangamook, now form Grand Lake Matagamon. On the south west shore is Horse Mountain. The cliffs of this mountain are Traveler Rhyolite.

---

> Horse Mountain is one of the smaller mountains in Baxter State Park with a summit of 1,589 ft. However, from an outcropping close to the summit, hikers get an expansive view of the mountains at the north end of the park.

*

## Connection to the Aroostook River

If the canoe-man's course be now towards the Aroostook River, he must toil up the main East Branch (sometimes called Thissell Brook), nearly one half of a mile through rapid water to a dam, and about two miles beyond, through dead-water and past a fall, to the mouth of Bog Brook. After wading a few rods up the brook, a good "carry" will be found on the left, which runs about a mile to a large beaver dam, from which for a mile and a half a canoe can be paddled up the brook to a bog. From this point the tourist may find a "spotted line" which runs over high ground on the right, and which will lead him in two miles and a half to Milnokett Pond.[103] It is another mile and a half over the pond to the thoroughfare, a few rods through the latter, four miles and a half over Milnokett Lake to the dam and outlet, and four miles and a half more down the stream to the junction with Munsungan Stream. See section, *Down the Aroostook*.

---

### 2020 Edition

In the text Hubbard refers to what is now Millinocket Lake as Milnokett. On his map it is labeled Millnokett.

What he labelled as Little Millnokett Lake is now Millimagassett Lake (Gazetteer maps 56 & 57, ed. 28). And the unlabeled pond is Little Millinocket Lake.

---

[103] **2020:** Now Little Millinocket Lake

The waterway to the Aroostook would now best past Millinocket Falls, down Millinocket Stream, and around the Devil's Elbow.

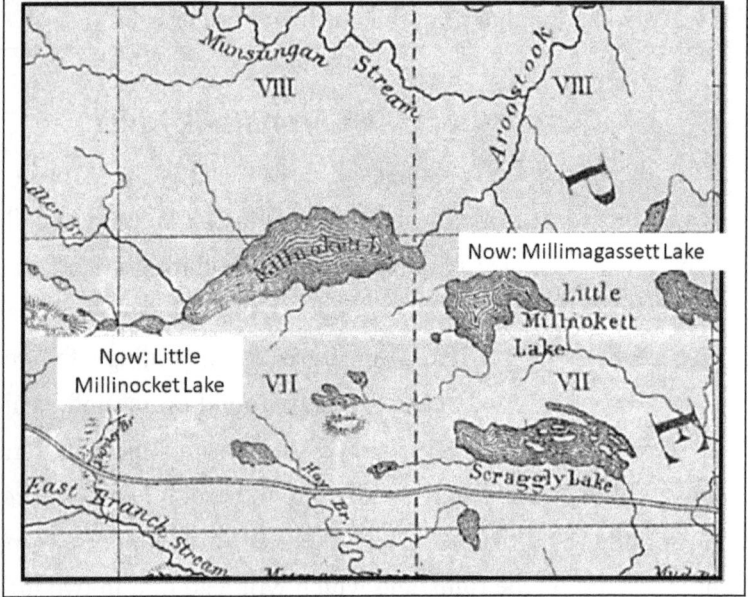

Now: Millimagassett Lake

Now: Little Millinocket Lake

*

## Nesowadnehunk Lake

The easiest way to reach this place is by way of Patten and Trout Brook farm. From the latter point a team can haul canoes and outfit through to the lake, twenty miles, in a day and a half, or less. The lake is shallow, its water clear, and free from vegetable growth; the immediate shores are flat, and in general rocky. A fine view is had from the north shore and from the upper end of the lake, and among the mountains Double Top (Ootop, or Outop) with its pyramidal form is one of the most striking. The northern part, or tableland, of Ktaadn is also very conspicuous.

In 1892 the writer found trout abundant in the lake, but saw none that would weigh over a pound, while, beside those of deer, the signs of game were not abundant. Below the lake proper, the outflowing stream bulges out into a good sized pool, narrowing as it approaches the dam, three-fourths of a mile down. Vegetation on the banks here has been largely destroyed by fire and by high water.

From the lake to the mouth of Nesowadnehunk Stream is about seventeen miles: five and a half miles to Smooth Ledge Falls (granite), one and a half miles more to "Slide" Dam opposite Double Top, three and a half miles to the mouth of Slaughter Pond Stream, about three and a half miles more to the third, or lowest dam, and three miles more to the mouth. The upper parts of the road, in 1892, were very good. Immediately above the "Slide" dam the water is dead for about half a mile. The "slide," east of the dam, appears on cursory examination to be the bed of a brook, worn down through a thin layer of drift into the bedrock granite. From the lake to "Slide" dam a loaded canoe could probably, at high water, be taken down the stream without much carrying, except around Smooth Ledge Falls, — the difference in altitude being about a hundred and seventy-five feet. Below "Slide" dam there are a few rough places, but as far as the mouth of Slaughter Pond Stream,[104] the limit of the writer's explorations, and probably as far as the third, or lowest dam, navigation would probably not be irksome, — with a good pitch of water. The total fall from the lake to Slaughter Pond Stream is about three hundred feet. Below the third dam for

---

[104] **2020:** Sometimes labeled Slaughter Brook.

three miles the stream is said to be very rough and the road wet and steep

The intervale immediately above and below the "Slide" dam, largely of hardwood growth, is very pretty, and is surrounded by mountains easy of ascent. Double Top seems to be most accessible from the north. In 1892 there was an old logging camp just below Smooth Ledge Falls and another half a mile above Slaughter Pond Stream.[105]

## Matangamooksis Lake * Grand Lake

Matangamooksis Lake[106] is three miles long, and from its bosom the Trout Brook and Traveller Mts., which have long been hidden from the tourist's view, come again into prominence, and seem to accompany him on his journey down the river, from which circumstance the latter group take their name. Matangamook Mt., the finest and most conspicuous peak, lies west of Matangamook, or Grand Lake.

---

**2020 Edition**

The Traveler was named by loggers using the East Branch of the Penobscot River in reference to its appearance moving with them up and down the river.

The Traveler Mountains are comprised of North Traveler, Traveler, and South Traveler. Also, along this course within Baxter State Park are Trout Brook, Billfish, Bald, and Sable Mountains. The Traveler Mountains are a deposit of unusual dark gray rock, the result of an ancient volcano. Traveler Mountain is the largest cooled lava mountain in Maine.

---

[105] **2020:** The Nesowadnehunk Stream from the lake to the Penobscot has sections of class III and IV white-water rapids.

[106] **2020:** Second Lake, now forms part of Grand Lake Matagamon.

The mountain Hubbard references as Matangamook may be Horse Mountain – described earlier.

*

The thoroughfare between Second Lake and Grand Lake is four miles or more long, and leaves the former at the right of the rocky bluff near its foot. It flows sluggishly between grassy banks, widens here and there into broad "logons," — enticing ground for game, large and small, — and finally merges into the larger lake. About half a mile from the head of the thoroughfare Hay Brook empties into it from the east. At its mouth the banks are high, but half a mile above they recede, and wide grassy meadows appear, which in times of high water are submerged and form a shallow "logon" several miles in extent. A similar "logon" on the same side of the stream, lower down, erroneously serves, on some maps, as the outlet of Hay Brook, and has been dignified with the name of "lake." Except in seasons of high water this "lake," according to the testimony of men that have worked near it for years, is simply a piece of swampy meadowland. Two miles and a half below Hay Brook the tote-road from Webster Lake crosses the stream over a floating bridge, around which canoes must be carried. From this point a branch-road runs a mile and a half to Trout Brook Farm, where provisions can be obtained.

Another mile of paddling takes one to Grand Lake (or Matangamook Lake) which is, on the whole, a more attractive body of water than those previously traversed. Its shores are in some places high and consequently more interesting, and on the tourist's left, as he enters it, lie several islets and a very pretty island of larger dimensions, from whose rocky top a fine view is had of the lake and surrounding mountains. "Louse Island" is the pleasing name given to this spot. A mile up Trout Brook on the left is the landing of Trout Brook Farm, a farm which has been cultivated since 1837. The tote road runs from here to Patten,[107] thirty-four miles, crossing the floating bridge before mentioned. At the mouth of the brook fine trout may still be taken in the season.

It is not more than three miles across Matangamook Lake to the dam, and on the right, near the outlet, one passes Moose Cliff, and near the dam a rocky point which, with the water, makes a pretty foreground to the mountains beyond. Lifting over the dam one comes again into quick-water, which, however, is not hard to run. It is nearly a mile to Bill Fish Brook, on the right, where good fishing can be had; thence 1½ miles to Webster's Landing, on a high bank on the left; thence nearly two miles more through quiet water between fine hardwood forests to Stair Falls. This stretch of water is particularly pleasing. The stream is rather wide, and sweeps now and then to the right or left, disclosing a bit of grassy shore lined with lily-pads, and above it a fine prospect of the Traveller Mts. A few rapids are easily run just above Stair Falls, where, should the water be low, canoes must be carried, as the river bed is filled with sharp ledges of sandstone. The "carry" is on the right bank, and is little more than an eighth of a mile long. Just below the falls there is a good spring near an old pine

---

[107] **2020:** Patten, Maine is home to the Patten Lumbermen's Museum. The multi-building site includes a replica of an 1820s logging camp. The museum actually has a photo of Joseph Reed's Depot on Trout Brook (which Hubbard references) from the late 1880s.

stump.[108] The falls are best appreciated from below, and show two sets of steps, over and beyond which Matangamook Mt. looms up, six miles away to the north.

Leaving Stair Falls, the river soon widens again, and in its sluggish course forms grassy "logons" on either side almost to Haskell Rock and Pitch, one mile below. Here there are two principal "pitches" in the river, neither of which can be run. The "carry" extends along the right bank past both pitches, and is one hundred rods long. The formation is a coarse conglomerate.

## Grand Falls - East Branch

Rips and quick-water intervene for two thirds of a mile to Pond Pitch, where there is a short "carry" on each side, that on the right being 17 rods long. Another strong half mile of quick-water brings one to Grand Pitch and rapids below. The water here rushes over a broken ledge of grits and clay-slate some twenty feet high, and flows between two walls which extend a few rods to the end of the "carry." The latter is on the left bank, and is forty-five rods long. Three-quarters of a mile of rapid water intervene between Grand Pitch and Hulling Machine Falls, the "carry" around the latter lying on the left bank and being about ninety rods long. The river here makes a double turn, and the falls consist of a series of heavy "pitches" close together, not so high as Grand Pitch, but well worth seeing, the mountains up the stream adding much to the grace of the picture.

---

[108] **2020:** In the Maine woods good luck distinguishing one old pine stump from another. Not that it matters, this particular stump is long rotted away.

Smoother water occurs immediately below Hulling Machine Falls, two miles, past Bowlin Ledges to Bowlin Falls, where the river curves and flows around a rocky island and some isolated rocks. Gravel beds predominate here, and while it is an easy stretch of water to go down, it is quite hard to go up it, on account of the current. The "carry," about a hundred yards long, lies on the right bank, but canoes can usually run the falls, which are but a succession of "rips" and small "pitches." Bowlin Stream joins the river at the foot of Bowlin Falls. The four falls last named, Pond Pitch, Grand Pitch, Hulling Machine Falls, and Bowlin Falls, are sometimes collectively known as Grand Falls of the East Branch, to distinguish them from their namesake on Webster Brook. By at least one writer,[109] Grand Falls is said to embrace, in addition to those just named, the others up to and including Stair Falls.

Below Bowlin Falls there is some quick-water, and a mile and a half below them Spring Brook joins the river from the west behind one of two large islands. At and below Bowlin Stream granite boulders occur in the river. Soldiers' Field Rips and Spencer Rips are passed in quick succession, followed by more quick-water. Opposite Spencer Rips the river banks converge and are covered with a black growth. Above and below they open again and hardwood appears. From Spring Brook and Soldiers' Field Rips the view down the river is very pretty. Lunksoos Mt. looms up in the distance. Twin Islands and Sufferers' Rock follow next, then four islands, opposite the lowest of which, on the right, is Hathorn's High Landing.

---

[109] Prof. C. II. Hitchcock. Report of the Secretary of the Maine Board of Agriculture for 1861, p. 401.

Lunksoos Brook joins the river on the east just above a ridge that separates it from the Seboois.[110] From this point, which is over eleven miles from Bowlin Falls, it is three and a half miles to the mouth of the Seboois River {Sipoo, "river," and *es*, diminutive, "little river") over a stretch of dead-water which continues to Patterson's on the left bank, three miles below. From Patterson's it is three-quarters of a mile to the mouth of Wassataquoik Stream.

### Wassataquoik Stream * Whetstone Falls

The name Wassataquoik, or Wassa-tegwe-wick, according to the Indians, belongs properly to the main East Branch of the Penobscot from Nickatow (the "Great Forks") up to and possibly beyond the mouth of the stream which now bears the name. That the two forms are identical in meaning seems probable, although the writer understands their identity of application to be denied by one of the oldest living members of the Penobscot tribe, who insists that Wassa-tegwe-wick is the name of the main stream, while Wassataquoik is that of the smaller one. Further investigation may solve the difficulty. "Wassa-tegwe-wick" comes from *wassay*, "to take fish by torchlight" (Râle), *tegwe*, "stream" (Râle), and *wick*, a form of the locative, — "at the stream where they take fish by torchlight," or, more broadly, "at the salmon-spearing stream." Greenleaf, in a list of Indian names published in 1824, applies the name, "Wassataquoik" to the great "East Branch."

Opposite Patterson's (the old Dacey farm) the road to Mt. Ktaadn leaves the river and runs for some distance along

---

[110] **2020:** Seboeis River.

Wassataquoik Stream. Three-quarters of a mile below the mouth of the stream on the opposite bank is the Hunt farm, formerly kept by Patterson, but recently bought by S. B. Gates. It is here that visitors to Ktaadn used to cross the river and take the road opposite, to the mouth of Wassataquoik Stream, which they also had to cross.

Below the Hunt farm three miles of deep but not sluggish water bring one to Whetstone Falls, which consist of two 'pitches' a hundred rods apart. These rapids are caused by the water flowing over blocks of granite. Canoes can run the upper, and usually the lower "pitch," although they may have to be "dropped" over one bad place with the aid of the "painter." There is a good path on the right, and easy walking on the left.

From Whetstone Falls to the mouth of Mud Brook, nine miles, the water, except for a mile, past Burnt Land Rips, is smooth and canoeing easy. Three miles more of very pretty country with a short string of rapids intervene before Grindstone Falls are reached. The carries are nearly a mile long, on both the right and left banks. The falls consist of a succession of "pitches," which cover perhaps a mile or more, and in the aggregate make quite a descent. The formation along the river is strata of clay-slate, grits, and quartz tipped on edge, and very sharp and ragged, while here and there are scattered boulders of granite which add to the difficulties of navigation. However, it is possible by wading, and by letting canoes down with the "painter," to accomplish the passage at some seasons without "carrying."

From Grindstone Falls to Ledge Falls it is six miles. Rocky Rips and Scratch Rips are passed during the first half of the distance, the river being otherwise almost entirely free from rapids.

Houses and farms begin to appear at Scratch Rips, and grow more numerous in the two and a quarter miles between Ledge Falls and Medway. These falls can be run by canoes, if care is taken to keep out of the "boil" of the water and avoid swamping.

Medway, or Nickatow, is at the junction of the two branches (East and West) of the Penobscot, and it is twelve miles from there to Mattawamkeag.

---

**2020 Edition**

In his 1881 description of the "oldest route" to Katahdin, Charles Hamlin, who espoused that the East Branch should be called Mattagamon (from its source waters), wrote, "From Mattawamkeag a stage runs the first eleven miles to a little village at the mouth of the Mattagamon, formerly designated upon the maps as **Nickatow** (the *forks*), but some years since incorporated as the town of Medway, its significant Indian name being dropped for one threadbare and unmeaning."[1]

1. Charles E Hamlin, "Routes to Katahdin," 1881.

---

\*

Patterson calls it twenty-four miles from his house to Matangamook Lake, and twenty-three to Nickatow, — the entire distance being forty-seven miles.

For wildness and picturesqueness of scenery this route is equal to, or perhaps surpasses, that down the Ket-tegwe-wick or West Branch of the Penobscot, if we except the gorge on the latter below Ripogenus Lake. Its falls are on the whole much finer than those on the West Branch. It is fully as difficult as the other route, and offers many a good trout pool, and not infrequently an opportunity to secure large game. It is a strange fact, however, that among all the mountains visible from its course Ktaadn does not once appear. Wassataquoik and Lunksoos Mts., the latter 1,378 feet[111] above the river, are prominent above Hunt's, on the west side of the Wassa-tegwe-wick.

It takes ordinarily four days or even less to go from Matangamooksis Lake to Nickatow.

### RÉSUMÉ

| | | |
|---|---|---|
| Apmoojenegamook Lake (Mouth of Mud Br.) to Telosmis Lake . . . | 6 m. | |
| Telosmis Lake to Telos Dam . . . . . . . . . | 4 ½ m. | 1 day |
| Telos Cut . . . . . . . . . . . . . . . . . . . . . . | 1 m. | |
| Webster Lake . . . . . . . . . . . . . . . . . . . . | 2 ½ m. | |
| Webster Lake Dam to Indian Carry . . . . . | 8 m. | 1 day |
| Indian Carry to Matangamooksis Lake . | 2 m. | |
| Head of Mat'sis Lake to Head Matangamook Lake . . . . . . . . . . . . | 7 m. | 1 day |
| Across Matangamook Lake . . . . . . . . . | 3 m. | |
| Matangamook Dam to Stair Falls . . . . . . | 4 1/8 m. | |
| Matangamook Dam to Bill Fish Brook . | ¾ m. | |
| Bill Fish Brook to Webster Landing . . . . | 1 3/8 m. | 1 day |
| Webster Landing to Stair Falls . . . . . . . . | 2 m. | |
| Stair Falls to Haskell Rock Pitch . . . . . . | 1 m. | |
| Haskell Rock Pitch "Carry" . . . . . . . . . . | 5/16 m. | |
| Haskell Rock Pitch to Bowlin Falls . . . . | 4 ½ m. | |
| Haskell Rock Pitch to Pond Pitch . . . . . . | 2/3 m. | |
| Pond Pitch to Grand Pitch . . . . . . . . . . . | 5/8 m. | 1 day |
| Grand Pitch to Hulling Machine Falls . . . | 7/8 m. | |
| Hulling Machine Falls to Bowlin Falls . . | 2 1/3 m. | |
| Bowlin Falls to Seboois River . . . . . . . . | 14 ¾ m. | |
| Bowlin Falls to Lunksoos Brook . . . . . . . | 11 ¼ m. | 1 day |
| Lunksoos Brook to Seboois River . . . . . . | 3 ½ m. | |
| Seboois River to Patterson's . . . . . . . . . | 3 m. | |

---

[111] According to the late Professor Hamlin.

Patterson's to Whetstone Falls . . . . . . . . 3 m.
Whetstone Falls to Burnt Land Rips . . . . 3 m.
Head of Burnt Land Rips to Mud Brook . 6 m.
Mud Brook to Crowfoot Falls . . . . . . . . 1 m.
Crowfoot Falls to Grindstone Falls . . . . . 1 ¾ m.
Head of Grindstone Falls to Rocky Rips . 1 ¾ m.    ½ day
Rocky Rips to Ledge Falls . . . . . . . . . . . 4 ¼ m.
Ledge Falls to Nickatow . . . . . . . . . . . . 2 ¼ m.
                                              85 m.

# Moosehead Lake.

## HOTELS, STORES, AND STEAMER.

## ROACH RIVER HOUSE,

Twenty miles by road from Greenville, at the foot of **Roach Pond.** Reached comfortably by steamer to Lily Bay, thence by team, seven miles, over a good road.

The Trout-Fishing in its neighborhood is unexcelled by any on Moosehead Lake.

The hotel, a new and commodious two-story building, can accommodate a goodly number of guests, and the wants of visitors will receive careful attention.

## TERMS EASY.

*Canoes and Boats to let.*

**LEVI DAVIS, Proprietor.**

# TOURS EAST OF GREENVILLE

---

**2020 Edition**

In this section, Hubbard describes regions east of Greenville and then travels south.

To arrive here from where we last were in Medway, routes 157/11 run to Millinocket from which connections to the Golden Road, Jo-Mary Road, and Katahdin Iron (KI) Works Road can be made. Registration and fees may apply on portions of these private roads.

Hubbard includes information on the tourism in what were more populated areas; as well as, the mountain terrain.

---

*

## *Katahdin Iron Works*

This township is northwest of Brownville, and the focus of the mining operations carried on in it is on Ore Mt. and at a small pond a mile east of it, whose Indian name, or rather that of the West Branch of Pleasant River, which flows through it, is by Greenleaf[112] given as Mun-olam'mon-un'gun, "very fine paint, or place where it is found, or great quantity of it." From a recent christening this pond is called "Silver Lake," and it is about 604 feet above sea-level. At its outlet are the blast furnace and charcoal kilns of the Katahdin Iron Company, while on the opposite or west side of the stream is the Silver Lake Hotel, recently enlarged and refitted, — a pleasant stopping-place for the constantly growing throng of health-seekers and tourists,

---

[112] Report of American Society for Promoting Civilization of the Indian Tribes, 1824.

who are but now beginning to appreciate the natural attractions of this vicinity.

---

**2020 Edition**

The Katahdin Iron Works operated from 1845 to about 1890 in this very remote location of Maine, that wasn't so remote back then. The ironworks made high quality iron for railroad cars and the U.S. Navy. Men came to the site to cut timber to feed the furnaces or to mine the ore.

The community of Silver Lake was reached by a railroad and the site had a 100-room hotel. When the iron company went out of business, the village transformed itself into a recreation and sportsman's destination. Newspaper advertisements touted Silver Lake as, "Absolutely the healthiest spot in Maine," and, "Where hay fever is unknown."

Today only a skeleton of one blast furnace and a charcoal kiln survive at the site. Inside the blast furnaces raw materials of iron ore, limestone, and charcoal were mixed together to form pig iron. The iron bars were called pigs because as the ore ran into troughs dug in the sand, the ore oozed and made a sound like a pig.

The site can be reached from Greenville through the Hedgehog Checkpoint, or from Route 11 and the Katahdin Iron Works Road. Fees for access apply, check latest information online.

Roads in this area are active for logging. Yield to logging trucks.

**Blast Furnace**

**Silver Lake with view of Saddleback Mountain**

**West Branch Pleasant River**

Milo Station is the southern terminus of the Bangor and Katahdin Iron Works Railway, a standard gauge road, now operated by and forming a part of the Bangor and Piscataquis R. R. From Milo Station the road runs six miles, past Brownville, its northern terminus in 1881, to the Iron Works, connecting daily with the regular trains to and from Bangor and Moosehead Lake. At North Brownville it also connects with the International Railroad, for Mattawamkeag on the east, and Greenville and Montreal on the west.[113]

From Milo Station to Milo Village it is a mile and a half, and four or five miles from the latter place to Brownville, according as one takes the straight road over a high hill or the more level road east of the former, which crosses Pleasant River and turns northwest along its left bank. Brownville Village is scattered, so to speak, among a number of little hills, dotted with groups of pretty shade trees, and within its limits are some of the oldest slate quarries in this section of Maine, still in active operation.

From Brownville the wagon road to the Iron Works soon climbs a hill, and discloses to view the pretty valley of Pleasant River below, and the mountains, which are now rapidly approaching from the northwest, their chain extending from Ebeeme (pronounced Eb-ee-my) on the east to Boarstone[114] on the extreme west.

Seven miles from Brownville, or half-way between that village and the Iron-Works, the road enters the "Prairie," a wide flat tract of ground at the confluence of the three branches of Pleasant River, — East, Middle, and West. A mile beyond, or

---

[113] **2020:** Passenger lines no longer run these routes.
[114] **2020:** Now Borestone Mountain.

at the upper end of the "Prairie," the road crosses the Middle Branch, having previously crossed the East Branch half a mile above its junction with the West Branch, and enters the woods. Six miles more of execrable riding bring one to the Iron Works hotel, store, furnace, and settlement.

From this point and from farther up the valley fine views are had of Saddlerock, White Cap, Spruce, Baker, and Chairback Mountains, a succession of peaks which give to the place its chief charm. Far to the east is Ebeeme Mt. with its rounded top, next to which, northwest, is Saddlerock Mt.

### Saddlerock Mountain

Saddlerock Mt., is 3,054 ft.[115] high, and whose summit is between six and a half and seven miles from the hotel. Three-quarters of a mile east of the summit, and only a little below it, is a pretty little pond between two cliffs which flank it on the north and south. Saddlerock may be ascended from the west by following an old road which leaves the Brownville road a quarter of a mile below the hotel, or from the north by following the Chesuncook road around the west end of the mountain. The mountain lies nearly east and west, and from the west looks quite peaked.

Next towards the west is Little Spruce Mt., 3,274 feet high, with the twin Spruce Mt. Ponds at its southern base, 1,802 feet above sea-level.

---

[115] The elevations given here and elsewhere in these pages, except when otherwise stated, are calculated from observations made by the writer with a Green's mountain barometer on the several peaks, simultaneously with others made by President M. F. Fernald at Orono, in July and August, 1881.

**2020 Edition**

In the **1894 Report of the Forest Commissioner of the State of Maine,** then Forest Commissioner, Charles E. Oak, in reference to a study on the growth of trees based on exposure, referred to this mountain as Saddle Rock.

Hubbard consistently refers to a Saddlerock Mountain as one word, and not as Saddle Rock. Hubbard was not incorrect in his time.

On my edition of the *Maine Atlas and Gazetteer*, map 42, the mountain is labeled as Saddleback. The current elevation is given as 2,999 ft. On the Gazetteer, the 'little pond,' Hubbard refers to is likely Crater Pond, which is east of the summit.

Also, on the Gazetteer map there is a small pond south west of the summit, Saddlerock Pond, that feeds into Saddlerock Stream, which flows down into Silver Lake.

I cannot find when, or why, the mountain name was changed to Saddleback and why the pond and streams remained as Saddlerock. It must have happened between Oak's 1894 report and an article that appeared in the 1926 Brownville H. S. Reflector by Pauline Green. Green wrote, "Over the broken back of Saddleback Mountain lies Silver Lake, far from city habitation, hemmed in by mountains and thick, black woods that crowd close to the water's edge."

There is also a Saddleback Mountain (4,120 ft) in Sandy Plantation, Maine, in the Rangeley Lakes Region.

## White Cap Mountain

North of Little Spruce Mt., is old White Cap, the monarch of the group, 3,707 feet[116] above the sea, its rounded dome covered with bare patches of mica-schist detritus and rock in place, alternating with scrub spruce and other stunted vegetation. West of it extends a spur divided into two peaks, and southwest is Big Spruce Mt., all of which must be considerably over 3,000 feet high. The main summit of White Cap is fourteen or fifteen miles, by road, from the Iron Works hotel, and is best reached from this point by taking the "Gulf" road for five miles to White Brook, along whose rapidly descending course a branch road comes down from Gaffney's Camp (1880). This road, although steep in some places, is uniformly good (or was in 1881), and leads to within two miles or less of the summit. Gaffney's logging camp in 1881 was on this road, four miles from the summit, and Clark's three and a half miles below that. From both Saddlerock and White Cap fine views are had of the surrounding country, not the least of which is that of Ktaadn and Joe Merry Mt., there being no intervening ridges or peaks to belittle them.

## Chairback Mountain

On the other side of Pleasant River, and somewhat more than two miles from the hotel, is Chairback Mt., with its three principal peaks, of which that peak which forms the top or back of the "chair" is 2,219 ft., and the next peak, southwest, is 2,371 ft. above sea-level. The most practicable route to the summit

---

[116] **2020:** White Cap Mountain (3655 ft.) is a part of the 100-mile Wilderness, a stretch of the Appalachian Trail along which there are no towns or places for hikers to resupply.

lies two miles up the "Gulf" road to "The Farm," where one can cross the river by means of a rope ferry. Entering the woods, one may, if fortunate, find a "spotted line" leading up to a sort of tableland which runs along the north side of the mountain, about two hundred feet below the summit. A short, steep climb takes one up to the summit. From this point good views are had of the northern and eastern mountain peaks and a broad sweep of open country to the south and east.

North Chairback Pond lies nearly west. From the next peak, a mile or more to the southwest, Long Pond, West Chairback, and the small ponds on the Houston headwaters are near at hand, with Benson, Boarstone, Barren, Elephant, Lyford, Baker, and other mountains near Moosehead Lake conspicuous. The formation of the north peak of Chairback is mica-schist, which changes, about halfway across the second peak, into granite. One day is enough in which to make the ascent of Saddlerock or Chairback and return to the hotel, and two days for that of White Cap.

Big Houston Pond lies southeast of Chairback Mt., with Round Mt. and Houston Mt. east of it, the latter lying between Big and Little Houston Ponds. Little Houston Pond is two miles from the hotel, by a good road partly over Ore Mt., which road continues two miles further to the dam at Big Houston Pond. Another path to the head of the latter pond runs west through an old clearing, and diverges from the main road a quarter of a mile from Little Houston Pond.

### Ore Mountain

Ore Mt., one mile from the hotel, is a small eminence, and is reached over an easy but dusty road, and by paths leading from it. A number of excavations, none of them very deep, are being made, and from them the ore, which lies in beds nearly horizontal, is taken to the furnace below. The ore is a limonite, the result of the oxidation of a singular formation of pyritiferous rock, which on exposure to the air gives off a light smoke. Several springs near the top of the hill discharge water highly impregnated with iron and copperas,[117] some of them so much so as to be extremely nauseating, and the extent to which the mining is continued seems to affect the character and taste of the water.

From Ore Mt. a pretty prospect opens out before the beholder. The intervale below, with its bright patches of cultivated land, "Silver Lake's" extended waters nestling passively among the forests, and on all sides lofty and imposing mountain peaks, near and distant, varying in their lights and shadows, make a scene of ever-increasing interest.

From the Iron Works a road leads north along Saddlerock Brook past B Pond, which is ten miles away. There is said to be good trout fishing here, and at one time caribou frequented the shores of the pond in large droves. Indeed, on the summits of many of the neighboring mountains are well-worn paths made by these animals, which still rove through the woods, when not disturbed by the loggers' presence.[118]

### The Gulf

Perhaps the greatest natural curiosity in this section of Maine is a gorge known as The Gulf.[119] It is a narrow chasm some

---

[117] **2020:** Hydrated ferrous sulfate, typically from green crystals.
[118] **2020:** South west of Big Houston Pond is a place called Caribou Bog.
[119] **2020:** Gulf Hagas

three and a half miles long, through which flows the West Branch of Pleasant River, the "Mun-olam'mon-un'gun." From the hotel a good road runs along the west side of "Silver Lake," and beyond it for half a mile along the top of a "kame" or "horseback," about thirty feet high, which has a brook on one side and a low meadow on the other. This "kame" is north of the river and about midway of the valley. From the hotel to a large clearing known as "The Farm" it is two miles, and rather more than a mile beyond to the edge of the forest, near where three townships corner, the road by the way touching the river at Horse Eddy. At the end of another mile is an old logging camp, from which branches off the road up White Brook to White Cap. Two miles more bring one to Pugwash, a small "logon" opposite the foot of the Gulf. The road thus far has been passable for buckboards; the latter half of it, however, is very rough, and one can better walk than ride over it. Rather more than a mile above the foot of the Gulf the road crosses a bridge under which flows Gulf Hagas Stream.

### Gulf Hagas Stream

This little brook is a gem. For a quarter of a mile below the bridge it is an alternation of bright sparkling cascades and shady pools. The fall of land in its bed between the bridge and river must be one hundred and twenty-five feet, and there are no less than seven or eight "pitches," varying in height from four to twenty-six feet, some falling over the ledges in an even mass, others divided into two or three branches or arms, and — others still, broken in their fall by obstructing rocks, all of them, when over four feet high, as white as milk. The most interesting one is "Screw-Auger" Fall, the third from the bridge. It is twenty-six feet high, the entire body of water passing through a part of the rock about four feet wide, which it has worn into the shape of an S. The water strikes the lower part of the S with such force that it is precipitated about twelve feet in a plane at right angles with the wall. Just below it is a pool surrounded on three sides by a square chamber of perpendicular walls, — a great curiosity. The walls of this miniature gulf are ragged, and in many places a descent to the water's edge is dangerous and in others impossible, while in only a few is it at all practicable.

The main road in no place comes within sight of the river, but branches lead from it, here and there, to "landings" used by the loggers, from which to roll their logs into the stream. One of these branches, over half a mile above Gulf Hagas, leads down to what has been dubbed "Hammond Street Pitch," a precipitous bank some ninety feet high, with a ledge or shelf five feet wide jutting out two-thirds of the way down its side. The view from here is quite impressive. The stream foams and froths down its straight course of eighty rods or more, while the opposite cliff, with its profile of the "Old Man," rises perhaps sixty feet higher, or to a total height of one hundred and fifty feet above the stream. The latter turns sharply to the south at its base, and soon again to the east, flowing past the end of a rounded spur or ridge of solid slate, which extends back some thirty or forty rods from the stream, and rises gradually from a height of sixty feet or more some hundred feet additional. This is probably the highest part of the Gulf; that is, the cliffs are here highest above the bed of the stream.

From this point a good path runs over the ledges above the stream, and from it many points of interest below can be reached where the cliffs descend abruptly to the stream, while at others they are too precipitous to admit of descending them or of walking along their base.

---

**2020 Edition**

While all trails need to be respected and the hiker must be prepared, Gulf Hagas is especially challenging. It is a spectacular place to hike and not someplace for the casual walker, or for those who do not respect the danger of the woods. The cliffs here are high and often slippery. Due to the location of the trail and the terrain, an injured hiker may wait for hours for help to arrive.

Furthermore, there is no cell service in this area to call for help. There are no roads close to the trail. Hovering a helicopter over the gorge is challenging as the trail is narrow and leaves few places where a basket can safely be lowered. This means, disabled hikers must wait for a rescue party to arrive on foot.

Carrying someone through the woods for miles is not a job for one or two people. These rescue parties more typically are a dozen or more first responders from the Maine Warden Service, local fire departments, police, and volunteers. The rescue party must continuously alter who is carrying to ensure they maintain their own stamina to get everyone out safely. Making a rescue at dusk or in the dark makes for an even more treacherous situation.

During a hike here in the summer of 2018, one of the editors came upon a hiker in distress near Billings Falls. The hiker had broken an ankle on a slippery rock that had a basin full of water. We had heavy rain the night before. The day was overcast and chilly. The hiker, who was with a companion, had been stranded for more than two hours. A prior party of hikers, that reached them before we did, had gone for help. They had no poles, no warm clothes, no rain shelter, or ways to keep warm once darkness fell.

Another danger here is the rushing, cold water. On a hot day, the pools below the falls can look inviting for a swim. In his book, "A Good Man With A Dog," Maine Game Warden Roger Guay tells the story of two brothers who drowned after diving into the pools along the stream. The reason had to do with the aeration of the water from the force of the falls. The water wasn't dense enough for them to push themselves out. Guay calls The Gulf, "the most spectacular, and deadly, place," he's ever had to do rescues.

Be careful here – at The Gulf – and everywhere you explore. Be aware. Be prepared. Be safe.

A mile above Gulf Hagas is a logging camp (1880), the name of which appears on a painted sign, nailed high up to the trunk of a small birch tree, — "Gulf House." A few rods from here a rustic bridge has been thrown over the river some twenty-five or thirty feet above its bed, for the use of the "river-drivers." From this bridge to the head of the Gulf it is about a mile and a quarter, and one point of interest succeeds another at short intervals along the entire distance. First in order, and visible from the bridge, is a remarkable full-front face of an Indian, formed by the overhanging cliff on the south side of the stream. This rock is one side of what is called the "Lower Jaws," a point made memorable by the death of an Indian who was killed there in May, 1882, in a "jam" of logs. A short distance above, at the "Main Jaws" the channel was only seven feet and seven inches wide, until blasted out to a width of twenty-six feet.

A few rods from this point is Duck Pitch, about fifteen feet high, over which the water pours with great force, being churned to the consistency of buttermilk.

A short distance above this fall is another very narrow passage, where before it was blasted out the channel of the stream for ten feet could not have been more than five feet wide, and below it a pool and eddy have eaten into the cliffs and formed an irregular chamber with overhanging walls. The contraction of the opposing walls at this point is known as the "Upper Jaws," and from the ledge on the north side may be seen, lower down, on the opposite side, a pretty good profile of an individual wearing a cap with a long and clumsy visor. Next above is Billing's Fall, sixteen feet high, which with the "pitch" just above it makes one of the prettiest sights of the Gulf, and is well seen from a high cliff just below it, a few steps from the path. A few rods above here and around the bend are Stair Falls, the head of the Gulf.

The formation along this remarkable chasm is slate. Rocks jagged and rounded, cliffs perpendicular and overhanging the stream, the former where the cleavage is parallel with, and the latter where it is at right angles to, its course; huge blocks stripped off and lying in confusion below, others partly detached from the parent mass and separated just enough to leave an ugly chasm between; rounded spurs sloping down to the water, solid masses, patched with moss and lichens, all these hard and rugged ledges covered with a scattered growth of fir and spruce, — such are the characteristics of the Gulf. In places the tourist can find a difficult descent to the water's edge, where he will get a much better impression of the marvels of the place, and from its many pools he may take an abundance of fine trout.

The Gulf road leads up the stream past Baker Mt. to Big Lyford Pond and the West Branch Ponds at its head, some ten or twelve miles distant. These waters, heretofore practically inaccessible, abound in trout.

From the foot of the Gulf, on the south side of the river, a fairly good path leads two miles to Long Pond.

## Long Pond

Long Pond is the main source of the Sebec River, and the home of the trout and land-locked salmon. It is a pretty lake, three and a half miles long, affording many fine views of distant mountains, and runs nearly to the base of Barren Mt., around which its waters are discharged to the south and west. A thoroughfare separates the upper or principal part from the lower and narrower part, and a short stretch of quick-water intervenes before the end of the pond and the dam are reached. From here it is about three miles through the woods to Indian Pond (otherwise called "Rum" Pond); thence three miles more to Greenville over a good wagon road. A path leads from the dam down the stream to Elliotsville and Monson.

**The Gulf**

| **2020 Edition** |
|:---:|
| Maine poet, Frances Parker Laughton Mace, wrote a poem about Silver Lake, c. 1887. Included here is the first stanza. |

### At Silver Lake

WOULD you feed on the strength of the hills, —
   Would you drink of the wine
That is poured from the balsamic boughs
   Of fir-tree and pine?
Then into the wilderness come
   And the feast partake,
While you linger and rest on the shore
   Of fair Silver Lake.

# MT. KINEO HOUSE.

## MEALS.

*Breakfast*, 7.30 *to* 9 A.M.; *Dinner*, 1½ P.M.; *Supper*, 6½ P.M.

## BOARD AND LODGING.

Single person, $8.00 to $15.00 a week, according to location of
   room.
Man and wife, $15.00 to $25.00.
Children, usually half price.
Nurse and young child (under two years), $1.00 to $1.50 a day.
Transients, $2.00 to $2.50 a day.
Single meals, 75 cents; Lodging, 50 cents.

   *In July, a discount of 15 per cent is made on the above prices.*

## BOATS.

Row-boats to let, at 50 cents a day, or $2.50 a week.
Canoes, 25 cents a day, — for long trips, less.

### The "DAY-DREAM," $10.00 a day.

To Head of Lake, $10.00.   To Lily Bay or Spencer Bay, $5.00.
To East Outlet, $3.00 to $4.00, — large parties, 25 cents apiece.
To Socatean or Tomhegan, $3.00 to $5.00, — according to size of
   party.
Around the Mountain, parties of twelve or fifteen, 25 cts. apiece.

## FARES ON STEAMERS.

Greenville to Kineo, or reverse, $1.00; round trip, $1.50.
Kineo to Greenville and return, not necessarily on same day
   (guests of hotel), 75 cents.
Kineo to Head of Lake and return on same trip (guests of
   hotel), $1.00.

# EAST OF THE GULF

## *Schoodic Lake * Ebeeme Ponds*

A mile beyond Brownville a branch-road leads to Schoodic Lake, and also into a logging road, which in turn runs past Lower Ebeeme Ponds to Jo Merry Lakes.[120] A pair of horses could formerly haul canoes and luggage through from Brownville to West Jo Merry Lake in one day, but such a feat is now impossible, owing to the badness of the road.

The upper and lower Ebeeme ponds lie about four miles apart, measured on the east branch of Pleasant River, which flows through them before its junction with the other branches. A canoe can be paddled and poled up the connecting stream for two miles without much difficulty, but above that point will have to be carried half a mile, and poled the rest of the way to the upper pond. The ponds and surrounding country are quite picturesque, several wooded mountain peaks being near at hand on either side.

The lower group of ponds consists of West Ebeeme, connected by a narrow thoroughfare with Horseshoe Pond, into which empties, by a small brook on the north, Pearl Pond, and on the east. East Ebeeme Pond, the latter being three-quarters of a mile from Schoodic Lake, and connected with it by a good path. There are numerous coves and inlets around the shores of these ponds, which, besides being pretty, make good shooting-ground. A good farm, cultivated by Elisha Norton, lies on the Jo Merry road near Schoodic Lake.

---

[120] **2020:** See earlier note in section, "Tours Beyond Moosehead" for Jo-Mary lakes.

Into the Upper Ebeeme empties, on the north, Wongun Brook, which for two miles from its mouth is navigable by canoes. From the head of the dead-water a good road leads into the Jo Merry road, and it is only four miles to Jo Merry Lake.

Horace Falls, two miles above Upper Ebeeme, is a pretty little cascade fifteen feet or more high, with a small island perched in the middle of it.

### East Branch of the Pleasant River

On the East Branch of Pleasant River, six miles above upper Ebeeme pond, there is a gorge similar to the Gulf, and called the "Gauntlet," — very wild, but not quite equal, either in extent or picturesqueness, to the former. A tote road runs from Lower Ebeeme pond, from the mouth of Babel Brook, to the Gauntlet.[121]

Persons who visit Ebeeme Ponds leave the stage at the house of William Tufts, at the "Prairie," seven miles from Brownville.

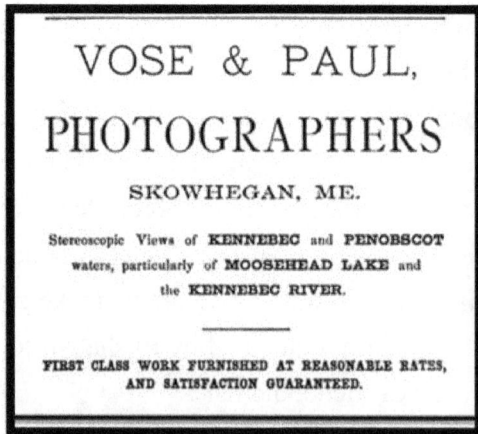

# VOSE & PAUL,

# PHOTOGRAPHERS

SKOWHEGAN, ME.

Stereoscopic Views of **KENNEBEC** and **PENOBSCOT** waters, particularly of **MOOSEHEAD LAKE** and the **KENNEBEC RIVER.**

**FIRST CLASS WORK FURNISHED AT REASONABLE RATES, AND SATISFACTION GUARANTEED.**

---

[121] **2020:** No such tote road appears on a current map. Best access is from Jo-Mary Rd., to Johnston Pond Rd.

# SOUTH OF GULF HAGAS

## *Sebec Lake*

Sebec Lake (same as Sebaygook, "large body of water"), an oddly shaped lake, and in some respects a pretty one, lies near the line of the Bangor and Piscataquis Railroad, and can be reached conveniently by either of three routes. The first is by way of South Sebec, the second lies through Foxcroft, and the third leaves Monson Station (formerly Abbot), — all stations on the B. & P. R. R.

From South Sebec to Sebec Corner is a mile and a half, and thence it is three miles and a half to Sebec Village at the extreme end of the lower lake, or "Pond," though some people call it two and three miles respectively. About three-quarters of a mile before reaching the village the road forks, the right branch lying straight over Moulton Hill, and the left one circling around its base. From Moulton Hill, and from other points on the road, fine views can be had of Saddlerock, White Cap, Chairback, and other mountains to the north and east, and in clear days of Ktaadn also; while off to the west rises Boarstone, a rugged, peaked mass. Stages to Sebec Village connect with the regular trains of the railroad. Fare, twenty-five cents.[122]

From Foxcroft one can go by private conveyance, or stage, at 7 a.m., due north four miles and a half to Blethen Landing, at the west end of the lower pond. There is a saw-mill here, and several farm-houses where one can get a meal if needed, and await the arrival of the steamer, which is due at 8.15 a.m. The

---

[122] **2020:** The road that reaches Sebec at the east end of the lake is today named, "Stage Coach Road."

fare from Foxcroft to the head of the lake is fifty cents, or about a dollar if by private conveyance.

The road from Monson Station leads through a pretty and more or less cultivated valley, nine miles to the Lake House, at the mouth of Wilson Stream. At last accounts no regular stage ran over this road oftener than once a week; and should the visitor select this route, which in some respects is preferable to the other two, he will have to depend on private conveyance from Monson, which place he will reach by railroad.

Blueberries grow in profusion near Sebec Lake, especially on Granite Mt. on the western shore; and during the time when they are ripe a small steamer makes the round trip up and down the lake every day, and runs pretty regularly during the rest of the summer season, say from July 25th to September 1st, leaving Sebec Village in the morning and returning from Wilson Stream in the afternoon.[123] Campers will find the ordinary articles of an outfit at Sebec Village, and at reasonable prices; but guides are scarce, and canoes not to be had anywhere on the lake, unless by the courtesy of some inhabitant, who may happen to own one for which he has no immediate use. Mr. Frank M. Ford, at the village, owns a sailboat which is generally at the service of visiting sportsmen.

In the spring, when the ice first breaks up, the fishing at Sebec Lake is quite good at the outlet of the lake, at the mouth of Ship Pond Stream in Buck's Cove, and up Wilson Stream as far as the falls. Landlocked salmon abound in its waters, and furnish capital sport to the angler; but their "run" lasts only a

---

[123] At present discontinued. (**2020:** Of course, this applies in the modern day as well.)

short time, and during the summer the fisherman must be content with pickerel and white perch.[124]

Sebec Village was settled about 1802, and incorporated in 1812, and the visitor must therefore be prepared to see more or less cultivation on the shores of the lake. A good road runs up the north side of the lower pond, some five or six miles, past a number of farms, while the south side seems to be still an unbroken forest. The lake is eleven or twelve miles long, the lower part being narrow and rather commonplace. From the village it is three miles to Little Pine Island, which consists of eight stumps, one cedar bush, and a lot of driftwood. One mile beyond is Big Pine Island, whence it is three miles to the Narrows. The latter are about forty-five rods wide, and from thence the upper or main lake opens to view with its hilly western shore, and Boarstone and Barren Mts. prominent at the north.

The shores of the upper part of the main lake are one mass of granite blocks, and are covered with a hard-wood growth; and only at and near the mouth of Ship Pond Stream and on Green Point, three-quarters of a mile below it, and a mile and a quarter from Wilson Stream, can good camping ground be found.[125] An old deserted fish-hatching house stands at the mouth of Ship Pond Stream, just below the falls and an old burnt dam. From it an old decayed tramway leads up the west

---

[124] **2020:** Landlocked salmon still thrive in the lake. For an excellent summary of this water body and fishery, see, "Fisheries Progress Report Series 13-02, Sebec Lake Fishery Management," by Timothy C. Obrey, April 2013. Available online from Maine.gov.

[125] **2020:** Campsites are available at Peaks-Kenny State Park.

bank of the stream, a mile and a quarter, to the quarry of the Howard Slate Co., abandoned some years ago.

Besides the lake there are a number of ponds and streams nearby, where the angler will be much more likely to find fish than in the lake. One of these is Buttermilk Pond, which is accessible over two good roads which lead from two "landings," one above and the other below a burnt ledge on the east shore of Buck's Cove. The lower road takes one, after ten minutes' walking, almost within sight of Bear Pond, a pretty little lakelet half a mile wide. A mile beyond Bear Pond this road runs through a clearing filled with sawdust and trimmings made by cutting up birch for spools; thence a mile and a half more to the east end or head of First Buttermilk Pond, the latter part of the way through a fine beech and maple grove.

### *Buttermilk Pond*

Buttermilk Pond is two miles long, and rather narrow except where a cove indents the south shore, midway of its length. The road touches the pond soon after leaving Sawdust Clearing. The upper end of this pond, near the inlet, is said to be a rare spot for trout and landlocked salmon, in the season. The outlet is three-quarters of a mile long to its junction with Ship Pond Stream,[126] and for the last half-mile of its course tumbles over innumerable slate ledges, making one of the prettiest succession of falls in that section of country, some of the "pitches" being over twelve feet high. An old path leads from Sawdust Clearing, a mile and a half, nearly to the mouth of the stream, which is opposite the old Howard slate quarry.

---

[126] **2020:** Ship Pond Stream runs from Lake Onawa to Bucks Cove in Sebec Lake.

From Sawdust Clearing another logging road leads west, two and a half miles, to Millbank Pond,[127] which empties its waters into lower Sebec Lake just west of Big Pine Island. It lies south of Third Buttermilk Pond, which is quite pretty, while Buttermilk Pond, No. 2, is marshy and uninteresting. The latter is a quarter-mile, or more, from No. 1, and three-quarters of a mile from No. 3. No.2 is a mile and a half long.

The Lake House, formerly a hotel, but now seldom used as such, kept by Captain A. G. Crockett, is situated near the mouth of Wilson Stream. It is the terminus of the road from Monson, and from it one can be conveyed to within three-quarters of a mile of Grindstone Pond, formerly one of the favorite fishing grounds. Half a mile above the mouth of Wilson Stream, at the falls, are the mill and buildings of the Willimantic Linen Co., where they make their spools from the birch which grows in abundance in this region.[128] The red-painted boarding house of this company and its little Queen Anne cottages, on the brow of the opposite hill, are very picturesque, and are decidedly unique in these forest wilds.

Ship Pond Stream is impassable for canoes except in high water, and the best way to reach Ship Pond is over the wagon road, three and a half miles, to Welch's Mill, thence over the Elliotsville branch to Greenwood Pond.[129] From Welch's Mill to Monson is five miles, the way being along the outlets of Monson and Hebron Ponds and over Norton Hill, from which

---

[127] **2020:** Now labeled, "Millbrook Pond." Gazetteer map 32.

[128] **2020:** Not far from the town of Guilford, the home of Puritan Medical Products where they produce cotton swabs from Maine birch.

[129] See section for Greenwood Pond – a few pages hence.

the mountain views to the north and northeast are very fine. It takes about three hours to drive from Crockett's to Monson.

### Monson * Elliotsville

Monson Village, in the middle of the township of the same name, is six miles northeast from Monson Station, on the Bangor and Piscataquis Railroad, and about fourteen miles south of Moosehead Lake. Several large slate quarries have been operated here for ten years or more; and since their opening, the village has, from a quiet farming community, sprung into an enterprising and busy trade-centre. It lies on high ground, among the hills which skirt the east side of the Piscataquis Valley, and from many points within its limits fine views are had of the more distant and pretentious mountains, which are prominent on the west, north, and northeast. The best outlook, by all odds, for the lover of natural scenery is from the top of Homer's Hill, above the slate-quarries. The latter, opened from one hundred and twenty to one hundred and fifty feet below the surface, and disclosing a mass of solid rock which extends to unknown depths, are objects of great interest to all who visit them. Should the quality of the slate in them continue as good as at present, they will probably furnish work to many men for several generations to come.[130]

Hebron Pond, west of the village, is a very pretty body of water, and contains many large and luscious trout. On summer evenings its surface is dotted with boats of merry villagers, seeking recreation, after the toils of the day, among its lovely islands or near its wooded shores.

---

[130] **2020:** Slate companies still operate in the town.

Monson lies on the old stage-road from Dexter and Dover to Greenville, as former visitors to Moosehead Lake will remember. A narrow-gauge railroad from Monson now connects with the Bangor and Piscataquis Railroad at Monson Station. Comfortable hotel accommodations combine with the natural surroundings to make Monson an attractive and favorite resort for people who love quiet and the healthful tonic of a bracing atmosphere.[131]

Childe's Falls, on Goodale Brook, the outlet of Spectacle Ponds, are two miles north of the village, just east of the road which divides the town. They are twenty feet or more high, and although the amount of water which leaps from ledge to ledge is not large, the cascade is a very pretty one.

Northeast of Monson is the town of Elliotsville,[132] much wilder and, for that reason, more attractive to many people than its more thickly settled neighbor. Following the old "centre-road" from Monson Village for a mile and a half, then turning to the right and skirting the north side of Monson Pond, in five and a half miles one comes to the Elliotsville line, and in another two and a half miles to Elliotsville Falls on Wilson Stream. From this point a road runs up the west side of the stream about a mile, crosses the Little Wilson (of Shirley) and

---

[131] **2020:** In 2017, the Libra Foundation of Maine began a multi-year revitalization of Monson. The town, the last supply point before the 100-mile Wilderness of the Appalachian Trail, and once just a pass-through on the way to Greenville, is again becoming a destination location.

[132] **2020:** Elliotsville, as a town, had a rather short existence. Elliot T. Bridge, who built a gristmill on Wilson Stream, set forth to incorporate the town in 1835. By 1858, with few habitants (around 50 or so), the incorporation was repealed. It became a Maine unorganized territory in March of 1983.

ascends a steep hill until it is lost in a large farm. Entering the woods opposite the house far up the hill on this farm, and walking three-quarters of a mile in a southwesterly direction, one comes to the Little Wilson again, and to a deep gorge through which it flows. A very steep and narrow ridge divides the stream from a tributary north of it. At the head of the gorge, some sixty rods from its mouth, is a waterfall fifty-seven feet high, of surpassing loveliness and well worth a visit. From the farm, as one descends again to the road, a fine view is had of Boarstone and Greenwood Mountains.

**2020 Edition**

**Little Wilson Falls**

At Elliotsville Falls the road crosses the stream on a bridge, and on the east side forks, one branch leading north to

Bodfish's, and the other running southeasterly to Chas. C. Hill's farm, where teams will be stabled, and meals provided for hungry tourists. Mr. Hill owns boats on Greenwood Pond and Ship Pond, and, besides being reasonable in his charges, is a kind and attentive host.

### Greenwood Pond * Ship Pond (Lake Onawa)

From this point the road to Greenwood Pond leads through hay fields, and camp equipage can be transported thither by team, while campers can walk or not, as they please. It is about half a mile to the shore of the pond, across which to its outlet it is perhaps a mile further. From the landing a fine view is had of Boarstone Mt.[133] and one of its spurs, called the "Calf," which cast their lengthened shadows into the marvelously clear water of the pond. Indeed, so bright and clear is this water that it is difficult to take fish from it, although they are said to be very abundant there.

The "carry" into Ship Pond, or "Onaway Lake," as it is sometimes called, begins west of and near the outlet. The path is a good one, open, and for the most part dry, although in places rocky, and is about three-quarters of a mile long. It comes out on Ship Pond, opposite a granite ledge which juts out into the water nearby. The shores of this pond, like those of Sebec Lake, are covered with granite detritus, and there are very few good sites on them for a camp. The best of these is at Haynes's Beach, on the south side of the cove of the same name, and another on the northwest shore of the pond, at a point just

---

[133] **2020:** What is now known as, Borestone Mountain, was originally named "Boarstone." The loggers had given this name due to resemblance, when viewed from the north, of a boar's anatomy.

below Long Pond Stream. An iron bridge of the International Railroad spans the ravine just below the outlet of the pond, and is 125 feet high, affording a magnificent view of the pond and its surroundings.[134]

Ship Pond is so called from an island (Schooner Island) which formerly had several trees on it, looking collectively, and from a distance, like the masts of a vessel. The name "Onaway" is borrowed from Longfellow's "Hiawatha."[135] The original Indian name is Oberneetsombeck.[136] This pond is one of the most strikingly situated ponds of its size in this part of Maine. On the northwest rises Boarstone Mt., abruptly almost from the water's edge and a thousand feet above it. South of Boarstone is Greenwood Mt., insignificant only by comparison with its neighbors. Across the outlet from Greenwood Mt. is Benson Mt., more impressive perhaps from a distance than from near its base; and joined to it on the north, completing the encircling chain, rises majestic Barren, several hundred feet higher than Boarstone. All of these mountains rise rapidly from the shores of the pond, and instead of having a sameness, offer quite a variety of scenery, and make the pond and its neighborhood objects of widespread admiration.

On top of Boarstone, below the principal or eastern summit, are three small ponds whose waters flow into Greenwood

---

[134] **2020:** The Onawa trestle is Maine's longest and highest.

[135] **2020:** Given the poem by Longfellow was published in 1855, this reference is most likely in error. Onaway is the English derivation of the Indian word "*onawa*" which has the meaning "awake." At some point the maps changed from using Ship Pond or Onaway, to Lake Onawa.

[136] Bangor Hist. Mag., 1889, Vol. IV., No. 8.

Pond.[137] There is also a small pond high up the slope of Barren Mt.[138] At the dam below Ship Pond, and in different parts of the pond, trout and landlocked salmon may be taken, and in some places also freshwater smelts.

From near the outlet (of Lake Onawa) a path leads east a quarter of a mile into the old Chesuncook or Thissell road, thence three-quarters of a mile past the end of Big Benson Pond to the north shore of Buttermilk Pond.

### Big Benson Pond

A spotted line leads from it down to Big Benson Pond, which is a mile and a half long. Its water is very clear, the shores being covered with a pretty sand, and the water near them shallow. Very large trout and togue have been taken from this pond, and its stock of fish is said to be by no means exhausted yet. Benson Mt. lies north and northeast, and Little Benson Pond is a mile to the eastward.

From the east shore of Moore's cove (southeast corner of Ship Pond) it is but a few miles to Sampson Pond and Caribou Barren[139] beyond, — good ground for deer.

From the head of Ship Pond one can paddle nearly two miles up Long Pond Stream to Bodfish's Bridge, from which Brown's clearing, a mile beyond, is reached by a road through the woods and fields on the west side of the stream. This road continues from Brown's, some five or six miles, to Long Pond. About a mile and a half up the stream from the clearing is a very pretty succession of falls, called "Slugundy," a name elsewhere found

---

[137] **2020:** Sunset, Midday, and Sunrise Ponds.
[138] **2020:** Cloud Pond.
[139] **2020:** Caribou Bog.

in Maine. They are best reached from the road. A fine view of the end of Barren Mt. is had from Brown's Clearing.

The ascent of Boarstone Mt. may be made from the south side, over the "Calf," or more easily from the north through the hardwood forest which covers the northern slope.

Parties who visit this locality will do well to secure a canoe at one of the neighboring farms in advance, or bring one with them. Camp-outfits and teams can be obtained at Monson.[140]

## Fishermen, Attention!

## FINE SALMON AND TROUT RODS,

Made of Split Bamboo, Greenhart, Ash, or Lance-wood. Every rod thoroughly tested before it leaves the shop.

### Split Bamboo Rods a Specialty.

*Prices Reasonable, and Satisfaction guaranteed.*

————◆————

Orders are particularly desired from WHOLESALE DEAL-ERS, to whom the very best of terms will be offered.

## JAMES REED,
### 26 Banks Street, Cambridge, Mass.

---

[140] For information and guide, apply to E. R. Hayncs, Postmaster, Monson, Maine.

# FORKS OF THE KENNEBEC AND VICINITY
## *First Route – North Anson*

Another way of reaching Moosehead Lake and the headwaters of the Kennebec is by way of Skowhegan, or North Anson, and thence up the Kennebec valley. The tourist leaves Boston at 7: 30 a.m. by the Eastern, or by the Boston and Maine Railroad, and, connecting at Portland with the Maine Central Railroad, continues by way of Lewiston and Auburn to West Waterville. At this place those who wish can connect with the Somerset Railroad, and go to North Anson, or one can without change of cars continue to Skowhegan.

By the former route one crosses the Kennebec at Norridgewock, an interesting old town on its banks, which was settled early in the eighteenth century. A short distance above it the cars pass, on the left, a granite obelisk erected to Father Rasles[141] and the Norridgewock Indians, who were slaughtered there in 1724. The pious father had come from Canada, a missionary to this wild tribe, and had succeeded in gaining a great ascendency over them. At his instigation they committed depredations on the settlers nearby, at the time when the French and English were not on very good terms. Finally, Captains Harmon and Moulton were sent with two companies of soldiers to punish them. Coming on to the high ground east of their village, they divided the party, surrounded the unsuspecting Indians, and, after a brief resistance, killed most of them, and burned their chapel and village.

---

[141] **2020:** The spelling on the monument is Sebastian Rasle.

The railroad runs along and near the left bank of the river, crosses to the right bank at Madison, where there is quite a waterfall, and continues on the same side to North Anson. It takes about an hour and a quarter to go from West Waterville to North Anson, and the fare is one dollar.

North Anson, at the junction of the Kennebec and Carabassett Rivers, is a thriving little village, and at present the northern terminus of the Somerset Railroad. It lies on both sides of the Carabassett, a stream which runs noisily through it, over rapids of considerable length and interest.[142] From the village a fine view is had of Mount Abraham and Mount Bigelow, to the west. The cars arrive here about half past five, and the tourist can have supper, and push on, the same evening, seven miles, to Solon, or he can stop here over night and leave for Solon the next morning at half past seven. It is forty miles from here to the Forks, the junction of Dead River with the Kennebec, and teams connect at Solon, in the morning, with the regular stage from Skowhegan, or vice versa from Solon, with the morning train from North Anson to West Waterville. The fare to Solon is fifty cents. Parties can procure, at reasonable rates, a team to carry them through to the Forks, the same night.

### Dead River & Flagstaff

From North Anson a good road runs twenty-seven miles to Dead River. Here, at Parsons's hotel, in Dead River Village, one can get canoes and staple provisions, and go up the river eleven miles, or by land nine miles, to Flagstaff Village, which is between the pond of the same name and Dead River.

---

[142] **2020:** North Anson Gorge.

## 2020 Edition

The Flagstaff Village, Hubbard mentions here is no longer. The village, along with Dead River Village, was flooded by a dam in 1950 to provide hydroelectric power.

The town of Flagstaff originally took its name from the flagpole erected in the fall of 1775 by the men of Benedict Arnold's army on their way to Quebec.

The song, "Below" by Slaid Cleaves tells the story of Flagstaff Village and Dead River Village. The song has been set to a music video and includes photographs before the flooding. The video is available on the internet.

Hubbard's 1899 map shows the land before the construction of the dam that created the Flagstaff Lake of today. It is Maine's largest man-made lake.

*

Seven or eight miles up the river from Flagstaff is Eustis, a small village with a mill, above which on the north branch of Dead River one can paddle twelve miles to Chain Ponds. Only one carry, and that only twenty rods long, has to be made, about four miles above Eustis, around Ledge Falls.

From Chain Ponds one crosses the Canada line, and soon descends into Lake Megantic. This is the route taken by Arnold in his famous march to Canada in October and November of 1775, he having come up the Kennebec until opposite Carrying Place Ponds, over which he crossed to Dead River, camped some time at Flagstaff, and then proceeded up the north branch through Chain Ponds into Canada.

Below Dead River Village there are six miles of "dead" water to Long Falls, one mile to the west of which is Long Pond, a good fishing ground. In fact, the whole of this Dead River region, being out of the usual range of sportsmen, affords very good trout-fishing.

Around Long Falls there is a carry of three quarters of a mile; then come six miles of "dead" water, at the foot of which are Grand Falls and a dam. Below the dam there are wild rapids for seventeen or eighteen miles, — all the way to the Forks.

### Second Route - Skowhegan

The route through West Waterville and Waterville to Skowhegan is perhaps more convenient than the first named, as it involves no change of cars. Skowhegan is the headquarters of the regular and only Kennebec stage line, and one is more likely to get a good seat in the stage there, than if one should connect with it at Solon.

The night train from Boston fails, by two hours, to connect with the stage, unless there should be at least six persons aboard who are going up the river, and who shall have previously notified the stage to await their arrival. By this plan, however, one who wishes to buy an outfit at Skowhegan has no time to do so, and for such a person the morning train from Boston is the better, provided one can afford to lose the day spent on the cars.

Skowhegan is quite an attractive place, and the falls in the Kennebec there are well worth seeing. The Turner House, a spacious hotel, is well kept and comfortable, and within pistol-shot of the depot.

The stage leaves the hotel, for the Forks, forty-six miles away, at half past six o'clock every morning. The road up to Solon — fifteen miles — runs through broad and undulating country, and discloses now and then pretty glimpses of distant mountains and hills. One of the prettiest views is from Robbins Hill, ten miles from Skowhegan. Moxie Mountain[143] stands out prominently, to the north.

From Solon the road follows the course of the river up its left bank to Bingham, eight miles beyond, where stage-passengers dine. This is the terminus of the telegraph line.

Above Bingham the hills which flank the river approach it more nearly, and the road winds around its pretty curves, now through stretches of woodland, and again through "dugways," on the very edge of the bank. It is comparatively level all of the way to the Forks, and in good weather the entire distance through Solon, Bingham, Moscow, Carratunk, and the Forks Plantation, is made in about ten hours, stops included.[144]

Between Skowhegan and the Forks, a stage runs each way every day. From the Forks to Hilton's, in Sandy Bay township, a stage runs every Tuesday, Thursday, and Saturday, arriving at Moose River Village at three o'clock p.m., and at Hilton's,

---

[143] **2020:** Elevation 2,936 ft.
[144] **2020:** In your automobile on Route 201, less than an hour.

fourteen miles beyond, the same evening. The stage returns on the alternate days of the week. Should the amount of travel render it expedient, the proprietors are ready to run a stage every day over this route, both ways. Passengers to Canada connect at Hilton's with the Canada stage down the Riviere du Loup to St. Joseph, thence they go by rail to Quebec.

From Solon a stage runs every morning, and connects with the cars at North Anson, at 7: 45 a.m. The stage from the Forks reaches Skowhegan in the evening, in time, if required, to catch the night train for Boston. Excursion tickets from Boston to the Forks and back, by this route, cost fourteen dollars.

### The Forks of the Kennebec * Moxie Pond

The Forks of the Kennebec has long been a favorite resort for fishermen. A well-kept and commodious hotel is prettily and conveniently located in the centre of a large tract of fine trout country, and the smaller game of the woods abounds in its vicinity. One of the best fishing-grounds near at hand is Moxie Pond, which is between ten and twelve miles long, and from a mile to a mile and a half broad. Two roads lead to it from the Forks, one on either side of Moxie Stream. That on the south side is five miles long, and the more direct; the other is two miles longer, and passes near Moxie Falls, a cascade ninety-five feet high, which should by all means be visited.[145] Both roads come together at the dam which is at the outlet of the pond. Moxie Stream is "dead" from its mouth almost up to the falls, sixty rods above which is another fall of fifteen feet,

---

[145] **2020:** A recommended location to see one of New England's highest waterfalls. The two-mile round-trip trail is well-traveled, but includes some stairs that could be challenging for some.

called Rankin's Falls. From the latter point to the lower dam it is a hundred rods. Two miles intervene between the lower and upper dams, three fourths of which is "dead" water. At the lower dam there is a farm and a very neat cabin, kept by Tom Morris; at the upper dam Frank Heald has a camp.

**Moxie Falls**

*

Going up the pond one comes, at the end of a mile and a quarter, to Caribou Narrows, a charming spot for camping. Tall pines stand out above their forest companions, and with the mountains and rocks look wild and weird. Black Narrows are two and a half miles further up the pond, and Mosquito Narrows about two miles beyond them. A canoe can run up Mosquito Stream to Mosquito Pond.

Bald Rock is a mile above Mosquito Narrows, just opposite Sandy Stream, which is navigable for about a mile from its mouth. Baker Brook empties into the pond at its head, and is unnavigable. The Devil's Table, nine miles up the pond, is a large flat rock in the middle of the water. For two or three miles the upper part of the pond is narrow, and boulders and sharp rocks lie concealed just below the surface of the water.

Good fishing is to be had in Mosquito, Sandy, and Alder Brooks. Cranberries and blueberries grow in profusion on the shores of the pond, and deer and caribou are frequently seen near it.

## *Pleasant Pond*

Nine miles below the Forks a good road leads from the Kennebec, three miles, to Pleasant Pond, where there is quite a settlement. The water of this pond is deep and clear, so clear that one can fish successfully until quite late at night. The trout in it are of a peculiar kind, very silvery, round, plump, and delicious eating. The road continues from the north end of the pond four miles to Mosquito Pond.[146]

---

[146] **2020:** The Appalachian Trail crosses the north end of Pleasant Pond and subsequently passes between the south end of Moxie Pond and Baker Stream.

## West of the Kennebec * Otter & Pierce Ponds

Carrying-Place Ponds, and Otter and Peirce Ponds are reached from Carratunk,[147] and are said to afford good fishing, the trout in them running as large as four and five pounds.

## North of Moxie Pond - Fish & Black Ponds

Fish Pond,[148] six miles from the Forks, and two miles from the lower dam on Moxie Stream, also affords good fishing.

Black (Brook) Pond,[149] a mile from the Kennebec, has some togue in it, but few brook trout.

## Indian Pond – Headed to Moosehead

A convenient way of reaching Indian Pond from the Forks, by canoe, is through Black Pond, then two miles, partly by carrying, to Knight's Pond, thence one mile over a carry to Little Indian Pond, and through its boggy outlet, without serious difficulty, almost down to the mouth of Indian Stream, where some more carrying will have to be done.[150]

## West of Indian Pond – Wilson's Hill, Long, Horseshoe, Ellis, & Ten-thousand Acre Ponds

A group of ponds which furnish good fishing, and which lie pretty near together, are Wilson's Hill, (or Tomhegan Pond), Long Pond, above it, Horseshoe and Ellis Ponds, and the Ten-thousand-Acre Ponds. The first named is reached by going up

---

[147] **2020:** Now spelled, Caratunk.

[148] **2020:** Tiny pond off the Kennebec, south of yet another Mud Pond. This area has many small ponds. Public access these days is unknown.

[149] **2020:** Less than a mile below Black Brook Pond on the Kennebec is the Kennebec River Gorge.

[150] **2020:** From Indian Pond Moosehead Lake can be reached by way of the West Outlet. Caution is needed on all waters controlled by the dams as releases may occur at any time.

the Canada Road three miles from the Forks, then turning to the right up the lower Cold Stream Road through the Coburn field, and thence walking seven miles. A good way is to camp on the old farm on the border of Wilson's Hill Pond, and to make excursions thence, on different days, to the other ponds named, which are within a radius of two miles or less.

From the Forks to Indian Pond is fifteen miles, thence ten miles to Moosehead Lake. The better road is on the left bank of the Kennebec.

## *Parlin Pond*

Fifteen miles north of the Forks, on the Canada Road, is a group of buildings, a custom-house, post office, and hotel, which are a mile from the head of Parlin Pond, and which for many years have been a stopping place for sportsmen. The fishing in the pond is good, and canoes and guides can be had at reasonable rates.

Five miles beyond, on the Jackman-Parlin line, is a hotel kept by A. F. Adams, the proprietor of the stage line which runs from the Forks to Hilton's. This house is said to be very well kept, and its proprietor is attentive and obliging. It is only three miles from the foot of Parlin Pond, to which a good road runs from it. This road crosses at the dam just below the pond, and continues down the stream, and up Lang Stream to Lang Pond, where trout are abundant. Good fishing is also to be had at Parlin Pond dam. A good path runs four miles directly from Adams's to Long Pond.

## Moose River Village

Moose River Village[151] is fifteen miles from the head of Parlin Pond, on the same Canada Road. Two small hotels flourish here, together with all the appurtenances of a well-regulated New England village. Provisions and outfit can be obtained here for a trip into the woods, but, as has been remarked elsewhere, one must not be disappointed if one does not find on the verge of the forest everything that is needed.

## Holeb Pond, Heald Pond, and Bald Mt.

The International Railroad of Maine has made easily accessible a large number of ponds along the course of Moose River. Holeb Pond and the upper parts of Moose River, as far as the latter is navigable, are within immediate reach from Holeb Station. An island in Holeb Pond was, in 1890, the site of a permanent camp for sportsmen. From Jackman and Moose River Village, which offer fair hotel accommodations, one can go by team to Heald Pond under the shadow of Bald Mt., to the camps of Alick Dutelly. From this point a number of ponds are accessible, and canoes can be taken across to the head of Alder Brook, and thence into the West Branch of the Penobscot.

The height of Bald Mt. above the river at Moose River Bridge (Jackman), as determined by the writer with an aneroid barometer, is 2,302 feet. If we agree with Wells,[152] that Wood Pond and Long Pond are seventy-one feet above Moosehead Lake (too little, if anything), and consider the latter as 995 feet

---

[151] **2020:** North of Jackman, Maine.
[152] Water-power of Maine, p. 88.

above sea-level, that makes Bald Mt. 3,368 feet high, thus outranking all the Moosehead peaks except White Cap.[153]

## Moose River * Wood Pond * Attean Pond

Leaving Moose River Village, and paddling up Moose River, one soon comes into Wood Pond, along whose eastern shore one goes four miles to the head of the pond. One McKinney has a farm and house here, and he can provide parties with boats, and, if need be, with a guide, too.[154]

On the west of Wood Pond are Little Wood[155] and Big Little Wood Ponds. The latter is half a mile from the former, and a mile wide and nearly three miles long. A good road leads from Moose River Village to the latter, and, touching it midway of its length, runs up to its head. Both ponds contain trout in abundance.

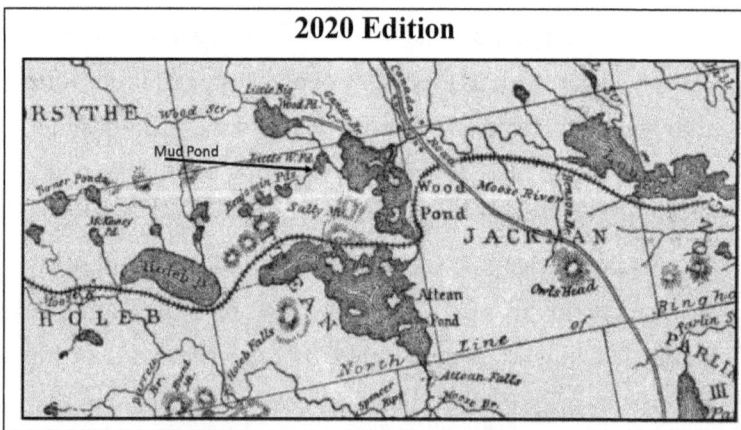

**2020 Edition**

---

[153] **2020:** Current estimate of Boundary Bald Mountain is 3,638 ft. (Not to be confused with Bald Mountain near Rangeley Lake.) White Cap is 3,655 ft.

[154] **2020:** Much of this tour is on the current Moose River Canoe Trail.

[155] **2020:** Little Wood is labeled, "Mud Pond," on Gazetteer map 39. *Big Little Wood Pond* is labeled, *Little Big Wood Pond* on both Hubbard's map and the Gazetteer.

A half or three quarters of a mile of river separate Wood Pond from Attean Pond, which is rather larger than the former, and much prettier.[156] It contains many islands, and has good shores covered with a generous amount of hardwood. From its western extremity a very good road, a mile long, runs across to Holeb Pond, and, by carrying across this one mile, one saves about twenty-seven miles of travel around the "bow."[157]

Three miles south from the outlet of Attean Pond Moose River again resumes its course, and is "dead" for half a mile up to Attean Rips, just below which is a pretty little island. The carry around the "rips" is on the left, and not more than twenty rods long. There are two principal "pitches," either of which can at times be run on the setting-pole, the upper one being perhaps the more difficult.

The river is substantially smooth for eleven miles, between Attean Rips and Holeb Falls, except at Spencer Rips, three miles below the latter, and in ordinary seasons its navigation will give the canoe-man little trouble. Spencer Rips can be run on the setting-pole.

At Holeb Falls (twenty-five feet) the river forms an island. The old carry was on the left bank of the north channel; that now in use, twelve rods long, is on the left bank of the south channel, near the head of the island.

Lookout Mt., four hundred and twenty-five feet above the river, southeast of the falls, affords a fine view of the

---

[156] **2020:** Between these ponds is Burnt Jacket Mountain. Not to be confused with the mountain of the same name between Sandy Bay and Beaver Cove on Moosehead Lake.

[157] **2020:** Of the Moose River.

surrounding country. A good road from Parlin Pond touches Holeb Falls and continues up the stream to the north branch.[158]

Above Holeb Falls, as far as Campbell Rips (smooth ledge), the water is dead; above the latter point it shows some current. From the falls to Holeb Stream the distance is between ten and twelve miles, the upper part of the river being very crooked, and, in places, shallow. In the upper parts of the river the banks are high and clayey. Barrett Brook is rather less than half way from the falls to Holeb Stream. The latter can generally be navigated by canoes, and is about a mile long.

Above Holeb Stream, the first brook on the right is Big Gulf Stream, and the second, — a fraction of a mile beyond, and on the same side, — Little Gulf Stream. Both are so named because of the gorges through which they flow. The mouth of Little Gulf Stream is near the town line,[159] three quarters of a mile west of which are Lowell Falls. A short carry lies on the right bank. A short distance above the falls, on the left, is a small pond, half a mile from the river, which used to be a famous moose-ground.

So tortuous is the stream between Holeb Falls and the town line near Lowell Falls, that the distance between the two, by canoe, is about eighteen miles, while in a straight line it is less than half that number.

*

---

[158] **2020:** This specific road is no longer.
[159] **2020:** Somerset and Franklin County Town Line.

## THE END OF THE TOURS

*

---

**2020 Edition**

Here is where Hubbard ended his tours. Today, the Moose River Canoe Trip along this route includes primitive camp sites. Continuing back to Jackman, a tour by water may take the paddler down the Moose River and ultimately to Moosehead. Or by vehicle, "carrying" your canoe on a rack, via Routes 6 & 15 towards Rockwood and Greenville.

If you have done a few of these tours, you deserve a stop for a nice meal in a local inn or tavern. The inns and establishments Hubbard recommended are no longer servicing the traveler, but many restaurants suitable for all tastes are available in the area.

And so, my paddling friends we have traveled throughout the north woods and into Canada. The tours covered parts of Aroostook, Piscataquis, Penobscot, Somerset, and Franklin counties. The area in square miles would encompass more than the states of Massachusetts, Rhode Island, and Connecticut combined.

I've often wondered, once Hubbard left the east coast and his summering in the Moosehead region for Michigan's Keweenaw Peninsula, if he returned and how many times. He does not tell us, but I am thankful he meticulously documented his exploring and journeys through Maine's North Woods.

## APPENDICES

### *Legend of Kineo and Squaw Mountain*

---

#### 2020 Edition

In the section of this book titled, *Moosehead Lake and Immediate Vicinity*, under the *Legend of Kineo*, Hubbard notes he omitted the legend from his fifth edition text. The legend of Kineo is re-added to this 2020 Annotated Edition as it is an excellent story of historical perspective.

Before we can cover the historical legends of Squaw Mountain and Mt. Kineo, we must first understand why Squaw Mountain was renamed to Big Moose Mountain. In the early 2000s, when the Maine legislature passed a bill (LD 2418) to remove the word, squaw, from place names in Maine. The mountains Big Squaw and Little Squaw, referenced in this book, were subsequently renamed to Big Moose Mountain and Little Moose Mountain.

The word squaw caused Native American people pain because the meaning of the word had been corrupted, and a generation only knew it as a slur or derogatory term. Since there are no Native American words with the spelling as "s-q-u-a-w," it probably makes sense for it not to be used in that spelling if it is offensive to the people of that race.

However, since the word is used in this book from the 1800s, in its original unoffensive meaning, we have included here some references for historical purposes with regard to sharing the legends for Squaw Mountain and Mt. Kineo.

To begin, the following explanation of the word 'squaw' is from Ives Goddard, Senior Linguist, Emeritus (Ph.D) at the National Museum of Natural History. The quoted text is from his letter titled, "Since the Word Squaw Continues to Be of Interest," that was published in the April 1997 issue of News from Indian Country. While Dr. Goddard, states, "I have always tried to emphasize that squaw is now generally considered disparaging, as current dictionaries rightly indicate," he provides the linguistic derivation and meaning of the word "squaw," along with how it became corrupted officially through incorrect claims of the word's origin.

Goddard notes, "The use of the word squaw is now generally considered disparaging and everyone would regard its use to refer to a Native American woman as demeaning, though it should be noted that terms like squaw bread and squaw dance are still pretty widely used in Indian Country."

Goddard continues, "In its historical origin, however, the word squaw is perfectly innocent, as current dictionaries also correctly indicate: squaw comes from a language of the Algonquian family in which it meant woman." *(It should be noted that the editor has now found some dictionaries incorrectly referencing the word as only being a slur, without any reference at all to the original common meaning and linguistic correctness. Dictionary entries have changed over time, not because the origination or meaning of the word had changed, but because perception has overruled.)*

In his article, Goddard goes into the languages of the Algonquian, as well as the techniques of comparative linguistics, which is his specialty. He explains the various words (used) for "woman" in these native languages and notes the exception was for the Massachusett language in their use of squa, which had become specialized to mean "female, younger woman."

Goddard notes, "Massachusett squa appears in the Massachusett Bible (printed in Cambridge, Massachusetts, in 1663) in Mark 10:6, translating "female," and in the plural form squaog in 1 Timothy 5:2 and 5:14, translating (as) "younger women." It is found in the writings of Massachusett Indians, including a will written in the Massachusett language by a native preacher from Martha's Vineyard who uses it to refer to his unmarried daughters. Massachusett squa was an ancient and thoroughly decent word." He adds additional references and notes before summarizing, "These published examples show that the English settlers in eastern Massachusetts had learned the word squa(w) as "woman" from their Massachusett-speaking neighbors by [1621] and were using it as an English word by 1634."

Goddard then explains the corruption of the word and misunderstanding of Native American languages, which isn't all that hard to imagine considering these languages are no longer spoken. Goddard writes, "A competing claim (to the linguistics he provided) has been made in recent years, despite the clear evidence that squaw comes from an Algonquian word for "woman," and in fact without discussing this evidence." He continues, "This is the claim (often somewhat garbled) that squaw actually comes from the Mohawk word ojiskwa', which we can politely translate `vagina'. Mohawk was spoken some 200 miles from Plymouth in the Mohawk Valley by the principal enemies of the Massachusett Indians. It is, of course, a language of the

Iroquoian family, which is completely distinct from the Algonquian family." He provides the reference that this interpretation is, "probably a French corruption of the Iroquois word otsiskwa meaning `female sexual parts.'"

Goddard writes, "This (incorrect) claim has more recently become widely known because of the following statement made on the Oprah Winfrey television show in 1992 by Suzan Harjo, (who said) "The word squaw, for example, is an Algonquian [sic] Indian word meaning 'vagina,' and that'll give you an idea what the French and British fur-trappers were calling all Indian women, and I hope no one ever uses that term again." (From the Oprah Winfrey program "Racism in 1992: Native Americans," as transcribed from a videotape by Jim Rementer at the request of a Delaware tribal member who knew from his knowledge of his own language that it was incorrect.)"

In Goddard's conclusion he states, "It is as certain as any historical fact can be that the word squaw that the English settlers in Massachusetts used for "Indian woman" in the early 1600s was adopted by them from the word squa that their Massachusett-speaking neighbors used in their own language to mean "female, younger woman," and not from Mohawk ojiskwa' "vagina," which has the wrong shape, the wrong meaning, and was used by people with whom they then had no contact. The resemblance that might be perceived between squaw and the last syllable of the Mohawk word is coincidental. Such partial resemblances between words of different meanings in different languages are common and of no significance. I suppose someone might claim that the meanings of these words are similar, but to do that would be to adopt the viewpoint that those "fur-trappers" are being accused of."

This linguistic definition of two different Indian languages is important because the use of the word squaw in this book is not disrespectful, in fact, the following stories show the reverence and use of a word from the 1600s to the early 1900s that had no demeaning connotation whatsoever. The only corruption may have been the English adding the ending 'w,' to 'squa' in oral and in written language.

Now that we've covered the word squaw, which means woman, and nothing different unless you choose otherwise and thus take the viewpoint noted above by Goddard, let's cover the history of the word as used in legends of the Moosehead Lake Region.

There is a legend of Mt. Kineo, which has been told over the years, but is becoming difficult to find. A version of this legend appeared in Hubbard's, "Summer Vacations at Moosehead Lake, fourth edition," (the earlier book that he later titled as this book, "Hubbard's Guide to Moosehead Lake and Northern Maine.") Hubbard removed the legend from the fifth edition of his book because he could not verify it directly from the Indians he was in contact with at the time.

During the 1800s, the story had been repeated enough that it became part of the folklore of the region. The legend tells a story of a chief, a wife and their son. The version here is as written in, "Farrar's Illustrated Guide Book to Moosehead Lake and Vicinity the Wilds of Northern Maine," by Charles A. J. Farrar (1884). I've chosen this one as it is the longest and most complete of the writings I can find on the legend. Farrar noted the legend had appeared in print sometime before he published his book, but he was unable to learn who authored it.

* * * * *

## The Legend of Mount Kineo

As one sails over the calm bosom of Moosehead Lake, and casts a glance towards Mount Kineo, it awakens a desire to gather what there is of legendary lore connected with this wonderful spot; and when one has climbed to the summit of this steep bluff, and gazes over the enchanting scenery before him, diversified by mountain, lake, and stream, the desire is heightened many fold, — a desire to know something of the beings who in days gone by had chased the moose and deer over these mountains and through these forests; who had paddled over these waters, and caught from them their supply of fish. Feeling thus, we gathered, from one and another, the main facts connected with the old Indian tale known as the legend of Kineo.

Some two centuries since, when all the north of Maine was one great forest, and before the "pale-face" had hardly thought of exploring it, there belonged to the tribe of Indians inhabiting this region an old chief named Mackae. Reserved, morose, and repulsive, he abstained from mingling more than was necessary with other members of the tribe, and seldom engaged in any of their many expeditions except when matters of a decidedly hostile nature required it. He had taken to wife a squaw of marked beauty, and one whose nature was the very opposite of his own. While Maquaso, the wife, cheerfully cooked his fish and game, and performed those many menial duties which devolved upon the wife of a chief, he sat upon a pile of skins in his wigwam's corner without even a smile brightening his countenance.

Kinneho, their only son, was the centre of attraction for Maquaso. From the time of his birth she had watched over him with that instinctive affection common to the women of her race. With her own hands she had taught him the use of the bow and arrow, and had prepared him for the chase and the war-path. As the years passed, she saw her labors rewarded in this direction; for among all the braves of the tribe there was none swifter to lead in the chase, none more daring in battle, or more certain of achieving success over the savage foe. Among the warriors he was the leader, and their courage was wont to fail them in battle if Kinneho were not there. His foes feared him, and they dared not make expeditions in small companies, lest Kinneho should surprise and slay them in a hand-to-hand contest.

But a feeling of terrible sadness took possession of the proud spirit of Maquaso, when, in watching her idol, she found that he had inherited much of the sullen nature of his father.

While at home from the chase and the war-path he spent his time in solitary wanderings about the little Indian village, caring little for the scenes around him, and doing nothing in return for those favors which his mother was constantly bestowing upon him. This produced a feeling of alienation between mother and son.

The wigwam became a prison to Maquaso, life a burden. She was too proud to own her grief, but it was nevertheless apparent to all observers. One morning they found, by the side of a smouldering fire, a few articles of clothing which they knew to have been the possessions of Maquaso, but she herself was nowhere to be found.

Strong suspicion rested upon Kinneho. His weeping and lamentations were in vain, and the earnestness with which he prosecuted the search was not sufficient to prove to the tribe that Kinneho had not been the murderer of his mother.

About this time hostilities broke out between the Indians along the Piscataquis and those dwelling on the Androscoggin. A council of the leading men of the tribe was called. Kinneho met with them. Hitherto he had been the foremost to advise, and his advice had been most frequently acted upon. Now he was held in such disgrace that he was not permitted to speak, nor was he permitted to become one of the war-party which was then organized. He left the council, made a few hasty preparations, took his arrows and tomahawk, and silently stalked forth into the forest.

Hardly two moons had passed before the two tribes met in active warfare. The tribe of which Kinneho was a member sorely missed his able council, his wonderful daring, his bloody action. In the enemy's country it had suffered many surprises, and many times had been sadly repulsed. In a bloody encounter, which was likely to determine the result of the war, Kinneho's friends were greatly surprised to see him come suddenly upon the field of battle. With an unearthly yell he dashed upon the foe; one after another they fell before him, and shortly the enemy were driven from the field. Cheer after cheer for Kinneho rent the air. Gladly would they have borne him from the field in triumph, but he, without speaking a word to his old companions, silently left the field, and betook himself to the forest.

Nothing further was heard of Kinneho until it became noised abroad among the Piscataquis Indians that he had erected his wigwam on the summit of the mountain in Moosehead Lake, which still bears his name. Of savage disposition, and of mighty power in a hand-to-hand contest, the Indians gave him a wide berth. As they looked towards the ragged crag by night and saw the blaze of his campfire, or saw the smoke wreathing upwards by day, a sort of mystic awe took possession of their minds, and they shrank from nearing his solitary abode. Superstitious traditions still lingered in the minds of the tribe in regard to the mountain, and so Kinneho was left to himself as if he had been superhuman.

To the south of Kineo is Squaw Mountain. While Kinneho had looked towards it by night, his eagle eye had discovered upon its side a bright light. Evening after evening it appeared, and burned until far into the night. Finally, he decided to make an excursion in that direction, and ascertain if possible whose fire it might be.

Over the lake and through the forest he journeyed, then up the side of the mountain, following in the direction of the light. At last he came upon a rude lodge, built of bark and skins.

Kinneho's heart beat wildly within him, as, bending over the fire, he saw the wasted form of his mother, Maquaso. Though he had known her in the days of her beauty, he did not fail to recognize, in the bent form and distorted features, his long-lost mother. He rushed forward and embraced her in his arms. She, overcome by his sudden appearance, would have sunk to the ground only for the strong arms which supported her. He hastily carried her to the lodge, bathed her face with water from a stream nearby, and forced some nourishment between her lips; but all to no purpose. Her eyes had looked once more upon her son, only to close in death.

On the side of Squaw Mountain he fashioned a rude grave heaped together a pile of stones to mark her resting-place. Each new moon he came to visit the lonely mound, and sprinkle it with tears.

In summertime a delicate white flower blooms in this forest, known as the Indian Pipe. The Indians affirm that this flower sprang from the tears of Kinneho. Wherever his tears fell, this flower is said to have appeared. During many moons the campfire of Kinneho could be seen on the dark bluff. The Indians still superstitiously shunned the spot. Sometimes they crept through the forest to the shore, which is now called Pebble Beach; but when they looked upwards against the perpendicular bank of solid rock they imagined that the form of the Great Spirit was hovering over them. And they thought they heard his voice pouring down imprecations upon their heads. Sometimes, they say, Kinneho made long journeys through the forest to Mount Katahdin, whose snowy sides were plainly visible from his own mountain. During these times they missed his campfire by night, and his smoke by day; and then they would summon almost the requisite courage to visit the spot, when of a sudden it would again appear.

But at last the fire died out, never to be rekindled by the hand of Kinneho. In vain did they watch for its reappearance. Stealthily they crept around to the northern side of the mountain, and up its sides, but they found not Kinneho. By the side of the spring which still bubbles up through the rocks they found a pair of moccasons; beside this a tomahawk and a few trinkets. Further on they found the traces of his fire, and the rocks charred and blackened, which even yet have not returned to their original color.

The Indians ever after believed that the mountain had opened and swallowed the form of Kinneho, and that he was doomed to remain in its bowels to the end of time. And so they called the mountain Kinneho, which in our day has been shortened to Kineo.

Such is the legend of Kineo. If any of our readers should visit the place (and we advise them to do so, if they wish to behold some of Maine's grandest scenery) they will find the tradition to be mainly as we have printed it.

\* \* \* \* \*

*(The above is directly as written in Farrar's book which is now in the public domain.)*

\* \* \* \* \*

The legend also appeared in verse in the November 11, 1881 issue of the Harvard (University) Crimson. In this retelling Kinneho's mother is immortalized when her son looks upon the mountain:

\*

*But once, when overhead a comet's tail,*
*Omen of strange import, illumed the night,*
*His yearning eyes descried upon the side*
*Of what has since been called "Maquaso's Mount"*
*A solitary fire. Then his heart*
*Gave one great bound, and quivered with intense*
*And dread excitement, while his flying feet,*
*Swifter than hers who spurned the lingering seas,*
*Bore him across the land that lay between.*
*And as her dear-remembered warrior son,*
*Once more her own, approached the wigwam low,*
*Maquaso gave one tender dying cry,*
*And fell, a happy mother, on his neck.*

\*

And this is, supposedly, how Mt. Kineo and Squaw Mountains came to be named. Whether true or not, folklore or fact, legend or fable, it is a story that inhabitants of the Moosehead region repeated, told, and wrote down to share with others, so much so it was published in numerous places over the years.

A second legend of Squaw Mountain speaks of a Penobscot Indian chief who was at Kineo with his tribe collecting the rhyolite rock to craft tools and weapons. When they noticed a Mohawk tribe approaching, he sent all the squaws and children to take refuge on a mountain down the lake. He told his squaw that he would send a signal when it was safe for them to return. She led her people down the lake and they climbed a high mountain. Once the signal from the fires was seen, she returned to him. The mountain they used for safety, was Squaw Mountain. As to which legend came first, I cannot tell.

Now, of course, these and many other area legends appear in texts from the 1700s and 1800s, relayed to various English writers. We have no way to verify completely, the way Goddard can conclusively tell us the true linguistic origin of the word *squaw*, but they sure make great stories.

Since Squaw Mountain has been named Big Moose Mountain for two decades, the story behind the mountain is shared with you here. Once the mountains, the places, and the dictionaries are changed due to a change in meaning of a word, these stories will have no reason to exist because the word may no longer be permitted to be uttered.

In addition, through the renaming of mountains most all of the original names the Native Americans had given to the local mountains, names that were full of history and legends and made for rich regional stories, have been changed.

When you hike Big Moose, or sit around a campfire, share the history of Squaw Mountain, share the legend of Kinneho and Maquaso. Explain how the original name for the mountain is derived from the Algonquin Native American word 'squa,' a respectful term for woman, not a slur; and that 'squaw' was the best pronunciation a white person could muster at the time for the Massachusett-language word.

The importance of the wife, or squaw, to the Native American family unit is illustrated in the book "Mothers of Maine," by Helen Coffin Beedy (1895). In her book she praised the women that made such a contribution to society and the family. She wrote, "The Indian brave had his duties, hunting, fishing and fighting. He would have thought his squaw out of place with a gun or fishing-rod. The women constructed the wigwams, cultivated the corn, prepared the food and reared the children. They were skilled in the manufacture of baskets and snowshoes; they braided mats and embroidered in beads; they made small cradles; the Indian women were the business agents, having the direction of the trade. The English noticed that whenever the Indians came with their furs, they were accompanied by a squaw, at whose nod the traffic was stayed or progressed. The women always had the care of the money."

A version of the legend of Kinneho and Maquaso is also given in Beedy's book. She includes a stanza from the poem titled, "Kineo," written by Maine poet, Frances Laughton Mace.

### Kineo
But wrathful, jealous, quick to strife,
He lived a passion-darkened life;
Even Maquaso, his mother, fled
His baneful lodge in mortal dread.

Lastly, keep your eye out when you are hiking in the region for Kinneho's flower (Monotropa uniflora), also known as Indian Pipe, and ghost plant. The plant is white since it does not contain chlorophyll to convert sunlight to energy, but rather is parasitic and tends to grow in darker areas of the forest.

## Further Reading:

1. Beedy, Helen Coffin., Mothers of Maine. The Thurston Print. Portland, Maine. 1895.
2. Bruchac, Marge. "Reclaiming the word "Squaw" in the Name of Ancestors." 1999. Cited from Nativeweb.org.
3. Goddard, Ives, Ph.D., Senior Linguist, Emeritus National Museum of Natural History, "Since the word squaw continues to be of interest," April 1997, News from Indian Country.
4. Farrar, Charles A. J., "Farrars Illustrated Guide Book to Moosehead Lake and Vicinity." Lee and Shepard, Boston. 1884.
5. Harvard Crimson. (no writer attributed) "Kinoe." 1881. (The Harvard Crimson, the nation's oldest continuously published daily college newspaper, was founded in 1873.)
6. Hubbard, Lucius L., "Summer Vacations at Moosehead Lake and Vicinity." Fourth Edition, 1889.
7. Maine Indian Tribal-State Commission, "Proposal to Drop "Squaw" from Place Names in Maine: Summary of Issues and Views. 2000." (2000). Indian Tribal-State Commission Documents. Paper 15. Cited from digitalmaine.com April 2020.
8. Schilling, Vincent. "The Word Squaw: Offensive of Not?" Indian Country Today. March 2017.

## *Tours for Campers*

**2020 Edition**

Within the book, Hubbard has provided what he titles, "Resume," for some of the trips. In this appendix he provided an additional supplement on duration of the itineraries.

When Hubbard wrote the book, camping for the most part was unregulated in most of the north woods. The reader is expected to review more up to date guidebooks and follow public and private land restrictions.

The following tables will show approximately the time needed to make several of the more usual tours, around and near Moosehead Lake. The night passed on the cars from Boston to Bangor is not reckoned in the tables, so that the "third night" means the night of the third day from Boston.

One must be on the move pretty much all the time, to carry out the programme laid down, and it may be well to add two or three days, in fourteen, for wet weather and other drawbacks. The enjoyment and comfort of campers will be greatly enhanced if they take half as much time again for each tour as is here thought necessary.

### No. I. —One Week
### MOOSEHEAD LAKE

Boston to Mount Kineo . . . . . . . . . . . . . . . . . . . . . 1 day

Head of lake and return . . . . . . . . . . . . . . . . . . . . . 1 day

Socatean River . . . . . . . . . . . . . . . . . . . . . . . . . . . . 1 day

East Outlet . . . . . . . . . . . . . . . . . . . . . . . . . . . . . . 1 day

Brassua Lake . . . . . . . . . . . . . . . . . . . . . . . . . . . 2 days

Mount Kineo to Boston . . . . . . . . . . . . . . . . . . . . . 1 day

## No. II. —Two Weeks
## MOOSEHEAD LAKE AND VICINITY

| | |
|---|---|
| Boston to Mount Kineo ..................... | 1 day |
| Mount Kineo House ....................... | 1 day |
| Brassua Lake ............................ | 2 days |
| Tomhegan and Socatean Streams ............. | 2 days |
| Mount Kineo Hous e ...................... | 1 day |
| Spencer Pond ............................ | 2 days |
| East Outlet ............................. | 2 days |
| Greenville ............................. | 1 day |
| Wilson Pond ........................... | 1 day |
| Greenville to Boston ...................... | 1 day |

## No. III. —Two Weeks
## UP THE WEST BRANCH OF THE PENOBSCOT

| | |
|---|---|
| Boston to Mount Kineo ..................... | 1 day |
| Nelhudus Stream, or Seeboomook Falls ........ | 2 days |
| To Forks of West Branch ................... | 1 day |
| To Hale Brook .......................... | 1 day |
| Hale and Alder Brooks ..................... | 3 days |
| To Penobscot Brook ...................... | 1 day |
| Back to Canada Falls ...................... | 1 day |
| To Gulliver Falls ......................... | 1 day |
| To Northwest Carry ....................... | 1 day |
| To Kineo .............................. | 1 day |
| To Boston .............................. | 1 day |

## No. IV. —Two Weeks
## DOWN THE WEST BRANCH OF THE PENOBSCOT

| | |
|---|---|
| Boston to Moosehead Lake ................ | 1st day |
| Greenville or Mt. Kineo to Moosehorn Stream . | 2d day |
| Weymouth Point, — Chesuncook Lake ....... | 3d night |

| | |
|---|---|
| Ripogenus Carry | 4th night |
| Sourdnahunk Deadwater. | 6th night |
| Sandy Stream, — Foot of Mt. Ktaadn | 8th night |
| Sandy Stream | 9th night |
| Ambajejus Lake | 10th night |
| Fowler's, or Medway | 11th night |
| Mattawamkeag | 12th night |
| Boston | 14th night |

## No. V. —Two Weeks.
### DOWN THE ST. JOHN RIVER

| | |
|---|---|
| Boston to Moosehead Lake | 1st day |
| Moosehead Lake to Moosehorn Stream | 2d day |
| Umbazookskus Lake | 3d night |
| Chamberlain Lock | 4th night |
| Thoroughfare Brook, or Chase's Carry | 6th night |
| Umsaskis Lake, or Long Lake | 8th night |
| Allagash Falls | 9th night |
| Edmundston | 11th night |
| Grand Falls | 12th night |
| Boston | 14th night |

## No. VI. —Fifteen Days
### CAUCOMGOMOC LAKE

| | |
|---|---|
| Boston to Moosehead Lake | 1st day |
| Moosehead Lake to Moosehorn Stream | 2d day |
| Lower Falls, —Caucomgomoc Stream | 3d night |
| Caucomgomoc Lake | 4th night |
| Avery Brook | 5th night |
| Round Pond | 6th night |
| Poland Pond | 1 day |
| Daggett Pond and Shallow Lake | 1 day |

Allagash Lake and return to Round Pond . . . . . . .    3 days

Caucomgomoc Stream  . . . . . . . . . . . . . . . . . . . .    12th night

Moosehorn Stream  . . . . . . . . . . . . . . . . . . . . . .    13th night

Mount Kineo House  . . . . . . . . . . . . . . . . . . . . .    14th night

Boston . . . . . . . . . . . . . . . . . . . . . . . . . . . . . . .    16th night


## No. VII. — TWO AND A HALF TO THREE WEEKS
## FORKS AND MOOSE RIVER

Boston to the Forks . . . . . . . . . . . . . . . . . . . . . . .    1 day

The Forks . . . . . . . . . . . . . . . . . . . . . . . . . . . . .    2 days

Jackman House  . . . . . . . . . . . . . . . . . . . . . . . . .    2 days

Moose River Village . . . . . . . . . . . . . . . . . . . . . .    7th night

Holeb Falls . . . . . . . . . . . . . . . . . . . . . . . . . . . . .    9th night

Lowell Falls . . . . . . . . . . . . . . . . . . . . . . . . . . . .    11th night

Attean Pond, via Holeb Pond . . . . . . . . . . . . . . .    13th night

Moose River Village . . . . . . . . . . . . . . . . . . . . . .    14th night

The Forks . . . . . . . . . . . . . . . . . . . . . . . . . . . . .    15th night

Boston . . . . . . . . . . . . . . . . . . . . . . . . . . . . . . . .    17th day

* * *

Moosehead Lake . . . . . . . . . . . . . . . . . . . . . . . . .    17th night

Boston . . . . . . . . . . . . . . . . . . . . . . . . . . . . . . . .    22d day


The following table gives the approximate expense of making each of the foregoing excursions from, or in the vicinity of Moosehead Lake, with one guide, and one or two tourists to a canoe. Under "R. R. Fares," there is included, in Tours 4, 5, and 7, besides meals and sleeping car berths, the cost of transporting guide and canoe from the end of the journey back to his home.

The car fare from Boston to Mount Kineo is $9.25; to Mattawamkeag, $9.10, — limited $7.60; and to Edmundston, $14.45, — limited $12.20.

| No. of Tour. | 1 | 2 | 3 | 4 | 5 | 6 | 7 |
|---|---|---|---|---|---|---|---|
| Tours. | Moosehead Lake . . . | Moosehead Lake & Vicinity | Up W. Branch Penobscot . | Down W. Branch Penobscot | Down St. John River . . | Caucomgomoc Lake . . | Moose River . . . . . |
| Duration of Tour. | One week. | Two weeks. | Two weeks | Two weeks. | Two weeks. | 15 days. | 2½–3 weeks. |
| Tourists. | 1 / 2 | 1 / 2 | 1 / 2 | 1 / 2 | 1 / 2 | 1 / 2 | 1 / 2 |
| R.R. Fares, incl. Meals & Sleeping-Cars. | $21.00 / 42.00 | 21.00 / 42.00 | 21.00 / 42.00 | 29.40 / 50.80 | 46.20 / 71.90 | 34.00 / 42.00 | 34.00 / 59.00 |
| M. H. Lake Steamer, Passengers & Canoe. | | | $6.00 / 8.00 | 3.00 / 4.00 | 3.00 / 4.00 | 6.00 / 8.00 | |
| Hotels. | $5.00 / 10.00 | 12.00 / 24.00 | 5.00 / 10.00 | 5.00 / 10.00 | 5.00 / 10.00 | 4.00 / 8.00 | 15.00 / 30.00 |
| Guide. | $9.00 | 22.50 | 36.00 | 39.00 | 43.00 | 39.00 | 25.00 |
| Provisions. | $4.00 / 6.00 | 8.00 / 12.00 | 12.00 / 18.00 | 12.00 / 18.00 | 12.00 / 18.00 | 12.00 / 18.00 | 12.00 / 18.00 |
| Carries. | | | $4.00 | 3.50 | 4.50 | 3.00 | |
| Total Expense. One Person, Two Persons, One Guide. | $39.00 / $67.00 | 63.50 / 100.50 | 84.00 / 118.00 | 91.90 / 125.30 | 112.70 / 150.40 | 85.00 / 118.00 | 86.00 / 132.00 |

## *Summer Vacations at Moosehead Lake*

\*

## *A Note on the sections of historical perspective*

### 2020 Edition Notes:

Hubbard issued five editions of this book. The first edition was 1879. In the later editions he added sections on additional ponds, lakes, and carries. For improved flow the tour sections from the third edition in 1882 and the fourth edition issued in 1889 have been incorporated into the main body of the text. These were writings about Chesuncook, Jackman, the North Branch of the Penobscot, and Neesowadnehunk Lake. No changes were made to the information other than to incorporate within the respectable sections.

A fifth edition was issued in 1893.

A major change in this *2020 Annotated Edition* is the placement on the sections titled,

- How to Camp Out
- Game and Fish of Northern Maine
- Digest of the Game and Inland Fish Laws
- Camp-Fires

from the main body of the guidebook, to this appendix.

Much of the information in these original sections has limited relevance, but is interesting nonetheless. Sportsmen and interested readers in the game and fish regulations are expected to consult the most current legal requirements for hunting and fishing in the State of Maine.

The sections are retained for the historical perspective and Hubbard's view of the times, and because it was part of his original text. The smaller font size used here indicates the original material.

The new updated information in these sections has mainly been compiled for this edition by editor Frederick Wilcox. Fred, in his career as a forester, has spent many years in the woods for both work and play. "The Forester," as I have come to call him, has an in-depth knowledge of the outdoors and he had a great respect for the writings of Lucius Lee Hubbard.

## How to Camp Out

**2020 Edition:**

The section, "How to Camp Out," was originally the first part of this guide with the title, "Part First." Hubbard likely included it at the start to give the explorer tips for preparing for their trip.

### Time of Year

All seasons have their respective advantages for the hunter or trapper, whether sportsman or not, according to the object he has in view. Each has its own disadvantages as well, but for general purposes of camping out, September and October offer the most attractions and have the fewest drawbacks. Blackflies and mosquitoes have then ceased their torments, the weather is apt to be settled and pleasant, the nights cool, and game is in its prime, and likely to be found everywhere.

The best fishing is undoubtedly to be had — at least in places of most frequent resort — in early spring, just after the ice breaks up in the lakes and streams. The larger game frequents the feeding-grounds on the banks of streams, and shores of ponds, and comes down to the water at night, in the hot weather of midsummer. But these are the halcyon days of the black-fly and mosquito, the one a constant attendant by day, and the other by night, both combining to make life miserable for the reckless sportsman. Besides, the days are sweltering and the nights oppressive.

Midwinter is not without its attraction, principally that of novelty for him who ventures into the woods too far north. He is soon disabused of the fascination which drew him thither, and learns that it is much more comfortable to put up at some hotel or cabin at the outskirts of civilization, and to make hunting excursions on snowshoes from these, and to fish through the ice under cover of a warm little fish house, than to camp under a shelter tent with the snow four feet deep around him, and the mercury at twenty-five below zero.[160]

## Number in a Party

The number of persons of which a party should consist will depend more or less on the characteristics of the individuals and the object in view. Travelling, especially in the woods, is apt to show up the least amiable side of one's disposition, and the larger the party, the more difficult will it be to have united counsels and action. If you are bent on having a jolly time, and are not particular about getting game and fish, nor where you go, you can well join a large party; but when you go mainly for the enjoyments of hunting and fishing such as can only be had in the wild woods, go with one friend, a tried

---

[160] **2020:** When hiking during the winter, the hiker is well advised to carry matches in a stay-dry container. When the ground is covered with snow, finding starter material can be challenging. Peeling birch-bark might be useful, if dry. Dryer lint is highly flammable for fire-starting material and is a light addition to your pack.

friend, on whose good sense and unselfishness you can rely.[161] The next best way, and you may prefer it, is to go alone, with a trusty and competent guide. Two men, each with a canoe and guide, is an advantageous combination, for the pairs can separate for a time, if advisable, and occupy different grounds near together. For a short trip two men and one guide can go in one canoe, but for a trip of two weeks or more a canoe will only hold two men and luggage, and will have an ample load at that.

## A Camper's Outfit
## Where and How to Get It

As Mr. Gould has happily suggested in his interesting book, "How to Camp Out," you should begin to make preparations for your trip two or three months before you intend to start. To make small purchases of useful articles to be taken with you, and to dwell in anticipation on what is before you, affords almost as much pleasure as the later enjoyment of the woods. There is great satisfaction in picturing to yourself what part this and that article will play in your adventures, or in what sort of a place, whether lake or brook, mountain or meadow, it will first be called into requisition. Then, too, if you put off all preparation until the last moment, you may forget some of the most important parts of your outfit, — a sine qua non, — and the thought of what "might have been" will be quite aggravating. Collect your outfit, piece by piece; appropriate a closet or a trunk to its exclusive use, and put the parts of your collection into it, day by day, keeping a list from which to check off each item as soon as obtained.

---

[161] **2020:** In *Woods and Lakes of Maine*, Hubbard travelled with his friend and artist, William Ladd Taylor. In that book he refers to Taylor as, "The Captain." Taylor was a successful illustrator who traveled the world. He and his wife, Mary Alice Fitts, had a summer home in Mooselookmenguntic, Maine.

Every time an article suggests itself to you as one that is likely to be indispensable, get it. Only be careful to make your load as light as possible. Remember that what one may consider a necessity at home may be regarded as a luxury in the woods, and that to carry one pound of extra weight fifty miles is equivalent to carrying fifty pounds one mile.

Get everything you need, in the way of personal luggage, at home. You seldom have time or inclination to stop over, by the way, and are not at all sure to find what you want at the last village on the verge of the forest. By "personal luggage" the writer means everything exclusive of food, and of the camp "kit," a term explained below.

It is very convenient, if you mean to use canned goods in the woods, to have them packed at home, in a box with rope handles on each end of it, and to take them with you as luggage.

## Camp "Kit" [162]

Parties who go into camp with guides do not usually have to provide what is termed the "kit." This includes, besides canoe and tent, axes, cooking utensils, and the like, —articles which nearly all guides own in quantities sufficient for parties of two or three.

For persons who may be about to go into camp without guides, the following list of articles will be found useful, if not indispensable:

| Party of Two. | Party of Four. |
| --- | --- |
| Axe, one 3 lbs | two |
| Baker, small | medium |
| Bread pan; 2 qts | 3 qts. |
| Can-opener | |
| Coffee-pot; 1 qt | 2 qts. |
| Forks, three | five |
| Firkins,or bags, for provisions | |
| Frying-pans, two, medium | |

---

[162] **2020:** Certainly, a kit as defined in 1893. The modern camper will want to update this list to accommodate your travel. See inset.

| | |
|---|---|
| Kettle, iron; 2 qts | two, large |
| Knives, three | 3 qts. |
| Molasses-can ; 1 gal. | five |
| Mop for dishes | |
| Pepper-shaker | |
| Potato bag | |
| Rope for canoe, — "Painter" | |
| Salt-shaker | |
| Sponge for canoe | |
| Spoon, one, large | |
| Teaspoons, three | two |
| Tent (A) 7ft. X 8ft | |
| Tin dippers, four | six |
| Tin pails; two, 2 qts. | |
| Tin plates, four | |
| White lead, for stopping leaks | three, 3 qts. |
| in canoe. | six. |

For parties of more than four persons, the capacity of the pails, pots, and pans will have to be proportionally larger, and the number of the more necessary table dishes increased, so that there will be two or three extra of each kind.

The cost of an outfit for two, such as is given above, will be about fifteen dollars, exclusive of tent, which may be bought for about five dollars.

Of course, persons *can* get along with fewer things than those above enumerated. The hunter often goes into the woods, in midwinter, and his outfit consists of a thin blanket, an axe, rifle, sheath knife, frying pan, and large tin dipper. With these, a bag of flour, a piece of pork, and what he shoots, he sustains himself, and makes no complaint. In like manner, a camper's "kit" can be crude, or elaborate, to suit his whims or his pocket; and he can direct his outlay in such a manner as to undergo a greater or less degree of "roughing it," — and to his entire satisfaction.

For the benefit of parties who go to Moosehead Lake, it may be well to say that all of the above articles can be bought at Greenville, except bags for provisions, which will have to be brought from home. These should be strong, made of stout drilling, and of various sizes, according to the bulk of the articles meant to be carried in them. Moreover, a large canvas bag, or rubber navy bag, should make part of the kit, to hold the smaller bags, and keep their contents dry.

It has been, and still is, quite common to carry provisions into the woods in wooden buckets or firkins[163]. They answer very well for trips where little or no carrying is to be done, but are very much of a nuisance when the contrary is the case. The principal advantage in having bags is, that, as fast as your food is consumed, the *bulk* of your luggage decreases, which with buckets is not appreciable. *One* bucket, for dishes, salt and pepper shakers, can-opener, condensed milk, and other odds and ends, will more than compensate, in convenience, the trouble of carrying it. Axes and hatchets should be provided with some sort of cover. They are then less troublesome and harmful, and can be thrown into a canoe or on shore without danger, either of cutting something else, or of being themselves nicked or dulled.

They can also be carried safely in one's belt, over carries and through the woods.

One or two kettle-holders will prove extremely useful, and easy to carry; a small whetstone and a crooked knife, too, may well be added to the kit.

An iron bean-pot will be found a great luxury, if it does not have to be "carried" much. Otherwise take *canned* beans, or cook your beans in a pail.

---

[163] **2020:** Small wooden vessel or cask.

A farina boiler, which consists of two pails, the smaller set in the other, serves well to cook oatmeal and mush, without risk of burning, either the food or the cook.

A shelter tent is warmer than an A tent, if a fire is kept blazing before it all night, but it is otherwise less convenient, especially in stormy weather.

## Personal Luggage

The writer first began to camp out in the year 1869. His preparations for his initial trip to the woods were crude. As beginners, we do not feel the need of many things, which want of experience, perhaps as much as lack of means, prevents us from getting; but after a series of summers spent in the woods, we learn how we can, in many ways, add materially to our enjoyment and comfort, at trifling expense, and with only a slight addition to the weight of our luggage.

Following is a list of articles the writer deems essential to a tolerable degree of comfort and ease, while out for a two weeks' canoeing excursion:

One pair stout shoes, well-greased.
One pair stout slippers.
One suit, old, but stout clothes.
One extra pair pantaloons (Scotch goods).
Two woollen shirts with collars.
One change of under clothes.
Slouch felt hat (gray).
Two or three pairs heavy woollen socks.
Two silk handkerchiefs
A cardigan jacket (gray), or "sweater."
A light rubber coat.
Two rubber blankets, —for each person.
One pair heavy woollen blankets, —for each person.
A blanket strap.
Two carrying straps, or knapsack bags.
Court and sticking plaster.
Small flask of brandy.
Bottle Jamaica ginger.
Box of grease for boots.
Bottle of mosquito mixture.

Piece of soap in small tin-box.
Sponge, tooth-brush, comb, and two towels.
Camp candlestick and candles.
Two or three haversacks, or a knapsack.
Mosquito net for the head.
A knit cap for sleeping.
Pieces of rope and twine.
Rags, and a small bottle of gun-oil.
Needles, thread, beeswax, and a small awl.
Compass, matches.
Broad belt, with strap for attaching tin cup.
Good sheath knife.
Cartridge-box (old army cap-box).
Magazine rifle, and from 50 to 100 cartridges.
Cheap fly rod, four leaders, and a dozen flies.
Six stout hooks.
Reel, and fifty yards oiled silk line.
Pack of cards — for rainy days.
Pocket-map of region to be visited.

## Comments on the Foregoing

Do not wear boots into the woods. They are cumbersome, and sure to get wet, and when in that condition are very hard to get off and on. A pair of loose-fitting brogans[164], such as can be bought for about two dollars, or an old pair of Waukenphast's shoes[165], if you have them, will be found most comfortable. Shoes should fit snugly, without pinching. If your feet are going to be out of order for want of proper covering, you would better go back home at once. A piece of leather may prove of service in your "kit." The writer has of late years found rubber boots, which come up half-way between knee and hip, almost indispensable where wading is necessary. However, a pair of stout shoes, well-greased, will answer the purpose, and when you return to camp with wet feet, the comfort of dry socks and slippers will be

---

[164] **2020:** As far back as the 16th century, Brogan shoes were used by the Scottish and Irish as work boots for wear in the boggy countryside.

[165] **2020:** Popular boots and shoes of the 1800s available in Britain and the U.S.A.

exceedingly grateful. If you take rubber boots, a change of pantaloons will not be necessary.

An excellent substitute for heavy shoes and slippers will be found in moccasons,[166] which when new are waterproof, and fit the foot easily. They are good either in a canoe, or when on the walk; an extra sole on the inside helps to protect the foot from roots and stones. In this connection, when you dry your shoes or moccasons, be careful not to expose them to too great heat. Greased leather, or the fatty hide of any animal, will, when exposed to the sun, or to a hot fire, burn very quickly, and before one would suspect it. It is a serious thing to lose one's foot-covering in the woods.

A heavy coat, or overcoat, will be found to be an incumbrance from its weight, and inconvenient when paddling. A good cardigan jacket and a thick vest will be all the extra clothing needed for cold days in September. The suit one wears should be such as one does not expect to use again. Scotch goods are preferable, as they dry easily after a wetting. Their color should be dark gray, if possible, to resemble that of the trunks of the trees. The wearer will thus be less likely to attract the notice of game that may come in his way.

A pair of suspenders is a comfort one should not be without. It does not matter if they do not look well over your woolen shirt.

A light rubber coat in the woods is invaluable, and two or three extra rubber blankets are apt to be quite serviceable, in more ways than one. Should a shower overtake you en route, one of them thrown over your canoe load protects it thoroughly. In camp two of them stretched overhead on either side of a horizontal pole make a good shelter both for your table and luggage, and they also make a warm covering to sleep under, on cold nights.

A good substitute for tent, and rubber blankets too, consists in pieces of cotton cloth, 7 ft. X 4 ft., soaked in boiled linseed-oil. If

---

[166] **2020:** Alternative early spelling of moccasin.

made with eyelet holes in the margin, they will answer the purpose of a tent, four of them being laced together in pairs, two side to side, and these pairs end to end. The two ends thus laced together are laid on the ridge-pole of the tent, and triangular pieces buttoned on at each end complete the dwelling.

One pair of stout uncut woolen blankets for each person is none too many. For cold nights in September more warmth and comfort can be had by having your blankets doubled over and sewed up on one end, and three quarters up the side, like a bag, so that when in it you have two thicknesses of blanket over and under you, and your feet cannot become uncovered during sleep. The top of the blanket can, if necessary, be drawn up over the head, while that part of the side left unsewed will furnish a good breathing-place.

Leather carrying-straps consist of a centre piece about a foot long and two inches wide, firmly sewed, at either extremity, to slightly tapering end pieces ten feet long and half an inch wide.

*

---

### 2020 Edition: Note on Camping Gear

Although Hubbard has described in detail the type and amount of camping gear, clothing, and food which is carried in his canoe and moved from campsite to campsite, he has made no mention of the combined weight of these various items.

Taking into consideration that the canoe camper of the time travelled with a canvas tent, heavy canvas packs, large ax, canned foods, cast iron pans, coffee pot, heavy cotton or woolen clothing, stout boots, and in Hubbard's case, a gallon of molasses and a bag of potatoes, the weight of all this gear had to well exceed two hundred pounds. When you combine the heavy weight of a birch bark or canvas covered canoe, the portaging of the canoe and gear must have a been arduous and time-consuming task. This excessive weight would have also increased the draft of the canoe which would be a disadvantage when moving across shallow water.

Today's canoe travelers have a very distinct advantage over Hubbard. The heavy canvas tents have been replaced with lightweight nylon tents with aluminum poles. Synthetic, fast drying material has replaced the heavy fabrics used in sleeping bags and clothing. The heavy leather footwear has been replaced by water resistant boating sandals. There are nylon watertight sea bags very suitable for packing your clothes.

Perhaps the biggest change over the years has been in what we choose to eat and how we prepare it. Found in today's outfitter stores or grocery outlets are a wide variety of dehydrated foods including entire meals suitable for each meal of the day. Meal preparation now takes little time and effort. For many canoeists and backpackers, preparation of their meals requires only the boiling of water. The dehydrated foods are packaged in cardboard boxes or light bags which have eliminated the need for metal cans that are too often left to litter the campsites.

The modern foods and their preparation and the use of small portable stoves fired by liquid fuels such as butane have greatly reduced our need for campfires. With the availability of lightweight tea kettles, and cooking ware, there is no longer a need for heavy pots and cast-iron frying pans. In Hubbard's list of tableware, he suggested tin cups and plates. Even these have now been replaced with durable lightweight products including insulated cups for that morning coffee.

It was also noted that Hubbard suggested carrying a three-pound ax. With the reduced need of large pieces of wood for campfires, most voyagers today prefer a lightweight camp saw.

With over 60 years of wilderness canoe camping, this editor has experienced the change in gear and clothing, as well as the food and its preparation. From the days of carrying in excess of 200 pounds of gear in the canoe, a party of two can now survive seven days of travel with well less than 100 pounds.

Other useful items:

- Band-Aids and first-aid kit.
- Sleeping bags – heaviness appropriate to the time of year.
- Duct tape.
- Kitchen sponge.
- LED headlamp.
- Gortex-type outerwear.
- Ropes of assorted sizes, including a painter rope for the bow of your canoe or kayak.
- Bear bag to hang your provisions high in a tree.

## Making a Pack

To make a pack, spread out on the ground your blanket, tent, or whatever you intend to use for the purpose, and double it over, more or less, to suit the size of your load. One or two trials will enable you to judge accurately of the extent of covering needed for the pack. Lay the strap on the blanket, &c.,[167] so that the centre piece shall be just over the edge of it, opposite the middle of the side, and the end pieces shall extend from the same side along the ends of the blanket, half-way from the middle of it to the ends. Then fold the ends of the blanket over the strap, letting them meet in the middle, or overlap, if necessary. The foundation of your pack is now ready.

Make a pile of your luggage, buckets, provisions, &c. on the blanket, and when you think you have weight or bulk enough, take the ends of your strap, one at a time, and knot each to the corresponding end of the centre piece; pull tightly, so that the ends of your blanket will be drawn together like the mouth of a bag. After the knots shall have been made, bring the ends of your strap together at the middle of the pack under the centre piece, cross them and carry them around to the opposite side of the pack, where they shall be firmly and finally knotted. The pack thus made is slung on the back; the broad part of the strap rests against the forehead, and by leaning forward, and holding the strap with both hands over the shoulders, a heavy weight can be carried with comparative ease. The Indians use this method almost altogether.

---

[167] **2020:** The use of &c., is another abbreviation for etc., from et cetera, for 'and other similar things,' or 'and so forth.'

**2020 Edition**

Indian Guide, Joe, Making a Pack.
Illustration by W.L. Taylor in
*"Woods and Lakes of Maine."*

\*

The foregoing list includes a small quantity of brandy. This should be used only in case of sickness. People are supposed to go into the woods for the purpose of gaining health and strength, and this inestimable privilege should not be prostituted by the use of liquor, merely to gratify an appetite for drink. The use of stimulants is sure to be followed by an unhealthy reaction, and in the woods, if nowhere else, there ought to be enough in Nature's charms to draw one away from a practice at once ruinous to health and to self-respect. For colds, or after a wetting of the body, Jamaica ginger[168] will be found an excellent remedy and preventive.

Parties who camp out in July or August will need some mosquito-repellent, to put on their faces and hands. Various compounds are put up, and are for sale, by druggists and others, which may answer the

---

[168] **2020:** Jamaica ginger, or Jake, was a medicinal extract that contained 70-80% ethanol by weight and was used in small doses mixed with water. Because of the high alcohol, some used in higher doses. In the 1930s users of Jamaica ginger were afflicted with a paralysis of the hands and feet.

purpose; but the writer has never found anything better than oil of tar, and sweet oil or glycerine, in equal quantities, and a little gum camphor and oil of pennyroyal mixed with it. At first, renewed applications are necessary at short intervals, until the skin becomes moist, and saturated with the odor of the mixture.

---

### 2020 Edition:

This mosquito-repellent is an 1800 remedy and not to be utilized today. Use over-the-counter repellents. A mosquito netting over a wide-brimmed hat is also recommended.

Hubbard makes no mention of ticks, as these pests were certainly not as prolific in his day. You are advised to wear light-colored clothing, spray the clothes, keep your pants tucked, check yourself often, and do a thorough inspection at the end of each day. Lyme disease and other tick-borne diseases are a serious problem whether you spend time in the woods or a suburban yard.

---

*

For ladies, a pair of thick buckskin gauntlets, and a good veil, are the best and most pleasant substitutes for the above mixture.

A mosquito net for the head, such as are for sale at sporting emporiums, will be a great comfort on warm nights, and especially about daybreak.

Matches should be kept in a small tight tin box, in a dry part of your luggage. A waterproof pocket matchbox you should always carry with you, well filled. You may need it once in ten years, but might fare badly that one time if caught without matches.

As to gun and fishing tackle, some prefer one kind and some another. Usually campers-out take just what they can conveniently get. There are many guns in the market that answer equally well the purposes for which they are wanted. The principal points to be considered in selecting a hunting rifle are its lightness, accuracy, rapidity of action, and the flatness of its trajectory, — all of which qualities will be found united in several well-known magazine guns. For a two weeks' trip, fifty cartridges will be found more than enough, unless one expects to ignore the possible presence of large game, and to shoot right and left at anything which may furnish a good target.[169]

A shot-gun will generally be found a useless encumbrance on a canoe trip in the Maine woods.

For fly rods, one made of ash and lancewood,[170] and which weighs from eight to twelve ounces, and costs about five dollars, will answer well enough for ordinary fishing. Higher priced rods can be had according to one's taste and resources, and afford, perhaps, more satisfaction to the scientific fisherman. They can well be taken care of, when the owner is at a hotel, but the camper-out will find it rather irksome to be continually putting his rod together, and taking it apart to avoid a rain-storm or the dews of night.

For flies, the best are the Montreal, red-ibis, brown-hackle, and blue-jay. For spring-fishing additional varieties may be found good, such as the Jenny-Lind, the grizzle-king, the professor, and the gray-drake.

Six-foot leaders are long enough. They should be of a pale bluish lint.

A map is desirable as a guide; it also serves to while away many an hour which might otherwise be dull. You become familiar with the character of the country, and, after study of the different water-courses, can often plan out trips, and post yourself upon their practicability, by questioning guides and others, whenever opportunity offers.

---

[169] **2020:** Reference all Fish and Game Laws and seasons accordingly.

[170] **2020:** Pseudopanax crassifolius, or lancewood, is a New Zealand native tree (family Araliaceae). Used for rods in the 1800s.

## Provisions

The following list of provisions will be found to contain all that is necessary for good camp fare, together with a little that may be regarded as a luxury. The acid in pickles, tomatoes, and dried or canned fruit, serves as a corrective to the large amount of fat unavoidably eaten by campers, and just enough of these articles should be taken to serve this purpose, and vary one's diet, without adding too much extra weight to the necessary canoe-load.

The fractions opposite each article in the list represent the amount of such article which a man of average "camp-appetit " will eat in one day, and are based on the writer's experience with ten different men on six different trips. To know approximately how much to take for a given time, it is hardly necessary to say, multiply the number in your party by the number of days you are to be in camp, and this result by the several fractions. Of course, there can be no absolute gauge of appetites, and during the last few days of your trip you may have to live on short rations; or you may take so much game as to have an overplus of provisions. In either case, however, this list will be found to be not wide of the mark.

### Hubbard's Recommended Provisions per Person

| Items | Daily Amount per Person | Items | Daily Amount per Person |
|-------|--------------------------|-------|--------------------------|
| Baking powder | 0.500 lb. | Lard | 0.100 lb. |
| Beans | 0.063 qt. | Molasses | 0.035 qt. |
| Butter | 0.085 lb, | Oatmeal, wheatgerm, rice, etc. | 0.080 lb, |
| Chocolate | 0.030 lb. | Onions | 0.050 lb. |
| Cocoa | 0.025 lb. | Pepper | 0.005 lb. |
| Coffee | 0.050 lb. | Pickles, maple sugar, raisins | optional. |
| Condensed milk | 0.075 can. | Potatoes | 0.020 bu. |

| | | | | |
|---|---|---|---|---|
| Corn, tomatoes, etc. | 0.100 can. | | Pork or bacon | 0.300 lb. |
| Corned beef | 0.080 lb. | | Salt | 0.040 lb. |
| Dried peaches, apricots, etc. | 0.050 lb. | | Sugar | 0.250 lb. |
| Flour, white and Graham | 0.500 lb. | | Tea | 0.025 lb. |
| Hard bread | 0.200 lb. | | Soap, matches | optional. |
| Julienne, dried (invaluable) | 0.020 lb. | | | |

**2020 Edition:**

The exactness of these provisional measurements are commendable.

Dried julienne refers to dried vegetable cakes. It is marked as 'invaluable' by Hubbard likely for a way to provide nutrients while on the trail.

In, *"Soyer's Culinary Campaign: Being Historical Reminiscences of the Late War,"* by Alexis Soyer, 1857, Soyer describes, "cakes of dried vegetables, to be called course julienne, for the army." In 1855 Soyer's aim was to prevent scurvy and malnourishment of the soldiers fighting in Crimea. The cakes were made up of carrots, turnips, parsnips, cabbage, celery, leeks, and pulverized seasoning of thyme, winter savory, bayleaf, pepper, and cloves.

As to whether soap, matches, or both were optional, this is a wonder. The editors recommend both.

\*

It must be borne in mind that, if any one of the above articles is not taken, more of something else must be substituted. Maple sugar, dried or canned fruit, chocolate, and corned beef are luxuries, and will have to be used sparingly, if taken in the quantities given above.

Canned meats will be found most acceptable for lunch, when you are on the move and do not or cannot stop long enough to cook. Flour will generally be found preferable to hard bread, as the latter is apt to become crumbled on being moved from place to place.

Some parties go into the woods with a notion that they are sure to get all the game they need for subsistence, and that it is therefore unnecessary to take more than enough flour, &c. to give a pleasant change to one's diet. This is a great mistake. Rely on your own larder, not on Nature's, and you will be much better off.

## Canoes and Their Usage

A good birch-canoe should be made of tough bark, the eyes of which are not easily broken, and there should not be any inequalities or "humps" on that part which is usually in the water, for the water by swelling them makes the "humps" more prominent, and thus more likely to be scraped or broken by contact with rocks. Nor should a canoe be what is vulgarly called "hog-backed," that is, lower in the middle than at the ends. For general use it should be flat-bottomed, rather than have a slight keel. It will then ride in shallower water, and be less ticklish and more manageable.

One can, with a little practice, learn how to *paddle* a canoe; the secret of keeping a straight course lies in feathering the paddle at the end of the stroke. To be able to use the *setting-pole* skillfully requires more study, not only to learn the effect on the canoe of each position and movement of the pole, but also the additional effect on it of the current or "set" of the water, and of gusts of wind, all of which must be "compensated."

At all times a canoe should be so loaded as to be "trim," or perfectly level. A slight displacement of equilibrium is very annoying.

When poling through rapids, the chief points to be borne in mind are to keep the bow pretty well loaded (more so when going up than when coming down), and to *keep it pointed in a line parallel with the current.* In sinking the pole into the water, it should be held away from the side of the canoe, and in pushing laterally it should be used from that side towards which you wish the bow to go. Much less strength is needed to *push* the bow around in this way, than to *pull* it around from the other side, besides which it is much less dangerous. In the latter case the current may swing the stem against and over the pole, and the jar and pressure may send the canoe-man into the water, or make him drop his pole. You should stand erect in the stern, with the left foot in front, and both feet on a line with the length of the canoe. Grasp the pole with both hands, the right uppermost, so that on the end of the push the left will be free to take hold higher up. This position is for poling on the right side. The pole may be shifted from side to side, and either end used, as emergency requires, but the end that is shod with a pick is alone reliable among slippery rocks.

The posture of the man in the stern of a canoe is usually sitting on the rear thwart and rails behind it. The bow-man's best position is kneeling on the bottom, his thighs supported by the second thwart. More work can be done in this position than if sitting on the thwart or on a seat behind it, although the latter is the more comfortable. The more highly a canoe is loaded, the more easily it can be overturned, and for this reason it is best for both the bow-man and stern-man to sit on the bottom of the canoe while on stormy water.

The scope of this work will not admit of more general discussion of this topic. A little practice, and a wetting or two, will give one sufficient insight into the theory to enable one soon to be quite at home in a canoe.

For leaks in the canoe a mixture of resin, and tallow or other fresh grease, is generally used. A small quantity of grease is needed, more or less, according as the water is cold or warm. If your mixture should be too soft, boiling will make it harder. It can be tested by putting a few drops on a chip, and dipping it in the water. The bark must be quite dry when it is applied, which condition is best produced by turning over the canoe and exposing it to the sun, or by holding a firebrand near the injured part. And in this connection, it may be said, that a canoe, when not required for use, should always be taken out of the water and turned over. While afloat, its bark becomes saturated with water, and increases very much in weight.[171]

For the same reason, do not get sand into your canoe. It gets down under the ribs, and cannot be removed. Wash off the soles of your shoes before you step in, and do not step in when by so doing your canoe will be depressed on to sharp rocks or gravel. This rubs the bark and makes the eyes crack. A canoe should be treated as carefully as if it were made of glass.

Many of the foregoing remarks now seldom have any practical application, for within the past ten years the birch-bark canoe has almost entirely given way to a canoe built on the same model, but covered with canvas. The latter is lighter, drier, and much more durable than the "birch," and will be found fully as serviceable in all respects. Patent folding canoes are not desirable for a tour through Maine.

It is dangerous to attempt to sail in a canoe. When your course is straight, you can sometimes profitably lash two canoes together, not so close that they will chafe, and, by means of a rubber blanket or coat, sail before the wind. In a single canoe a thick bush planted or held in the bow will greatly help to accelerate your speed before the wind.

It may not be out of place to say here, never allow the man in the stern of a canoe to have a loaded gun by his side while you are in the bow. The reason is too obvious to need explanation.

---

[171] **2020:** Current day explorers are certainly thankful for the Maine Old Town canoes.

## 2020 Edition: A Note on Canoes

Although canvas covered canoes were available at the time, it appears that Hubbard had a fondness for the more traditional birch bark canoe. No doubt the bark canoe was a very seaworthy craft but it was fairly heavy and a bit slow moving across an open body of water. It performed very well on open water or deep streams, but it was a bit fragile beating against rocks or going over ledges. In the list of items Hubbard suggested for travel he included white lead for stopping water leakage. In his book, *"Woods and Lakes of Maine,"* he frequently mentioned the need to make repairs to the canoe hull following a day paddling on shallow rocky streams.

As mentioned previously, canvas covered canoes were available at the time. This style canoe was a bit more durable than the bark canoe but they also were rather heavy and they had their limitations. In his early years of canoeing in Maine, this Editor had a twenty-foot wood and canvas canoe that was made by E.M. White in Old Town, Maine. This craft was extremely well constructed and durable and it had a dry weight of slightly more than one hundred pounds. The length, weight and shape of the canoe made it a great craft for crossing large lakes and handling rough water. It tracked extremely well but unfortunately the length and hull shape made it an unsuitable canoe for meandering streams. Hubbard may have made a similar observation.

The modern day canoes come in a wide variety of lengths, width, and hull design. They are manufactured from a wide range of material ranging from ultra-light carbon fiber to the heavy canvas coated wooden hull. Whereas Hubbard's birch bark canoe was a great all-around craft, many of today's canoes are not suitable for all situations. Some are very stable in rough open water while others are not. Some can survive a pounding on rocks and others are easily damaged under the same conditions. In selecting a canoe for use or purchase a careful decision has to be made in choosing a canoe to fit the individual needs.

Hubbard made no mention of personal flotation devices (PFD) being a part of the gear carried during his expeditions. Crude PFD's were available at the time but they were not widely used. On a trip today, it is mandatory that a wearable PFD is available for every person within a canoe or kayak. Hubbard, also, made no mention of a sea anchor being a part of his recommended gear. From his personal experience, this Editor strongly recommends having a painter on the stern of the canoe, as well as the bow, and having a sea anchor available if you plan to be in open water on a large lake such as Moosehead.

Today, kayaks, especially solo kayaks, are more popular than canoes. Like canoes they are available in various lengths, widths, hull designs and made from various materials. The kayaks tend to be more specialized in their design than canoes. Fortunately, there are kayaks well suited for wilderness travel. For the minimalist it is an excellent craft for a sojourn through the Maine Northwoods.

## Guides

Well-informed and reliable guides can be secured at prices ranging from one to two and a half dollars a day, according to the locality, and according to the length and difficulty of the trip in view. At Moosehead Lake, for services rendered parties staying at any of the hotels on the lake, the regular price is two dollars and a half and board, or three dollars, the guide to "find" himself. For services from Moosehead on a trip where a canoe is likely to receive hard usage, three dollars per day and board may be asked, while for a long and not difficult trip less than two and a half dollars and board may be reasonable compensation.

Away from Moosehead Lake, guide-hire is rarely more than two dollars a day, while at the Forks of the Kennebec and at Sebec Lake good guides may be had for from a dollar to a dollar and a half a day, and board.

The laws of supply and demand apply to guides and their compensation, as well as to other marketable "commodities," and good guides in the "season" are apt to have little spare time on their hands to dispose of at less than the usual local rates. Inferior guides, lacking in knowledge of the various routes and fishing grounds, can be had at a very low price.

Guides who receive the above-named prices furnish a canoe and the necessary camp "kit," except blankets. Sportsmen provide all the food needed.

Cases have been not uncommon where men of prominence in their own neighborhood have knowingly recommended as competent guides persons of notoriously bad character, temper, or incapacity. Again, some guides have willfully imposed upon parties engaging them, and by misrepresentation, apathy, or opposition to their wishes, have made an utter failure of what could otherwise have been a delightful trip, — one on which perhaps the participants had been building hopes of pleasure for months previously. Such practices do great injury to those guides who conscientiously try to make their employers realize their expectations of a pleasant vacation, and are apt to reflect on the entire fraternity, to their great discredit.[172]

In this connection it may not be out of place to say a word about the treatment of guides. They may picture in exaggerated language the hardships of this or that particular trip, and dwell upon the advantages of some others, which they well know will require much less labor on their part. You thus may be imposed upon, and may miss having a great deal of enjoyment. Get your information well digested before you start, and when your mind is once made up, push ahead. Let your guide understand, at the outset, where you mean to go, and that you expect him to devote all his energy and experience to getting there.

On the other hand, do not harass him in trivial matters. Some persons stand over a guide, when he is cooking, and object to this way of holding the frying pan, or that way of turning the flippers, and perhaps in a majority of cases thoughtlessly annoy him when there is no necessity for it.

Give your guide plenty of time to select a good camp-ground, and to prepare for the night. Favor him when you can. Keep your end of the canoe trim, and do not hesitate to get out and walk now and then, if by so doing you can avoid tearing or scraping the bark.

---

**2020 Edition:**

Licensing for Registered Maine Guides first began 1897. During that first year, over 1300 individuals became

---

[172] Within a year or two last past some of the Kineo guides have demanded as much as three dollars and a half and four dollars per day, and, besides, have refused to engage themselves for a less time than a month. By declining to submit to any such extortion visitors will render a service to the public.

licensed, primarily in the hunting and fishing disciplines. The first person in Maine to receive their guide license was Cornelia Thurza Crosby (1854-1946), or "Fly Rod Crosby," as she was better known. Crosby promoted Maine's outdoor sports at shows in New York City, and she wrote a column for syndicated newspapers.

The requirement to become a guide at that time, and for many years after, was basically for a local game warden to 'license' the person based on their "woods" knowledge. In 1975, a standardized test and procedure was established for licensing. Guides can be licensed in one or more specialized classifications of hunting, fishing, specialized recreational (watercraft, ATVs, snowmobiles, and the like), sea-kayaking, and tide-water fishing.

*1. Source on Maine Guides: Maine Department of Inland Fisheries & Wildlife. www.maine.gov, cited 2020.*

\*

## Campground

It is of the utmost importance for tourists to stop early enough, at the end of each day, to select a good site for their camp, to pitch their tent, and to get wood enough together to last overnight. Many people do not seem to think how hard it is to do all of these things in the dark. Only an absolute necessity should induce late camping. An hour before sunset is late enough to cease paddling.

A good campground will be one with a good landing, not a steep, muddy bank, where there is plenty of wood, good water, and where the ground is dry and level. A small tree or two may have to be cut down, and all roots and "humps" should be removed. They make themselves very prominent before morning, even when covered generously with boughs.

The tent should be pitched with the head to windward, so that the smoke from the fire shall not be blown into it. It should also be well under shelter, in anticipation of high winds or heavy rain, and in a position where a heavy rain would not be likely to flood it.

The ridge-pole and uprights should be well trimmed of all projecting twigs which might make a hole in the tent, except that the uprights may have left on one side several such, on which to hang belts, cups, and the like. The uprights should be cut about nine feet long, with a slight notch on the upper end, and the lower end sharpened. Drive them into the ground, by their own weight, and work them from side to side, thus enlarging and deepening the holes until the poles are sunk sufficiently to stand out of ground the height of the tent. Then lay the latter out flat on its side, put the ridge-pole in its place, along the top of the tent, take down the uprights and insert them under the side of the tent, up against the ends of the ridge-pole, and, with one person holding each of the two poles, lift into a perpendicular position, and set them into their holes. They will usually stand alone while the pins (notched sticks) are being driven into the ground.

*Campers and Lumbermen, Attention !*

A NEW AND VALUABLE INVENTION.

THE

## CROSBY PATENT AXE COVER.

NO LUMBERMAN NOR CAMPER SHOULD BE WITHOUT IT.

Made of stout leather, with brass trimmings. It is cheap, light, and durable; will not rust, and protects the edge of the axe from becoming nicked or dulled, and renders it safe to carry. Also,

INDIAN HATCHETS AND AXES,

With broad steel heads, made specially for campers, and adapted for use in the woods. Three sizes.

SEND STAMP FOR CIRCULAR.

A. S. CROSBY & CO., Manufacturers,
WATERVILLE, MAINE.

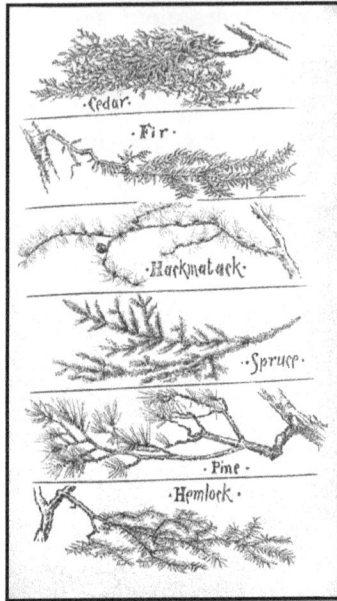

**Sketches of Various Coniferous and Evergreen Trees**

*

A string stretched across the tent, just under the ridge-pole, will make a good clothesline for socks, towels, and the like. Guns and rods can be stacked around the pole at the head of the tent, at night, and made secure by a strap.

The historic camp bed is made of fir boughs, laid down in rows with the underside up, and overlapping each other shingle fashion, the larger part, or stem, being covered by the adjoining layer. It requires some knack to break off boughs from fir-trees. A quick snap, accomplished by the thumb and fore and middle fingers, does it.

Tables and seats can be improvised, and with a small amount of labor a camp can be considerably embellished. Two rubber blankets stretched over a ridge-pole, which is laid on, and tied to, the branches of adjoining trees, make an excellent canopy for the table. To provide a seat, select two trees about four or five feet apart; with your axe cut into them on the same side for several inches, about a foot and a half above ground. Then make several perpendicular cuts into this part of the trees, into which drive a wedge, which shall project about a foot, and a little above a horizontal. On these wedges lay poles cut the proper length, and you have your seat.[173]

A candlestick may be made, by taking a stick as large round as your thumb, sharpening one end, splitting the other, and inserting the candle, which will be held in place by the elasticity of the wood. If not, it can be tied with a string or withe.[174]

## Campfire

The campfire should be built about six feet from the door of your tent. The large trunk of a tree, say five feet long and two feet in diameter, (or two smaller logs, one on top of the other,) makes your back log, or reflector, while two smaller and shorter ones, placed at right angles to it, about four feet apart, make your "hand-junks,"[175] all of them preferably of hard wood. The active or burning part of the fire will be between the hand-junks, and it may readily be lighted with birch-bark. Dry soft-wood is usually abundant. Dead wood found lying on the ground is apt to be wet and soggy, and will not burn readily. Pull down two or three small dead trees, which can quickly be cut or broken up in lengths to suit. This serves well to kindle your fire, after which hard wood will be found hotter and less crackly.

The following woods are good for cooking, when dry, substantially in the order named: pine, fir, cedar, hemlock, and spruce. The last four kinds crackle considerably, and make a great

---

[173] **2020:** Please do not employ this old technique at public campsites or those where you do not have permissions from landowners to cut into trees.

[174] **2020:** More typically spelled, withy. This is a tough, flexible branch of the willow (or like tree), used for tying, binding, or basket making.

[175] **2020:** The side logs. It is preferable to use stones. Only burn where permissible and allowed by law.

quantity of ashes. A dead and partially decayed hemlock will burn well, and will not crackle very much.

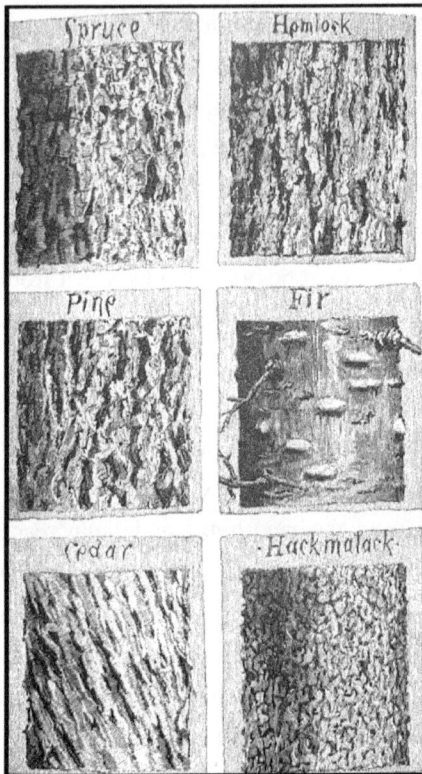

**Images of Tree Bark**
*

All of the foregoing, when green, have a good deal of gum in them, except cedar, which splits easily, and is much used for tables, skin-stretchers, and the like.

Of the hard woods, rock-maple and yellow-birch are the hardest found in Northern Maine. The latter, being very tough, and usually growing to a much greater size than rock-maple, is good for back-logs and hand-junks, while white-birch is easily split, burns freely, but does not give as much heat as rock-maple or yellow-birch.

## Cooking

Having given the kinds of food suitable for camp, and the quantities of each to be provided, it may not be out of place to give a few hints as to its preparation for the table.

Fish chowder is one of the readiest of camp dishes, as well as one of the most palatable. Clean your fish, cut it into pieces about an inch long, peel and slice your potatoes, not too thin, and put into your pail alternate layers of fish and potatoes, together with a small quantity of pork or bacon cut into small squares, and a quarter of an onion chopped fine. Season each layer, as you put it in, with salt and pepper, and cover the whole with water. Boil about fifteen or twenty minutes, after which stir in one or two table spoonful's of condensed milk, add hard-bread, soaked or not, to suit the fancy, and leave on the fire a few moments longer. After the hard-bread shall have been added, great care should be taken that the mixture does not burn.

For duck, partridge, or musquash stew,[176] cut the meat into small pieces, and place it in a pail, two thirds full of water, where it can boil gently. After half an hour or more, according to the tenderness of the meat, season to the taste, add two handfuls of pearled barley, and boil twenty minutes longer, taking care that the barley does not burn on the bottom of the pail. In the absence of barley, thicken with a little flour previously dissolved in cold water.

For white bread, a small quantity of baking powder, according to directions which accompany the latter, and a pinch of salt, should be thoroughly mixed with the flour, *dry*. Then add cold water, stir vigorously, and knead *ad libitum*. Bread can be baked in a regular baker, or in a frying-pan. The latter method requires good coals and a hot fire. Put the dough in the pan, which has been previously

---

[176] **2020**: Musquash, or muskrat, are medium-sized rodents with an omnivorous diet. They are not, however, members of the genus Rattus. Also, (*Ondatra zibethicus*).

greased, and set the latter on a small bed of coals, a foot or more from the fire. Leave it there a few moments, until the underside shall have hardened enough to retain its shape. Then tilt the pan up, and support it by a crotched stick stuck into the hole in the end of the handle. The bed of coals behind and underneath, and the fire in front, will soon cook the loaf, which will need watching and turning.

"Flippers," or "flap-jacks," are mixed like bread, except that a little more baking powder is used, and a good deal more water.

Graham bread is made like wheat bread, with two parts of Graham and one of wheat flour, and some sugar or molasses. A bread that contains sugar or molasses mil, when baking, burn much more easily than one without sweets, and therefore needs more careful watching.

A good johnny-cake, or suet-cake, can be made of equal parts of wheat flour and corn meal. First mix in your baking powder, then cut up into small squares a piece of pork, try out the fat, and pour the whole into your pan with molasses and a little cold water. Stir briskly, and bake before a hot fire.

Some persons prefer "prepared" flour for camp use, but the writer has always had the best of success with baking powders.

For baked beans you need an iron pot with close-fitting cover, and a good dry bean-hole. The latter can be dug with the blade of your paddle, near the campfire. A fire should be made and kept ablaze in it for an hour or more, so as thoroughly to heat the ground. Pine bark, cherry, or black birch sticks make good coals.

Pick over the beans, put them into a pail of water, and set on the fire after, or during, supper. Parboil until the skin can easily be rubbed off the beans, when the water must be drained off, and the beans transferred to their iron pot. Put a good piece of pork in the middle near the top, add two teaspoonfuls of molasses, and cover the whole with water. The coals should then be shoveled out of the hole, a few being left on the bottom, the covered pot set in and surrounded by coals, on top and on the sides. Cover the coals in turn with earth, to prevent a too rapid combustion of the former. In the absence of a bean-hole hang your pot or tin pail high over the camp fire for the night.

It is hardly necessary to add directions for making tea and coffee, boiling or frying potatoes, or frying fish, except that fish should be put into the frying-pan only after the grease is thoroughly hot. Everyone is supposed to know how these simpler dishes are prepared. Should any camper-out fail of the requisite knowledge, let him once become hungry, really "camp-hungry," and he will need no instructor. The art of cooking will come of itself.

## Dressing Game

The larger game of the woods is skinned by cutting through the hide, under the belly, from the tail to the neck, and laterally up the four legs and around the knees and hocks. The skin is then stripped or cut from the body, the animal lying on its back. The layer of flesh under the belly is deceptively thin. Therefore, in cutting through it to take out the entrails care must be exercised not to cut them. Their connection with the body is severed just back of the breast. The carcass should finally be washed thoroughly, and hung up by means of the sinews on the hind legs.

All refuse matter should be buried at a long distance from camp.

The brisket, or breast, the "back-half," a part of the fore-quarter which runs on the ridge of the back on either side of the spine and above the ribs, and the hind-quarters, are generally the best parts of large game, while in the moose the tongue, nose, and lower lip, and in the beaver the tail and liver, are considered great delicacies.

The smaller fur-bearing animals, such as otter, mink, and musquash, are skinned by cutting across the end of the body from the hock of one leg to that of the other; then the lower parts of the hindlegs are cut off without being separated from the skin, which is pulled down, on all sides, over the body of the animal, after the manner of a stocking.

Trout are prepared for the frying-pan by being cut lengthwise along the belly, and having the entrails removed and the head and tail cutoff. A pleasant flavor is imparted to them by hanging them where they will be in the smoke of the campfire for several hours.

## Hygienic Notes

Original Note:

[The following pages are taken, with the kind permission of Dr. Elliott Coues, U. S. A., from that gentleman's valuable work on "Field Ornithology," (Salem, Naturalists' Agency,) and the advice given in them cannot fail to prove serviceable, both to those who go into the woods to camp out, and to those who stay at home. It is here offered again to the public by the writer of this little book, with a grateful sense of the obligation he, in common with many others, is under to its author.]

## Accidents

*Always carry a loaded gun at half-cock*, unless you are about to shoot. Unless the lock fail, accidental discharge is impossible, except under these circumstances: a) a direct blow on the nipple or pin; b) catching of both hammer and trigger simultaneously, drawing back of the former and its release whilst the trigger is still held, — the chances against which are simply incalculable. Full-cock, ticklish as it seems, is safer than no-cock, when a tap on the hammer or even the heel-plate, or a slight catch and release of the hammer, may cause discharge. Never let the muzzle of a loaded gun point toward your own person for a single instant. Get your gun over fences or into boats or carriages, before you get over or in yourself, or at any rate no later. Remove caps or cartridges on entering a house. Never aim a gun, loaded or not, at any object, unless you mean to press the trigger. Never put a loaded gun away long enough to forget whether it is loaded or not; never leave a loaded gun to be found by others under circumstances reasonably pre-supposing it to be unloaded. Never put a gun where it can be knocked down by a dog or a child. Never forget that, though a gunning accident may be sometimes interpretable (from a certain standpoint) as a "dispensation of Providence," such are dispensed oftenest to the careless

The secret of safe *climbing* is never to relax one hold until another is secured; it is in spirit equally applicable to scrambling over rocks, a particularly difficult thing to do safely with a loaded gun. Test rotten, slippery, or otherwise suspicious holds, before trusting them. In lifting the body up anywhere keep the mouth shut, breathe through the nostrils, and go slowly.

In *swimming*, waste no strength unnecessarily in trying to stem a current; yield partly, and land obliquely lower down; if exhausted, float, the slightest motion of the hands will ordinarily keep the face above water; and in any event keep your wits collected. In fording deeply, a heavy stone will strengthen, your position. Never sail a boat experimentally; if you are no sailor, take one with you or stay on land.

In crossing a high, narrow footpath, never look lower than your feet; the muscles will work true, if not confused with faltering instructions from a giddy brain. On soft ground see what, if anything, has preceded you; large hoof-marks generally mean that the way is safe; if none are found, inquire for yourself before going on. Quicksand is the most treacherous, because far more dangerous than it looks; but I have seen a mule's ears finally disappear in genuine mud. Cattle-paths, however erratic, commonly prove the surest way out of a difficult place, whether of uncertain footing or dense undergrowth.

WINCHESTER

## REPEATING RIFLES,

*THE SPORTSMAN'S FAVORITE,*

Are unequalled for rapidity and accuracy of fire, ease of manipulation, simplicity, and strength of construction.

**FOR ILLUSTRATED PAMPHLET,**

With full description of these arms, and of METALLIC AMMUNITION of all kinds, PAPER and BRASS SHOT-SHELLS, &c., &c., address

*WINCHESTER REPEATING ARMS COMPANY, NEW HAVEN, CONN.*

## MIASM

---

**2020 Edition**

This section is retained in the text as a historical reference to the period. Miasmatic theory is no longer considered a viable medical theory. It was once believed that this so-called, 'bad air,' caused epidemics originating from rotting organic matter. By the late 1880s this theory was widely being replaced with the germ theory of diseases.

---

\*

Unguarded exposure in malarious regions usually entails sickness, often preventable, however, by due precautions. It is worth knowing, in the first place, that miasmatic poison is most powerful between sunset and sunrise, — more exactly, from the damp of the evening until night vapors are dissipated; we may be out in the daytime with comparative impunity where to pass a night would be almost certain disease. If forced to camp out, seek the highest and driest spot, put a good fire on the swamp side, and also, if possible, let trees intervene. Never go out on an empty stomach, just a cup of coffee and a crust may make a decided difference. Meet the earliest unfavorable symptoms with quinine, —I should rather say, if unacclimated, anticipate them with this invaluable agent. Endeavor to maintain high health of all functions by the natural means of regularity and temperance in diet, exercise and repose.

## "Taking Cold"

This vague "household word" indicates one or more of a long-varied train of unpleasant affections, nearly always traceable to one or the other of only two causes: *sudden change* of temperature, and *unequal distribution* of temperature. No extremes of heat or cold can alone effect this result; persons frozen to death do not "take cold" during the process. But if a part of the body be rapidly cooled, as by evaporation from a wet article of clothing, or by sitting in a draught of air, the rest of the body remaining at an ordinary temperature; or if the temperature of the whole be suddenly changed by going out into the cold, or, especially, by coming into a warm room, there is much liability of trouble. There is an old saying, "When the air comes through a hole, say your prayers to save your soul;" and I should think almost anyone could get a "cold" with a spoonful of water on the wrist held to a key-hole. Singular as it may seem, sudden warming when cold is more dangerous than the reverse; everyone has noticed how soon the handkerchief is required on entering a heated room on a cold day. Frost-bite is an extreme illustration of this. As the Irishman said on picking himself up, it was not the fall, but stopping so quickly, that hurt him; it is not the lowering of the temperature to the freezing point, but its subsequent elevation, that devitalizes the tissue. This is why rubbing with snow, or bathing in cold water, is required to restore safely a frozen part, the arrested circulation must be very gradually re-established, or inflammation, perhaps mortification ensues. General precautions against taking cold are almost self-evident, in this light. There is ordinarily little if any danger to be apprehended from wet clothes, so long as exercise is kept up; for the "glow" about compensates for the extra cooling by evaporation. Nor is a complete drenching more likely to be injurious than wetting of one part. But never sit still wet and in changing, rub the body dry. There is a general tendency, springing from fatigue, indolence, or indifference, to neglect damp feet; that is to say, to dry them by the fire; but this process is tedious and uncertain. I would say especially, off with the muddy boots and sodden socks at once, — dry stockings and slippers, after a hunt, may make just the difference of your being able to go out again or never.

Take care never to check perspiration; during this process the body is in a somewhat critical condition, and sudden arrest of the function may result disastrously, — even fatally. One part of the business of perspiration is to equalize bodily temperature, and it must not be interfered with. The secret of much that is to be said about *bathing* when heated, lies here. A person overheated, panting it may be, with throbbing temples and a dry skin, is in danger partly because the natural cooling by evaporation from the skin is denied, and this condition is sometimes not far from a "sun-stroke." Under these circumstances, a person of fairly good constitution may plunge into the water with impunity, even with benefit. But if the body be already cooling by sweating, rapid abstraction of heat from the surface may cause internal congestion, never unattended with danger. Drinking ice-water offers a somewhat parallel case; even on stooping to drink at the brook, when flushed with heat, it is well to bathe the face and hands first, and to taste the water before a full draught.

It is a well-known excellent rule, not to bathe immediately after a full meal; because during digestion the organs concerned are comparatively engorged, and any sudden disturbance of the circulation may be disastrous.[177]

The imperative necessity of resisting drowsiness under extreme cold requires no comment.

---

[177] **2020:** As per online information from the Mayo Clinic in 2018, it is noted there was no scientific basis for this belief. It may not be comfortable to swim on a full stomach, but disastrous consequences resulting from a 'bath' in a mountain lake is unlikely.

In walking under a hot sun the head may be sensibly protected by green leaves or grass in the hat; they may be advantageously moistened, but not enough to drip about the ears. Under such circumstances the slightest giddiness, dimness of sight, or confusion of ideas, should be taken as a warning of possible sunstroke, instantly demanding rest, and shelter if practicable.

## Hunger and Fatigue

Hunger and fatigue are more closely related than they might seem to be; one is a sign that the fuel is out, and the other asks for it. Extreme fatigue, indeed, destroys appetite; this simply means, temporary incapacity for digestion. But even far short of this, food is more easily digested, and better relished after a little preparation of the furnace. On coming home tired it is much better to make a leisurely and reasonably nice toilet than to eat at once, or to lie still thinking how tired you are; after a change and a wash you will feel like a "new man," and go to table in capital state. Whatever dietetic irregularities a high state of civilization may demand or render practicable, a normally healthy person is inconvenienced almost as soon as his regular mealtime passes without food; and few can work comfortably or profitably fasting over six or eight hours. Eat before starting; if for a day's tramp, take a lunch the most frugal meal will appease if it do not satisfy hunger, and so postpone its urgency. As a small scrap of practical wisdom, I would add, keep the remnants of the lunch, if there are any; for you cannot always be sure of getting in to supper.

## Stimulation

When cold, fatigued, depressed in mind, and on other occasions, you may feel inclined to resort to artificial stimulus. Respecting this many sided theme I have a few words to offer of direct bearing on the [bird] collector's case. It should be clearly understood, in the first place, that a stimulant confers no strength whatever; it simply calls the powers that be into increased action at their own expense. Seeking real strength in stimulus is as wise as an attempt to lift yourself up by the boot-straps. You may gather yourself to leap the ditch and you clear it; but no such muscular energy can be sustained; exhaustion speedily renders further expenditure impossible. But now suppose a very powerful mental impression be made, say the circumstance of a succession of ditches in front, and a mad dog behind; if the stimulus of terror be sufficiently strong, you may leap on till you drop senseless. Alcoholic stimulus is a parallel case, and is not seldom pushed to the same extreme. Under its influence you never can tell when you *are* tired; the expenditure goes on, indeed, with unnatural rapidity, only it is not felt at the time; but the upshot is, you have all the original fatigue to endure and to recover from, *plus* the fatigue resulting from over-excitation of the system.

Taken as a fortification against cold, alcohol is as unsatisfactory as a remedy for fatigue. Insensibility to cold does not imply protection. The fact is, the exposure is greater than before; the circulation and respiration being hurried, the waste is greater, and as sound fuel cannot be immediately supplied, the temperature of the body is soon lowered. The transient warmth and glow over, the system has both cold and depression to endure; there is no use in borrowing from yourself and fancying you are richer.

Secondly, the value of any stimulus (except in a few exigencies of disease or injury) is in proportion, not to the intensity, but to the equableness and durability of its effect. This is one reason why tea, coffee, and articles of corresponding qualities, are preferable to alcoholic drinks; they work so smoothly that their effect is often unnoticed, and they "stay by" well the friction of alcohol is tremendous in comparison. A glass of grog may help a veteran over the fence, but no one, young or old, can shoot all day on whiskey.

Thirdly, undue excitation of any physical function is followed by corresponding depression, on the simple principle that action and reaction are equal: and the balance of health turns too easily to be willfully disturbed. Stimulation is a draft upon vital capital, when interest alone should suffice; it may be needed at times to bridge a chasm, but habitual living beyond vital income infallibly entails bankruptcy in health. The use of alcohol in health seems practically restricted to purposes of sensuous gratification on the part of those prepared to pay a round price for this luxury. The three golden rules here are, never drink before breakfast, never drink alone, and never drink bad liquor; their observance may make even the abuse of alcohol tolerable. Serious objections for a naturalist, at least, are that science, viewed through a glass, seems distant and uncertain, while the joys of rum are immediate and unquestionable; and that intemperance, being an attempt to defy certain physical laws, is therefore eminently unscientific.

## *Game and Fish of Northern Maine*

Northern Maine, like all other hunting ground within easy reach of civilization, has been pretty thoroughly hunted and trapped over, among others by a class of men, to whom, in the face of quick returns even with small profits, the laws of the State and the rights of fellow citizens are of little or no consequence. Nor does it seem to matter much, that in killing off game indiscriminately and wantonly they are making away with the goose that lays the golden egg. Statistics show that for every moose killed in the autumn by tourists at least fifteen hundred dollars are brought into Maine and distributed among her inhabitants. No one can now report having seen a moose anywhere, cow or bull, in winter or summer, in season or out of season, but that some listener will quietly hurry off, to see if he cannot kill it. The immunity from punishment of persons that violate the game laws is due largely to the policy of the State, in not equipping itself with a well-organized and decently paid corps of wardens. Added to this, the widespread and self-confessed ignorance, even among the more intelligent citizens of the State, as to the game resources, their value and their needs, the general apathy among all classes, as shown by the absence of clubs for the protection of game and punishment of game law breakers, and the existence of a small but determined band of deer-hounders, who, when cornered, do not scruple even to shoot down the wardens in cold blood, — all of these causes tend to paralyze the efforts of the few friends of game protection, and, if not counteracted, will surely lead to the extermination of big game, and with it the loss of the fairest hunting ground east of the Mississippi River.

The game and fish laws of Maine have undergone some changes for the better within the past eight years. Every person may now take, at the proper season, one moose, two caribou and three deer. This liberal allowance is more than enough to supply the needs of any party of campers, and no true sportsman will wantonly kill more game than he can use, just for the sake of the excitement, or "sport," as it is called. The same rule of conduct should apply equally to fishing. Can any person with humanity in his nature continue to catch trout long after the needs of his table are supplied, only to see them spoil afterwards? "Oh, but I put back into the water all under a pound in weight," says an ardent fisherman. "I have the fun of playing them, and, you know, it does not pain them to be hooked." Is not this casuistry? Who has proved that the torn and twisted mouth, or the lacerated and bleeding eye of a trout does not pain? Let us even admit that the pain a trout is capable of suffering is very slight compared with that of more highly organized beings. Will not the fisherman's argument excuse the shooter when he inflicts a flesh wound on a deer, just to have the fun of seeing whether he could hit him? Moderation on the part of our shooters and fishermen, moderation well digested, so to speak, would produce enjoyment more satisfactory in the end, in that it would leave more room for the enjoyment of others.

The fish laws of Maine now prohibit the taking, or having in possession for the purpose of transportation, by any one person, of more than fifty pounds of trout at one time, and this measure bids fair to prevent the rapid depletion of Maine's ponds and streams.

The writer has not attempted to give, in these pages, exact directions as to the whereabouts of all the good fishing-pools in different ponds and streams, and for three reasons. First, and principally, he does not know where they are; secondly, they change from year to year, nay, even from day to day; and, thirdly, it would take away much pleasure from the camper-out, if he were not allowed occasionally to hunt after his game. One soon learns, without being told, that at the foot of rapids, below dams, at the mouths of cold streams, and in pools along their course, are the most likely places for fish. As to game, one should ever be ready to meet it. It comes when least expected, and may be off again before one can disengage his gun from a lot of rods and camp equipage. Keep it by your side, or in your hands, always while in the woods.

## Digest of The Game and Inland Fish Laws of Maine

It is unlawful to hunt, catch, kill, or destroy, with DOGS, any moose, deer, or caribou. Penalty for moose \ one hundred, for deer or caribou forty dollars. — 1891,

ch. 95, §§ 9, 10.

Close-time for moose, deer, and caribou, January 1st to October 1st.

"Any person may lawfully kill any dog found hunting moose, deer, or caribou, or kept or used FOR THAT PURPOSE. Any person owning or having in possession any dog for the purpose of hunting moose, deer, or caribou, or that is kept or used for such hunting,

forfeits not less than twenty nor more than one hundred dollars." —
Ibid. § 10.

The possession of any such animal or part thereof at a time when
its killing is unlawful, is presumptive, but not conclusive, evidence of
having killed it. — Ibid. §11.

Whoever takes, kills, destroys, or has in possession between the
first days of October and January more than one moose, two caribou,
or three deer, forfeits one hundred dollars for every moose and forty
dollars for every caribou or deer taken, killed, destroyed, or in
possession in excess of said number; and all such moose, caribou, or
deer, or the carcasses or parts thereof, are forfeited to the prosecutor.
Whoever has in possession, except alive, more than the aforesaid
number of moose, deer, or caribou, or parts thereof, shall be deemed
to have killed or destroyed them in violation of law. " But nothing in
this section shall prevent any market-man or provision-dealer, having
an established place of business in this state, from purchasing and
having in possession at his said place of business, not exceeding one
moose, two caribou, and three deer, lawfully caught, killed, or
destroyed, or any part thereof, at one time, and selling the same at
retail in open-season to his local customers." — Ibid. § 12.

Transportation of the above-mentioned game in close-time, or in
open-time unless open to view, tagged, and plainly labeled with the
name of the owner, and accompanied by him, is prohibited. Fine,
forty dollars. Any person not the actual owner, who, to aid another in
such transportation, falsely represents himself to be the owner, is
liable to the penalty aforesaid. Ibid. § 13.

Similar regulations, with penalties, apply to protected birds,
except that only fifteen may be transported at one time, and market-
men may purchase and sell, in open-season, to local customers. —
Ibid. § 21.

"Any person whose game or fish has been seized for violation of any game or fish law, shall have it returned to him on giving to the officer a bond ... in double the amount of the fine. . ." Failing to give such bond, he may lose his fish or game. — Ibid. § 14.

Game taken, etc., in violation of law is liable to seizure, and is forfeited "in case of conviction for such violation."— Ibid. § 15.

Any officer authorized to enforce the fish and game laws may, without process, arrest any violator of said laws. — Ibid. 16. §

### Fur-Bearing Animals, and Birds

| Open season for | Penalty |
|---|---|
| Mink, Sable,[178] Otter, and Fisher<br>Oct. 15 to May 1 | Ten dollars. |
| Beaver, not to be taken at any time! | Twenty-five dollars |
| Wood-duck, Dusky (black) duck,<br>Teal, or Gray duck<br>Sept. 1 to May 1 | Not less than five nor more than ten dollars for each bird |
| Partridge,[179] Woodcock<br>Sept. 1 to Dec. 1 | |
| Quail<br>Oct. 1 to Dec. 1 | |
| Pinnated grouse (Prairie-chicken)<br>Sept. 1 to Jan. 1 | |
| Plover<br>Aug. 1 to May 1 | |

---

[178] **2020:** The Sable ( Martes zibellina ) is a species of martin found in the Western Mountains of Europe most notably, Russia. The martin found in the forests of Maine is the American Martin ( Martes americana ). It is better known in Maine as the Pine Martin.

[179] **2020:** The Partridge is the common name used in Maine for the Ruffed Grouse (Bonasa umbellus).

During close-season the killing, sale, or possession of said birds (except alive) is prohibited.

In *any* season the exposure for sale, or the possession of said birds, except alive, or except for consumption as food within the state, and then, too, of not more than thirty of each variety at one time, is prohibited under a penalty of five dollars for each bird. (See paragraph above on transportation, and sale of game.)

No wild duck and none of the above birds, except plover, may lawfully be taken in snares or traps. Penalty, five dollars for each bird. —Ibid. § 22.

The wanton taking or destruction of the nests, eggs, or unfledged young of any wild bird, except of crows, hawks, or owls, or the taking of eggs or young from said nests, except to preserve the same as specimens or to rear said young alive, is punishable by a fine of from one dollar to ten dollars for each nest, egg, or young so taken or destroyed. — Ibid. § 24.

Indians are liable to the foregoing penalties equally with other persons.

SUNDAY is a close-time for game and birds of any kind. — Ibid. § 27.

### Fish

The close-time for land-locked salmon, trout, and togue is from October 1st to May 1st (except on the St. Croix River and its tributaries, and on all the waters in Kennebec County, where it extends from September 15th to May 1st); for black bass, Oswego bass, and white perch, from April 1st to July 1st. — R. S. ch. 40, § 487.

The penalty attached to the foregoing section is not less than ten dollars, nor more than thirty dollars, and a further fine of one dollar for each fish taken. In February, March, and April, however, citizens of Maine may "fish for and take land-locked salmon, trout, and togue, and convey the same to their own homes, but not otherwise." — Ibid. § 48.

The sale, possession with intent to sell, or transportation of trout, etc., during close-time is prohibited. Penalty, from ten to fifty dollars. —Ibid. § 49.

The possession of said fish in close-time (except alive) is presumptive evidence of violation of law. — Ibid. § 50.

"No person shall take, catch, kill, or have in possession, at any one time for the purpose of transportation, more than fifty pounds of land-locked salmon, trout, or togue, in all, nor shall any such be transported except in the possession of the owner thereof, under a penalty of fifty dollars for the offence and five dollars for every pound of land-locked salmon, trout, or togue, in all, so taken, caught, killed, in possession or transportation, in excess of fifty pounds ; and all such fish transported in violation of this section may be seized, on complaint, and shall be forfeited to the prosecutor. Whoever has in possession more than fifty pounds in all of such fish shall be deemed to have taken them in violation of this section." — Laws of 1885, ch. 271, § 54.

The use of grapnel, spear, trawl, weir, net, seine, trap, and set-line, except when fishing through the ice, and then with not more than five set-lines, in all fresh-water lakes, ponds, and streams, is prohibited.

Only hand-fishing, with a single-baited hook or line, or with artificial flies, is legal. The penalty for disregarding this section is twenty-five dollars for each salmon or land-locked salmon, and one dollar for each and every other fish so taken, etc., and all grapnels, etc., are forfeited if found in use or operation, any person being authorized in such case to destroy them. — Ibid. § 51.

The use of explosives or poison to destroy or take fish, is prohibited. Penalty, one hundred dollars fine, and two months' imprisonment in the county jail. — Ibid. § 52.

It is prohibited to kill or destroy sea-salmon or land-locked salmon less than nine inches in length, or any trout less than five inches in length. Penalty, five dollars for the offence, and fifty cents for each fish. Possession of said fish of less than said sizes is presumptive evidence of violation of law. — § 53.

## Special Laws for Moosehead Lake Revised Statutes 1885

§ I. No person shall take, catch, kill, fish for, or destroy any trout, land-locked salmon, or other fish in the Misery and Saccatien or Socatian rivers, which empty into Moosehead Lake, from the last day of September to the 1st day of May.

§ 2. Any person who shall violate the provisions of this Act shall forfeit and pay the sum of twenty-five dollars for the attempt and one dollar for each and every trout, land-locked salmon, or other fish so taken, caught, killed, or destroyed, to be recovered by complaint before any trial justice, one-half to the complainant and one-half to the county where proceedings are commenced.

---

### 2020 Edition: Notes on Game and Fish

Even though Hubbard appeared to enjoy the sport of hunting and fishing he appeared very concerned about the conduct of hunters and fisherman and their wanton killing of game and fish.

When Hubbard wrote this Guide, he stated that the game and fish laws of Maine had undergone some changes for the better within the recent years. In addition, the Maine Warden Service was established in 1880 and it may well be the time between the establishment of the Service, and his writing of the editions of this book that he was referring to. It would appear that prior to that period, even though there were laws relating to hunting and fishing, there were no official means to enforce them. Even at the time of the creation of the

Warden Service a license to fish or hunt was not required, and inhumane hunting practices, market hunting, and game exportation were all rampant. For example, during this period an estimated 4,000 caribou were being killed each year.[180]

In 1899, the Department, seeing a need to conserve fish and game enacted "The September Law." This early attempt at a hunting license program cost $4.00 for residents and $6.00 non-residents, and allowed license holders to kill one deer in the month of September. It was an extremely unpopular law and swiftly abolished. It wasn't until 1919 when residents actually began paying for a hunting and fishing license. The cost was twenty-five cents per license and it was good for a lifetime.

Hubbard refers frequently to the sighting and hunting of caribou during his trips. The north woods of Maine were once home to probably hundreds of thousands of Woodland Caribou (Rangifer tarandus caribou). Unfortunately, wild, free roaming caribou can no longer be found within the State of Maine. Certainly, there were several reasons for the elimination of caribou within Maine; over hunting and habitat destruction being the most prevalent. At the time of Hubbard's travels, hunters could legally kill two caribou per year.

The last legally killed caribou in Maine was in 1898 by "Fly Rod" Crosby.

---

[180] **2020**: Maine Department of Inland Fisheries & Wildlife: "History of the Maine Warden Service."

Efforts to reintroduce caribou to Maine were undertaken in 1963 and again in 1993 when a small number of caribou were released in Baxter State Park. Both efforts were unsuccessful due to possible poaching, predators, disease and migration back to Canada.

In Hubbard's list of fur bearing animals and birds he listed the Pinnated Grouse (Prairie-Chicken). It is not known specifically which bird he is referring to but the Greater Prairie-Chicken (Tympanuchus cupido) and The Heath Hen (Tympanuchus cupido cupido) were collectively referred to as Pinnated Grouse.

There is little documented information about the Heath Hen in the State of Maine but it likely was present along the coast. The Greater Prairie-Chicken was not known to be a native bird in Maine but an effort was made to introduce them in the 1870s.

The Heath Hen was a very common bird in the coastal plains of New England and was found in great abundance on Cape Cod. Though abundant, the bird became extinct in 1932, when the last bird named Booming Ben died. Over hunting has been largely blamed for the demise of the Heath Hen.

At the time of the creation of the Warden Service and for many years following, there was rampant fishing and exploitation of aquatic life within the rivers, streams and lakes. In 1885 it was permissible to take, catch, kill, or have in your possession up to a combined weight of fifty pounds of landlocked salmon, trout, or togue (lake trout). Today's limit on fish caught is now limited to the number of fish, not weight. Furthermore, there are now minimum and some maximum size limitations on the fish harvested.

In the 130+ years since Hubbard's travels, there have been many changes and improvements in the administration and enforcement of the State's fish and game programs. The State of Maine's wildlife program is considered by many to be one the finest in the Nation. The 125 +/- men and women which now comprise the Maine Warden Service and the many men and women who served before them are testimony to that fine achievement.

*

### Fires

Any person who shall build a camp or cooking fire in or adjoining any woods in this state, shall, before leaving such camp, totally extinguish such fire, and upon failure to do so, such person shall be punished by a fine not exceeding one hundred dollars, or by imprisonment in the county jail not exceeding one month, or by both such fine and imprisonment, provided that such fires built upon the sea-beach in such situation that they cannot spread into forest, wood or cultivated lands or meadows, shall not be considered as prohibited by this act. — 1891, ch. 100, § 5.

All persons engaged in hunting game on any of the woodlands within any town or unincorporated place in this state, shall use non-combustible wads in the loading of firearms used by them. — Ibid. § 57-

## Campfires
## Put Out Your Campfires!

The attention of campers is earnestly called to the subject of their campfires. Too much care cannot be exercised to see that these are *thoroughly* put out before the camps are deserted. The danger lies not so much in leaving a few smouldering brands in the middle of a bare fireplace, as in allowing to remain unextinguished a *single spark* in the turf at its side. It should be the tourist's last care, before leaving camp, to apply plenty of water to the soil around his fireplace, which nearly always is composed of dry moss, leaves, and other inflammable matter, frequently to the depth of a foot or more. A spark lurking in this mass for days undetected may be fanned into life by the next wind that blows, and the mischief which ensues may be irreparable. Too much stress cannot be laid on this matter. The writer knows of cases, where campers have taken the utmost care, apparently, to leave not a single live ember behind them, and yet ravaging forest fires have been proved to have originated from their camps. Thousands upon thousands of dollars' worth of timber have been thus destroyed; and if we only remember that in burning a man's trees we do him as much harm as if we burned his house, it will spur all conscientious men to treat the forests with perhaps even more consideration than they would their own property. It is no mean privilege we enjoy, of camping, hunting, and fishing on other men's land. Let us then render back at least this one duty of putting out our campfires.

### FIRE!

"Whoever kindles a fire on land not his own, without consent of the owner, forfeits ten dollars; if such fire spreads and damages the property of others, he forfeits not less than ten nor more than five hundred dollars, and in either case he shall stand committed until fine and costs are paid, or he shall be imprisoned not more than three years.

*

---

**2020 Edition: Notes on Campfires**

During the time period of Hubbard's travels through the North Woods it was rather essential to build a campfire for the cooking of meals and to provide some comfort on cool evenings. While there were portable stoves for camping available in sections of Europe, they were not popular in North America at the time. Unfortunately, the use of campfires often left unsightly scars on the forest floor or resulted in forest fires which destroyed large areas of the forests.[181] Public awareness of the impact of campfires may have contributed to the gain in popularity of portable stoves within North America in the beginning of the 20th Century.

Without question campfires have and will likely continue to be a popular part of the camping experience. In Hubbard's book he recognized the danger of campfires and spoke of the need to take extra time and effort to extinguish the fire before breaking camp. His message was a good one then and is a good one now.

At the time of Hubbard's wilderness sojourns there were laws in the State of Maine which allowed for the fine or imprisonment of individuals who kindle a fire on land not his

---

[181] **2020**: During the period from 2009 - 2018 there were 450 wildfires in the State of Maine classified as being caused by campfires. Eighty-one of these were in the Unorganized Territories. As a comparison, in the first eight months of 2020 alone there were 100 wildfires attributed to illegal, unextinguished campfires. (Source: Maine Forest Rangers.)

own, without consent of the owner, and not extinguishing a campfire or causing a forest fire. While the fines for violation of said laws may have appeared to be adequate at the time, they would not be a deterrent today.

Currently within the State of Maine, no person may kindle or use a campfire in the unorganized territory unless a permit has been obtained from the Maine Forest Service. The permit is not required if you are at an authorized campsite maintained by the Bureau of Parks and Lands or some other privately owned or authorized campsite. Campfires within organized towns also require the permission of the landowner.

The campfire permit, in unorganized territory, does not apply to the use of portable stoves which are fueled by propane, gasoline, or sterno or for recreational fires kindled when the ground is covered with snow.

In general, the state only writes campfire permits for a period of a few days. This can present a problem on long distance wilderness trips where there may be little or no contact with Forestry officials. However, upon application, the Maine Forest Service may issue a statewide yearly permit for out-of-door fires to resident guides licensed by the Department of Inland Fisheries and Wildlife,

Having a campfire without the required permit is a civil violation with a fine not to exceed $1,000 per day. Should the campfire result in a wildfire, the courts can require the violator to pay for the fire suppression costs; an amount not to exceed $125,000 per event, at the time of this writing.

**Special note from the Maine Forest Service:**

**"Keep the fire small, not tall."**

It is always easier to put a small fire out when it comes time to leave.

---

THE

# FORKS HOTEL,

### JOSEPH CLARK, Proprietor.

Newly built expressly for Summer Visitors, and contains seventy-five nicely-furnished rooms. It is situated on the banks of the Kennebec, near the mouth of Dead River, forty-six miles from Skowhegan, and on the mail road to Canada.

### First-rate Fishing & Hunting-Grounds close at hand.

The famous Moxie Pond, one of the finest fishing-ponds in the neighborhood, is only six miles from the hotel.

Guides furnished at $1.00 per day. Address HORACE ADAMS, JOHN ADAMS, or the Proprietor of the Forks Hotel.

## STAGE HOUSE,

### BINGHAM, MAINE.

After a year's absence, the subscriber has returned to his old quarters, and, with a house thoroughly repaired and refurnished, is ready to receive his old friends and the travelling public, to whom he extends a cordial welcome. TERMS REASONABLE.

### G. W. SAVAGE, Proprietor.

## *Original Table of Contents*

### PART FIRST

### How to Camp Out

### PART SECOND

### *Moosehead Lake and Immediate Vicinity*

### *Tours beyond Moosehead Lake*

## PART THIRD

# THE FORKS STAGE,

**W. G. HESELTON & SON, Proprietors.**

---

Runs daily (Sundays excepted), between SKOWHEGAN and the FORKS OF THE KENNEBEC, through *Madison, Solon, Bingham, Moscow,* and *Carratunk.*

Leaves Skowhegan at . . . . . 6.30 A.M.
,, the Forks at . . . . . . 6.30 A.M.

Round Trip Tickets can be bought, at reduced rates, in Boston, Portland, and on the line of the Maine Central Railroad.

---

Excursion Ticket from Boston to the Forks and Return, $14.00.

---

# CARRATUNK HOUSE,

## *SOLON, MAINE.*

### J. H. GRAY, Proprietor.

---

A good Hotel, with good Accommodations, and an *excellent Livery Stable.*

*Summer Boarders wanted. Terms Reasonable.*

## 2020 Edition - Selected References

While much of the added information in the form of insets and footnotes is from the knowledge and experience of the editors on northern Maine and the Moosehead Lake region, the following are selected as noteworthy sources cited or consulted during the 2020 edition writing.

1. Forest Commissioner of the State of Maine. Report Volume 2, Jan 1894. Cited for name of Saddle Rock Mountain near Silver Lake.
2. Green. Pauline. "Vacation Days." Brownville H. S. Reflector. 1926. Cited for article on Saddleback Mountain naming.
3. Hubbard, Lucius L., "Woods and Lakes of Maine. A Trip from Moosehead Lake to New Brunswick in a Birch-bark Canoe. 2020 Edition." Burnt Jacket Publishing. 2020.
4. Maine Department of Inland Fisheries & Wildlife. www.maine.gov, cited 2020.
5. Maine Forest Service. Correspondence between editor Frederick Wilcox and Bill Hamilton, Chief Forest Ranger and Kent Nelson, Forest Ranger Specialist. 2020.
6. Sprague, Francis John. "Sprague's Journal of Maine History." Vol. XiV, No. 2. Dover-Foxcroft, Maine, 1926. Cited for article, "Chadwick's Survey," by Fannie Hardy Eckstrom.
7. Ward, Julius H. (Rev.). "Moosehead Lake." In Harper's New Monthly Magazine. Vol. LI, No. CCCIII. August, 1875.

## Additional Advertisements from the Original Text

*2020 Note: Several advertisements were incorporated already into the body of the text. It was common at the time for travel books to include transportation, lodging, and supply advertisements such as these.*

### Bangor and Aroostook Railroad,

### (PISCATAQUIS DIVISION).

\*

### The Moosehead Lake Route,

The most direct route to KATAHDIN IRON WORKS, SEBEC LAKE, LAKE HEBRON, MONSON, and

### MOOSEHEAD LAKE,

Maine's great summer resort for sportsmen and tourists.

### TWO EXPRESS TRAINS EACH WAY DAILY.

Connecting at Oldtown with all trains to and from Bangor, Portland, and Boston, and at Greenville and Brownville Junctions with the Canadian Pacific Railway, for all points west.

Commencing with the Summer Schedule, June 26, passengers can leave Boston in the morning and arrive at Kineo for supper; returning, leave Kineo in the morning and arrive at Boston in the evening.

### EXCURSION TICKETS

Are on sale at all principal ticket offices in New England and New York City.

F. W. CRAM, General Manager.

*(2020 Edition Note: You may now find this map from Hubbard online)*

# NEW POCKET MAP

### OF

# MOOSEHEAD LAKE

### AND VICINITY,

Embracing the **Headwaters of the Kennebec, Penobscot, and St. John Rivers,** and giving routes for the tourist and timberman through the great forests, and over the intricate water-courses of

### NORTHERN MAINE.

It contains the latest geographical corrections of this great expanse of wild country, and will be found serviceable by all who contemplate a visit to these secluded localities.

### COMPILED AND PUBLISHED BY

### LUCIUS L. HUBBARD, CAMBRIDGE, MASS.

Printed on heavy bond-paper, and encased in durable envelope to fit the pocket. Price, 50 cents.

Will be sent by mail, post-paid, on receipt of price, by

### DAMRELL & UPHAM, BOSTON, MASS.

### D. BUGBEE & CO., BANGOR, ME.

*(2020 **Edition Note**: You may now find this map from Hubbard online)*

---

### MAP OF

### Northern Maine

(Now in Preparation.)

To embrace the entire northern part of the State, now covered by Hubbard's "Map of Moosehead Lake and Northern Maine," together with the whole of AROOSTOOK COUNTY and a part of WASHINGTON COUNTY.

It will show those eastern parts of the State accessible to the tourist from the

### Maine Central Railroad,

as well as the regions newly opened up by the

### Bangor and Aroostook Railway.

LUCIUS L HUBBARD.

Will be on sale by P. Bugbee & Co., Bangor, Me., and Damrell AND Upham, Boston, Mass.

Price, $1.00.          Ready about January 1, 1894.

| Time-Table | | | | | | |
|---|---|---|---|---|---|---|
| In effect daily, 1893 | | | | | | |
| GOING WEST (READ UP) | | | | | | |
| P.M. | P.M. | | | | P.M. | A.M. |
| 3:15 | 9:30 | Arr. East. Div. | Boston | De. East. Div. | 7:00 | |
| 4:15 | 9:30 | West Div. | | West Div. | | 8:00 |
| A.M. | | | | | A.M. | P.M. |
| 6:50 | 1:30 | De. | Bangor | Ar. | 5:20 | 3:22 |
| 6:25 | 1:20 | Ar. | | De. | 7:15 | 3:35 |
| | A.M. | | | | | |
| | 8:00 | | Greenville | | 11:35 | 7:25 |
| | | | | | P.M. | |
| | Abt. | | Kineo | | Abt. | |
| | 6:00 | | | | 2:00 | 10:00 |
| | | | | | A.M. | |
| 4:13 | 11:36 | | Mattawamkeag | | 8:25 | 5:20 |
| 2:15 | 10:00 | | Vanceboro | | 10:30 | 6:50 |

## JACKMAN HOUSE,

### Jackmantown, Somerset County, Maine.

#### A. F. ADAMS, PROPRIETOR.

Twenty miles above the Forks, on the main road to *Canada*, and three miles from *PARLIN POND*, one of the best trout-ponds in the County.

Guides furnished to parties, at $1.00 per day.

### GOOD HUNTING IN THE NEIGHBORHOOD.

The stage runs three times a week, on Tuesdays, Thursdays and Saturdays, from the Forks to Moose River Village, returning on alternate days. Fare $2.00. Passengers dine at Jackmantown.

*A. F. ADAMS, Proprietor.*

## . TOURISTS .

Going down the Penobscot, Allegash, or St. John Rivers,

OR TO ANY OF THE

Pleasure Grounds of Northeastern Maine,

will find good hotel accommodation
at either end of the

# NORTHEAST CARRY,

## MOOSEHEAD LAKE.

During the Summer Season several steamers touch at
the Carry daily. Within gunshot of the Penobscot House
flows the west branch of the Penobscot, with its miles of canoe-
able waters, and near at hand are the beauties of

### LOBSTER LAKE.

### United States Post-Office at the Carry.

CANOES HAULED PROMPTLY ACROSS THE CARRY;
ALSO TO RUSSELL POND.

FREE CARRIAGE FOR ALL GUESTS OF EITHER HOUSE.

GEORGE C. LUCE . . PROPRIETOR,

WINNEGARNOCK AND PENOBSCOT HOUSES.

# EVELETH HOUSE,

## Greenville, Moosehead Lake.

On the HIGHEST and COOLEST part of
the village, it commands a fine view of the
LAKE and its picturesque islands, near at hand,
and is conveniently located near the head-quar-
ters of the BLANCHARD STAGE LINE,
and directly opposite the POST-OFFICE, and
GROCERY STORE of J. H. EVELETH &
CO.

The House has ample accommodations for
fifty people ; and no pains are spared to make
its guests comfortable and at home. ..

### Prices Moderate. Teams to Let.

Stage Passengers en route for Kineo dine here,
and are conveyed to the STEAMER free of
charge.

*AMOS H. WALKER, Proprietor.*

## Acknowledgements

Thank you to Bill Hamilton, Chief Forest Ranger and Kent Nelson, Forest Ranger Specialist of the Maine Forest Service for their correspondence on the updated forest fires section.

We are grateful to Ms. Desiree Butterfield-Nagy, Special Collections Librarian, at the Raymond H. Fogler Library, the University of Maine at Orono. Ms. Butterfield-Nagy was instrumental in gathering images from an original printing of this book from 1893. Digital producing the original illustrations as they were first printed makes this a very special edition indeed.

Great thanks to our team of proofreaders. While much of the original text remains as it was written by Hubbard, the feedback received was invaluable for the newly added material.

Finally, thank you to all who will appreciate this book being re-released. We trust you will enjoy it as much as we have, whether you are reading from your living room chair or out on the trails exploring somewhere in Maine.

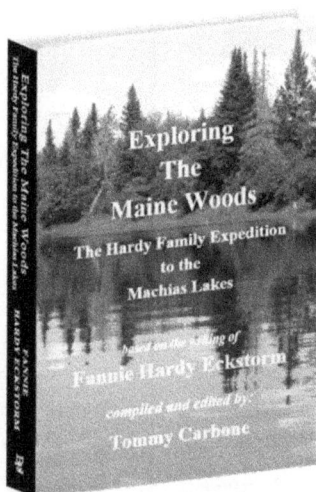

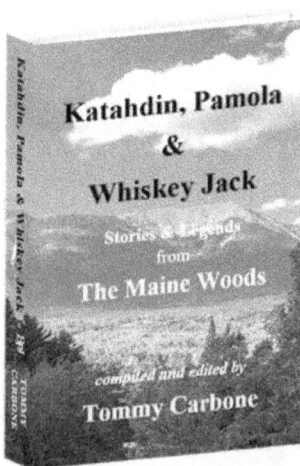

**Additional Reading on the Maine Woods – Machias to Moosehead**

# About Frederick Thomas Wilcox

*

Fred grew up in the vicinity of Warwick, New York. He describes his childhood as one spent mostly exploring the woods and surrounding areas. Following graduation from Warwick High School in 1957, he attended the University of Maine where he studied Forest Management. Following graduation from the University in 1962, he moved to Pennsylvania to work as a forester for the Commonwealth of Pennsylvania. After a long successful career of 39 years he retired in 2001.

Fred currently resides in Hershey, Pennsylvania and still spends time exploring the woods and surrounding areas. He still includes trips to Maine in his vacation plans.

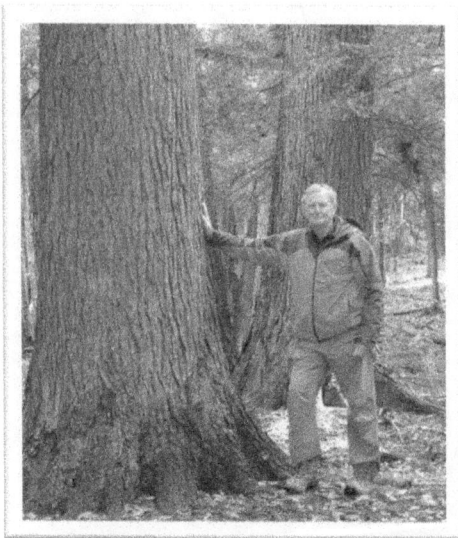

*Fred next to Eastern Hemlock in Cook Forest State Park, Pennsylvania*

# About Tommy Carbone

Tommy Carbone lives in Maine with his wife and two daughters. He studied electrical engineering and earned a Ph.D. in engineering management.

He writes fiction from a one room cabin, on the shores of a lake, that is frozen for almost six months out of the year, and moose outnumber people three to one. (I bet you can guess where that is...)

His first novel, "*The Lobster Lake Bandits – Mystery at Moosehead*," has made those 'from away' want to visit Maine. It's a big state – come explore.

# Woods and Lakes of Maine

## 2020 Annotated Edition:

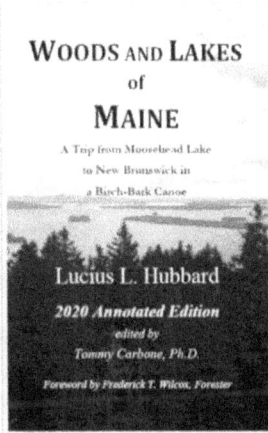

WOODS AND LAKES
of
MAINE

A Trip from Moosehead Lake
to New Brunswick in
a Birch-Bark Canoe

Lucius L. Hubbard

**2020 Annotated Edition**
edited by
Tommy Carbone, Ph.D.

Foreword by Frederick T. Wilcox, Forester

## Novels set in the Maine North Woods

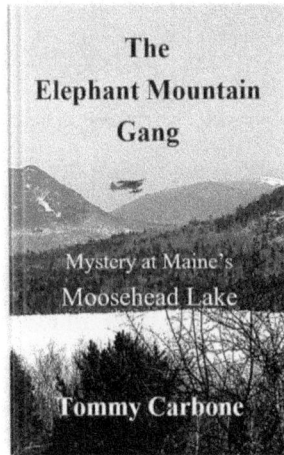

**The Lobster Lake Bandits**

*Mystery at Moosehead*

Tommy Carbone

"A real mystery thriller involving the north woods of Maine. A great read that will keep you hooked right up until the end."

John Ford Sr., Author of
Suddenly the Cider Didn't Taste So Good

**The Elephant Mountain Gang**

Mystery at Maine's
Moosehead Lake

**Tommy Carbone**

## Adventures from the Moosehead Lake Region

Thomas S. Steele wrote about his canoe trips through the Maine woods in these entertaining and informative memoirs.

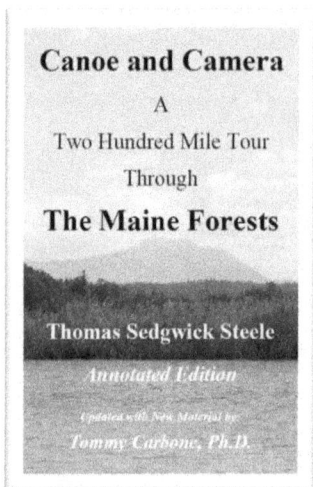

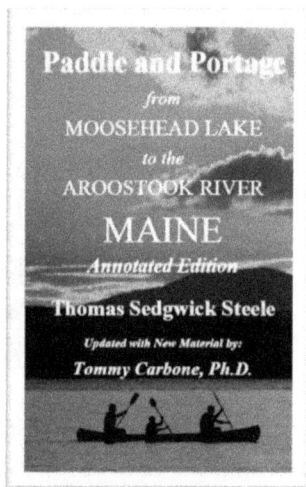

**Canoe and Camera**

A
Two Hundred Mile Tour
Through

**The Maine Forests**

**Thomas Sedgwick Steele**

*Annotated Edition*

*Updated with New Material by:*
*Tommy Carbone, Ph.D.*

**Paddle and Portage**

*from*
MOOSEHEAD LAKE
*to the*
AROOSTOOK RIVER

**MAINE**

*Annotated Edition*

**Thomas Sedgwick Steele**

*Updated with New Material by:*
*Tommy Carbone, Ph.D.*

The two-book commemorative hardcover edition of Thomas S. Steele's Maine Adventures.
A great gift for all lovers of the outdoors – or for yourself.
Updated with new information and maps.

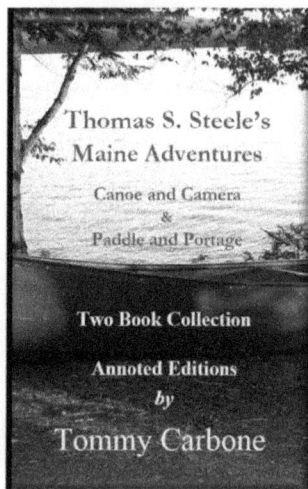

Thomas S. Steele's
Maine Adventures

Canoe and Camera
&
Paddle and Portage

**Two Book Collection**

**Annoted Editions**
*by*
Tommy Carbone

www.ingramcontent.com/pod-product-compliance
Lightning Source LLC
Chambersburg PA
CBHW031140020426
42333CB00013B/452